011307507

KU-205-939

THE NATURE OF POWER

THE NATURE OF POWER

Barry Barnes

Polity Press

First published 1988 by Polity Press
in association with Basil Blackwell

Editorial Office:
Polity Press, Dales Brewery, Gwydir Street,
Cambridge CB1 2LJ, UK

Basil Blackwell Ltd
108 Cowley Road, Oxford OX4 1JF, UK

British Library Cataloguing in Publication Data

Barnes, Barry
    The nature of power.
    1. Power (Social sciences)
    I. Title
    303.3   HM141
    ISBN 0–7456–0073–5
    ISBN 0–7456–0074–3 Pbk

Typeset in 10 on 12pt Times
by DMB (Typesetting), Abingdon, Oxon.
Printed in Great Britain

CONTENTS

CONTENTS

ACKNOWLEDGEMENTS

As always, my colleagues at the Edinburgh Science Studies Unit have been an invaluable source of commentary and criticism in the course of the preparation of this book. I owe a great deal also to other colleagues here in Edinburgh, who participated in seminars wherein much of the draft material of the book was presented and discussed. Christopher Bryant, Mary Hesse, Richard Jennings and Desmond McQuail all read and commented upon specific parts of the text to good purpose, helping me to clarify both my thinking and its presentation. Finally, I should like to thank everyone who has helped in the preparation of the manuscript. I am grateful to Carole Tansley in particular for producing a typescript from materials which not even the author always found easy to read.

INTRODUCTION

Power is one of those things, like gravity and electricity, which makes its existence apparent to us through its effects, and hence it has always been found much easier to describe its consequences than to identify its nature and its basis. Indeed, it is not at all clear that there is point and purpose in referring to 'the' nature and 'the' basis of power. We refer to many forms of power – political, military, economic, ideological and others: how far it is legitimate and useful to generalize about these as manifestations of 'power itself' is open to question. We refer to many bases for power – the possession of territory, of goods, of finance, of weapons, of skill: how far it is legitimate and useful to generalize about these as variations of a single basis – 'possession itself' perhaps, whatever possession may be – is open to question. Some social scientists believe that power is a motley and theoretically uninteresting, and that we should confine ourselves accordingly to discussion of its effects and consequences. I have eventually arrived at the opposite conclusion. I believe that power can properly be discussed in general terms and that much may be learned thereby, but by way of justification for this view I can only point to what follows, taken as a whole.

My explicit aim in this book is to set out, as clearly and straight-forwardly as I can, an account of what power is and what its basis in society is. The first two chapters are designed to prepare the ground: chapter 1 reviews some existing conceptions of power and its basis, and chapter 2 develops a view of social interaction and social order with which, I suggest, any satisfactory description of the nature and basis of power must be compatible. The third and central chapter comes to the heart of the matter by setting out reasonably systematically a particular view of social power: it is here that most of the explicit descriptions and definitions may be found. Finally, two chapters are devoted to illustrating and extending the analysis; in chapter 4, externally sanctioned activities are considered, and in chapter 5, actions directed to the collective good.

The material in these chapters is not designed as a survey of the forms of power or of the ways in which it typically manifests itself. Rather it is selected to highlight areas of possible difficulty for my account, and to allow the discussion of problems already well recognized as being associated with the sociological analysis of power. Unfortunately, many of these problems arise not from the generation of power through co-operative interaction but from the use of power against opposition and resistance, so that there is a tendency for the negative aspects of power relations to be dwelled upon and emphasized. I hope this will not draw attention away from the fact that specific distributions of power facilitate effective co-ordinated social activity, and that they may be sustained by genuinely co-operative social interaction precisely for this reason.

Let me now try to indicate some of the things that the book does not attempt to do. It takes an interest in how the term 'power' is actually used and in what is referred to when reference is made to power: to that extent it is an empirical study of a very general kind. But it is a study that employs only the perspectives of the social sciences. How other sciences may bear upon my subject I do not claim to know, and although what follows reads very much as a self-sufficient account of power in society I readily acknowledge its narrow viewpoint, and recognize that it may perhaps need to be modified or repaired in the light of work in other fields, now or in the future: social activity cannot be kept as the exclusive preserve of the social sciences. Moreover, even as a contribution to the social sciences the book is restricted in its scope and objectives. It says little of deep significance concerning the current distribution of power in particular societies, nor does it expound or evaluate any of the many current theoretical accounts of the power structures of actual societies or kinds of societies. It is also highly selective in its choice of illustrative materials. I have avoided detailed consideration of power in face-to-face situations and in small family-based contexts, largely because of a lack of expertise: there are a number of interesting accounts of power at this level that are compatible with what I have to say, but which of them holds the greatest promise and plausibility must be left for others to decide. Reluctantly, I have also omitted any discussion of the relationship of power to specialized knowledge, intellectual division of labour and the trust and credibility accorded to different forms of expertise. These are topics of immense interest and fascination, which for that very reason I decided would be best considered in their own right elsewhere. The effect of these omissions is to align the text quite closely with that existing body of work in the social sciences, and particularly sociological and political theory, which considers power on the large scale, as it exists in entire societies or social structures.

There is a sense in which all books are about more than their explicitly stated subject and in this sense my book is about more than power. Inevitably, it reflects some of my own very general attitudes and convictions, attitudes and convictions which at some points I am able to set out and defend, but which elsewhere are simply assumed and relied upon as the argument develops. It is worth making mention of one or two of these very general matters, since they play an important role in what follows and I doubt that a balanced evaluation of the book's claims can be made without considering them.

First of all I state a philosophical conviction. If one seeks to give a systematic account of social life or any of its aspects, there are two developed models of how ideally one should proceed. There is realism, which encourages reference to human beings as real entities with real properties and tendencies; and there is positivism, which enjoins attention only to observed behaviours, their sequence, their frequency, their predictability. I do not believe that it is possible to do social science rigorously and consistently on the basis of a positivist standpoint. In practice we are obliged to adopt a realist mode of speech. We have to be prepared to make reference to the objects of our enquiry and not just to signs of their possible existence. We may argue about the status of the objects to which we refer: we may assert a strong and uncompromising philosophical realism involving a firm metaphysical commitment to the reality of the objects we speak of; or we may, without inconsistency, take a fictionalist or an instrumentalist position and accept such objects as convenient constructs and no more: we may even take our references to real objects as a part of our own social activity, and seek to account for it and explain it sociologically. Such references remain, nonetheless, invaluable and irreplaceable. Consistent with this, power is referred to in what follows as something real, and an attempt is made to describe its nature. The reality described may be found somewhat diffuse and intangible, but it is important not to confuse reality, even material reality, with the presence of the solid state.

A second general point derives from my involvement in the sociology of knowledge. I have always found it difficult to accept the standard contrast between notions like 'society', 'social structure' or 'power' on the one hand, and 'culture', 'meaning' or 'knowledge' on the other. It is sometimes said that the distinction involved here is only an 'analytic' or 'theoretical' one, but in practice this is not so. The distinction is widely formulated as an 'analytic' one but almost invariably it is then used as an empirical one, even by the most sophisticated social theorists. It is asserted that social structural change *affects* culture, or that culture has feedback *effects* upon social structure, or that culture *mediates* between social structure and the individual. It is as if there is culture on the left and social structure on the right, and the 'interaction' between the two is between independently existing entities. I do not believe that culture and social structure are empirically separable in this way, nor am I aware of any useful purpose that can be served by marking an 'analytic' distinction between them. It is important to be aware that in what follows I never make reference to culture *as opposed to* social structure, or vice versa: to import the standard contrast into the reading of the text will only serve to mislead.

Finally, in common with an increasing number of writers today, I take the view that social actions have to be understood and explained by reference to the people who generate them, and not in terms of their functions or alleged functions in maintaining the stability of the society or the institution of which they may be a part. Functionalism continues to suffuse through the whole realm of social and political theory: much deeply insightful work has been developed in a functionalist framework. But functionalism, it seems to me, is irremediably teleological and hence, at whatever cost, has to be abandoned. We have to work our way toward an alternative mode of thought. Given that new thought always depends upon existing thought, the change can only be slow: no doubt there are many inadvertent instances of functionalism to be found in this book.

My hope and intention in what follows is nonetheless at all times to consider activity as being subject to the control and direction of the people who perform it. As a marker of this point of view I make continuing reference to action as the product of calculative human beings. Indeed, one of my major objectives is to show that the persistence of large-scale power structures is intelligible as the outcome of calculative action, and hence that functional explanations do not have to be employed in order to account for them.

It must be emphasized, however, that although there is considerable stress in what follows upon calculation and intentionality in social life, the text does not advocate an 'economic' as opposed to a 'sociological' orientation to the explanation of behaviour. We still tend to think that problems of explanation in the social sciences must be solved either by functionalism or by rational decision theory: what people do must be understood in terms of either a non-rational attachment to (functional) rules and customs, or a rational calculation of self-interest. But at the same time we are aware that both alternatives have fundamental defects, that neither of them will do. As I see it, the mainstream of sociological theory fails properly to get to grips with the reasoned and calculative character of human behaviour, whereas economic approaches are usually insufficiently sensitive to the extent of our interdependence on each other and to how far everything we think and do is shot through with custom and convention. We need to develop a view of social action as the customary activity of calculative agents.

Clearly, to argue in this way involves some revision in our standard understanding of the term 'calculative action': many of its existing connotations need to be set to one side. To refer to social actions as calculative is often taken to imply methodological individualism and a desire to explain what people do wholly in terms of their self-interest. Such references are not intended to have any such implications in this book. I am not an advocate of methodological individualism, nor do I believe that self-interest comes even remotely close to being a sufficient basis for human action. I emphasize this last point particularly, because in the text I occasionally assume the priority of self-interest for simplicity: the condition of extreme individuation wherein action is wholly oriented to self-interest never exists as an actual state of affairs but for the purposes of my argument it often provides the worst possible scenario, allowing the generation of conclusions which will stand even more securely where there is altruism and a willingness to give priority to the objectives of other people.

It is perhaps worth emphasizing also that in referring to people as calculative I do not deny that they may be creatures of habit. This needs emphasis because a false contrast is often made between action based on calculation and action based on habit. It is true that some actions have a tailor-made quality, as it were, and some are more off-the-shelf; some are specially planned and designed, some are not. But it is nonetheless wholly misconceived to treat calculation and habit, or calculation and resort to routine, as opposed bases for action. Rather, habit facilitates calculation and calculation sustains habit. Any attempt to take a self-consciously calculative orientation to a situation, and make a fully worked-out uncompromisingly thorough calculation of expedient action, immediately produces information overload. It is out of the question to calculate everything, all the time, taking account of every contingency. The best that can be done is to calculate a few things, some of the time, taking account of some contingencies. It is not even possible fully to calculate what is best omitted when one calculates less than fully. Not even in a society of intensely self-conscious and enthusiastic calculators can social action be based wholly upon direct calculation. All that we can confidently assert of such a society is that its ongoing activity is constantly vulnerable to adjustment and revision in the light of calculative appraisal and reappraisal. There is no prior reason for believing that this cannot be said of a society replete with habit and routine. Similarly, there is no prior reason for imagining that calculative individuals cannot at the same time be creatures of habit. Indeed, it must be recognized that, in order to be calculative, individuals have to be creatures of habit.

Some of my general attitudes and convictions may have hinted at iconoclasm. If so, let me conclude by redressing the balance and emphasizing the conservative character of the text. Needless to say, it relies heavily upon the literature of the social sciences, and asserts little if anything that is not prefigured in that literature. Its basic conception of power can be set in continuity with existing accounts of power as capacity and in its rudimentary form will surprise nobody already familiar with those accounts. Its underlying conceptions of social interaction and the nature of society are no less derivative. How could it be otherwise? To do work of this kind is to participate in a tradition. The point is worth mention here only because the main text takes little explicit interest in its own ancestry. It is predominantly ordered as a discussion of themes and ideas. It takes the literature primarily as a repository of concepts, images, procedures and arguments, not as a collection of recognized texts or authors. This, I believe, is the best way to keep a tradition alive and vigorous: the potency of the thought of the ancestors is greatest if one forgets that they are there. What this means, however, is that many major sources of inspiration are not commemorated properly in references and citations. It becomes necessary to do as I do now: to recognize deep and profound debts of many kinds which are marked implicitly in the text itself, but which cannot be given an adequate explicit acknowledgement.

1

THE CONCEPT OF POWER

1.1 COMMON SENSE USAGE

Specialized fields of study often try to solve problems that first arise in the context of everyday life, and they often draw their initial images and concepts from that same context. Sociology does both of these things. Its central problems, even those of its most arcane and esoteric branches, tend to be generalized versions of problems encountered and formulated by members of the wider society. Its central concepts – role, status, class, rule, sanction, power and so on – all originate in the everyday world, and most of the associations which make them an invaluable feedstock for the sociological imagination derive from their use in everyday contexts. Thus, it is far more than a ritual gesture to begin this study with a look at the common sense usage of the concept of power. Even though the intention is to move beyond common sense understanding, to develop it and add to it in worthwhile ways, that same understanding is nonetheless the major resource available for the task.

Let us then examine the common sense concept of power, and although our concern is to be solely and simply with power in society let us initially treat this as a part of a broader usage. That usage is in fact very broad indeed. Power is treated as an entity or attribute which all manner of things, processes, or agents may have. Natural forces and phenomena may have it, as when we speak of powerful currents or powerful magnets; artefacts may have it, and with some artefacts, engines and machines, their power may be their most important single feature; animals may have it, or even plants – as when tree-roots undermine buildings. People may be said to have power in a number of ways, of which three are worth explicit mention. First of all, the human body may be considered a repository of power, as when we refer to a powerful physique or powerful biceps. Secondly, there is a hard-to-describe spiritual analogue of physical power: we refer to powerful personalities or charismatic figures. Thirdly, we routinely speak of people possessing, or seeking to possess, the power of office or position. This is the mode of use which most clearly displays our awareness that power may reside in society, and somehow derive from social arrangements rather than individual natures.

The range of references may be bewilderingly large, but there is nonetheless considerable pattern and indeed integrity in common sense usage. People are, for example, consistently *realistic* when they speak of power. It exists. It is there. But what is the 'it' that is there? What kind of an entity or attribute is power? Common sense usage is again clear and consistent: it treats power as a *capacity*, not as something that is continually manifest and actual. A powerful magnet remains powerful when it is put away in the drawer; a 70 b.h.p. car engine remains a 70 b.h.p. when the car is parked; neither a powerful body nor a powerful office have to be put to use.

Thus, although 'power' is routinely taken to refer to something tangible and existent, it is nonetheless a deeply theoretical concept. It is always used to refer to a capacity, a maximum potential, and such a capacity is never clearly and obviously manifest. Perhaps a better mounting and transmission could squeeze a little more output from the engine; perhaps a little more concentration could drag a little more effort from the body. Actual observable behaviour can at best only set lower limits to the power that resides in something. How much power is 'really there' must always be a matter of conjecture.

The whole value of the concept of power in everyday life resides in its deeply theoretical character as a label for capacities. We use the term to set upper limits on capabilities of various kinds, and thus to calculate the possibilities and the risks inherent in various courses of action. The value of the concept in the natural sciences is of just the same kind. In thermodynamics and related fields of physics the concept has been refined and developed so that its proper use demands extraordinary care and precision, but it remains nonetheless a deeply theoretical concept referring most of the time to capacities. If the term is to be used in sociology – if sociologists are to speak of power in society – it would seem sensible to retain this same crucial feature of common sense usage. Power should be taken in the first instance as a theoretical term referring to distributions of capacities, potentials or capabilities.

There need be no fear of making sociology too abstract and theoretical by the use of a term of this kind. Even the most behaviourist of social scientists effectively think already of society as being so many capacities and potentials. Nor is there any need to apologize for such a mode of thought. The very term 'society' denotes a continuing, persisting pattern of interaction: strict behaviourism would forbid its use just as much as the use of 'power'. To use a concept like 'society' is to go quite beyond talk of specific behaviours or even specific actions; it is to think *dispositionally*, in a way that allows the existence of *continuing* capacities and capabilities. This is the right way to do sociology.

Power then is invariably a capacity. But what kind of a capacity is it? In the specialized usage of natural science, power is the capacity to do work: the power of an engine represents the maximum rate of doing work of which it is capable. Such usage is scarcely different from that of common sense. Our intuitive understanding of a powerful physique is precisely of one that is capable of getting more done in a given time. Similarly, our intuitive understanding of a powerful individual in society is of an individual who is capable of getting a lot of things done in a given time, because of who he is or where he stands in society. Such an intuitive understanding is one possible starting-point for sociological study: power might reasonably be thought of as an individual's capacity, deriving from where he stands in society, to get things done. More precisely, we might wish to speak of his[1] capacity to generate action.

Note also that power is often thought of as a *generalized* capacity: the car engine may also be used to drive a boat, or to generate electricity, or to pump water or compress air, and the deeply theoretical notion of its power gives some indication of its possible utility in relation to all these tasks and many more. Similarly, in assessing the power of a particular body we give ourselves a guide to its likely effectiveness in the performance of a great range of possible tasks. This is why it is out of the question to define the power of an engine, or of a body, behaviourally: such power may manifest itself in innumerable ways, including ways quite beyond what can be specified in terms of existing knowledge. Power in society is often considered similarly to be of a highly generalized nature, although this is not invariably the case. For some powerful agents, we are liable to think, scarcely anything is impossible; with others we may confidently specify the narrow limits of what we take to be their power.

In general, behaviour (or action) cannot be used to define power, but it is true nonetheless that power is manifest in behaviour. Particular behaviours are routinely taken as signs or indications of the existence and operation of power. The motion of the car is a sign of power in the engine; the movement of the body is a sign of power in the muscles; the movement of the muscles, it is sometimes said, is a sign of the power of the will; the obedience of subordinates, it is sometimes said, is a sign of the power of their superiors. As a matter of routine we refer to all manner of phenomena as the effects of power and hence as signs that the capacity referred to as power really exists.

There is a sense in which power as a capacity is only evident through its effects. It is emphatically not the case, however, that these effects are the only grounds for inferring the existence of power, or even the only means of measuring the magnitude of power. The car engine may be taken to pieces and analysed: its power in relation to other engines may be inferred from its bore and stroke, the number of its cylinders, its levels of friction and so on. It is possible to move from the nature of the engine to its power. (Needless to say, estimates and measurements made in this way will be unreliable. But all measurements are unreliable.)

In our common sense thinking we tend to assume that power can be understood by reference to the nature of its source, that the constitution of the source makes intelligible the capacity to work or act that inheres in it. Different kinds of powers are thought to inhere in differently constituted sources. Thus we understand the capabilities of the car engine in terms of its mechanical design and the chemistry of petroleum; we understand the capabilities of muscle in terms of the structure of its tissue at the cellular and the molecular level, and in terms of molecular chemistry. Other generalized capabilities exist, the nature and basis of which remain opaque to us, the sources obscure. Here we tend to speak of a 'power' residing in something, and await enlightenment as to its basis. As active human agents we have the capacity to move many of our own muscles. We do not understand how we get them to move, but we do. Accordingly, routine references are made to 'will-power', and an interest is taken in the nature of the will, the self or the soul, and in the relationship between mind and body. As members of society and occupants of social positions and offices we find ourselves with the capacity to affect the actions of other people. We are not quite sure how precisely it is possible, but we do it. Accordingly routine references are made to 'social power' and an interest is taken in the nature of social interaction and social hierarchy, and in the relationship between the individual and the social.

Powers, in routine common sense discourse, are capacities to do work or generate action, usually generalized capacities, which are possessed by or attributable to a diversity of sources, and the basis of which lies in the nature of those sources. As these things go, the basis of physical power in engines and artefacts is well understood, and that of the body only a little less well: the nature of machines and of the body is, we believe, reasonably apparent to us. On the other hand, the basis of will-power and of social power remains obscure, reflecting our acknowledged lack of understanding of the will and of society. It is interesting to see how far systematic study can throw light on these obscurely based powers, whether the nature of their sources can be illuminated or, alternatively, exposed and dismissed as chimerical. The study of the nature and basis of social power is of course a legitimate project for sociology, and the explicit objective of this book.

Unfortunately, beyond the reassurance that social power is 'really there', common sense discourse has not a great deal to contribute to such a project: it is notably thin in theories or conjectures concerning the nature and basis of power. Perhaps this is because in everyday life it suffices for many practical purposes to impute power purely on the basis of its supposed effects. Indeed, everyday discourse seems to spend much of its time within a closed loop, a cyclic sense-making system wherein not only is power inferred from its effects, but these same effects are only perceived for what they are because of their supposed relationship to power.[2] This point needs exemplification: an experiment carried out by the social psychologists Thibaut and Riecken (1955) brings out what is involved beautifully.

Every subject, X, in this experiment was introduced to a second individual, Y, and was required to request Y to perform a specific task of a very simple kind. Y, who unlike the subject was a party to the purpose of the experiment, invariably performed the task on request. This simple interaction was repeated time after time with many subjects in standardized conditions. Only one factor was allowed to vary. In some cases Y was introduced to X as a powerful individual of high social status; in other cases Y was described in terms implying low status and low power. How X perceived Y proved to be correlated strongly with how X described Y's behaviour – or, to put it another way, with how X perceived Y to act. Where Y was perceived as low in power, Y's behaviour was described as compliance. Where Y was perceived as high in power, Y's behaviour was described quite differently, as voluntary helpfulness.[3]

Although it may be perfectly satisfactory for practical purposes to infer power from effects and effects from power without any independent access to either, it is scarcely likely to be accepted as a legitimate procedure in a sociological study. Indeed, there must be many circumstances where it will not do even in the less demanding context of everyday life. There is a need for a direct attack on the problem of the nature and basis of power, one which if possible allows power to be understood independently of its effects and hence breaks the vicious circle of reasoning from the one to the other. Nonetheless, this circular reasoning should not be treated solely and simply as a weakness to be eradicated from our thinking. It is also an empirical social phenomenon in its own right and its existence must be borne in mind. We cannot dismiss the possibility that this circular reasoning and circular accounting is all there is to power.

1.2 SOCIOLOGICAL REFINEMENT

Needless to say, sociologists and other social scientists have produced an extensive literature on the concept of power. They have recognized the obscurity and imprecision of common sense usage and have sought to improve upon it. Unfortunately, however, the mainstream of this literature has not attempted to get to grips with the central problems of the nature of power and its basis. It has offered ways of defining power and of measuring power which, for all their merits, have managed to avoid any consideration of what is being defined or what is being measured.[4]

Definitions

Let us start with definitions of power, and take three well-known formulations which are typical of the currently predominant approach to the problem:

> Power is the probability that one actor in a social relationship will be in a position to carry out his own will despite resistance, regardless of the basis on which this probability rests. (Weber, 1947, p. 152)

> A has power over B to the extent that he can get B to do something that B would not otherwise do. (Dahl, 1957, pp. 202–3)

> Power is the capacity of some persons to produce intended and forseen effects on others. (Wrong, 1979, p. 2)

These three closely related definitions, for all their apparent simplicity, embody a whole array of attitudes and convictions about power in society.[5] First of all, they assign power to individuals rather than to institutions or entire societies. Although some sociologists, Parsons, Deutsch, Luhmann, Poulantzas and several others, think of power as essentially a structural property manifest in an entire society rather than its constituent individuals, the mainstream of sociologists and political theorists assigns it as a property of individuals just as the above definitions stipulate. Secondly, the definitions attribute power to individuals only in so far as those individuals enter into specific social relationships with other individuals: the power of the individual is indeed a property of the social relationships in which he participates. Here again other sociologists, notably Parsons, would beg to differ and would think of power as a generalized capability not tied to a few specific relationships. Finally, the power of the individual is manifest in its *effects* upon other individuals – in their compliance, whether willing or reluctant, with the will of the power-holder: power is defined as 'power over' rather than 'power to'. Once more Parsons is the outstanding deviant from the mainstream view.

What these definitions do, then, is to point us to an individual, to a social relationship in which he participates, and then to the *effect* of the power he is said to exercise – the effect being the compliance of the other in the relationship. We are brought to the point where power is said to reside and then, at the last moment, we are made to look away from the power itself, as it were, to its consequences. Whatever produces these consequences: that is power.

What is the source of the appeal of definitions of this kind? One source is their apparently 'scientific' quality. Individuals are more amenable to 'scientific' observation than are institutions or societies; there are fewer difficulties involved in producing generally acceptable descriptions of their characteristics and their actions. Similarly, the consequences of the operation of power are more visible and accessible than is power 'itself'; 'compliance' is not the most straightforward of notions, but an instance of it is much easier to observe than the theoretical entity, power, which is said to enforce it. To define power in terms of its consequences is to come close to an operational definition, to make 'power' more of a 'scientific' concept and less of a 'metaphysical' one: it is to manifest a positivistic prejudice.

Another attractive feature of these definitions, as far as many writers are concerned, is their individualistic formulation, which facilitates a range of moral and evaluative objectives. By defining power as a capacity exercised by individuals it is possible 'to fix responsibility for consequences held to flow from the action, or inaction, of certain specifiable agents' (Lukes, 1974, p. 56). Lukes notes how C. Wright Mills specifically favoured an individualistic conception of power, since it enabled him 'to make demands upon men of power and to hold them responsible for specific courses of events' (Mills, 1959, p. 100). It scarcely seems appropriate for social scientists to favour some definitions over others simply because of their greater utility in exhortation and homiletic, yet the opposite case is forcefully made in Lukes (1974), who asserts that it is in practice impossible to set aside normative considerations when selecting definitions. Certainly, it must be conceded to Lukes that discussion of the concept of power in the social sciences is shot through with evaluative considerations and profoundly influenced by political commitments. Anti-individualistic, structural definitions are adopted for their moral and political significance as much as any others. Lukes rightly quotes Poulantzas as an example: for him power is 'the capacity of a social class to realise its specific objective interests' (Poulantzas, 1973, p. 104).

Clearly then, there are significant incentives to the acceptance and use of the existing mainstream definitions of power. They encourage the virtues of positivism – attention to what is observable, caution in generalizing, suspicions of theory and theoretical entities – and they sustain an individualistic style of thought well suited to the currently accepted idiom of moral exhortation and condemnation. On the other hand, the definitions offer no insight whatsoever concerning the nature of power or its basis, and their wide acceptance testifies to an equally wide lack of curiosity concerning these questions. These are definitions that may appeal to those who think they know what power is already, and who merely seek to speak of it with more precision and more moral leverage. But what then is power? What is it that enforces compliance? It is a considerable feat of virtuosity to have defined power without saying anything at all concerning what power is, but that problem still demands an answer.

It might be said that there is no answer to be given. All kinds of diverse, unrelated factors might make people powerful, that is, induce others to comply with their demands. 'Power' may be merely a catch-all term for whatever myriad of diverse factors happens to be operative. It could even be that compliance in society is random and uncaused, like good fortune, and that powerful individuals are no more interesting than lucky ones. 'Power' and 'luck' may be strictly analogous terms, used to make sense of what happens to people *ex post facto*: where someone is obeyed he is said to be powerful; where someone chances upon his desires he is said to be lucky. I do not believe this. I think that power in society is an identifiable phenomenon, that an understanding of its nature and its basis is possible and that it can be identified independently of its effects. But even if this were wrong, even if 'power' were indeed a concept just like 'luck', we could only come to know this by an extended study presuming the opposite. Only by attempting to 'find' power as a phenomenon could we become convinced that it was in fact not there to be found: only by seeking to define power in terms of its essential characteristics could we be convinced that this was not possible and be reconciled to a less satisfactory definition in terms of the effects of power. In fact, there has been no sustained attempt to ascertain what the nature and basis of power consist in. Existing definitions reflect a lack of interest in the nature of power, not a failure to discover what it is.

Indicators

Only a small part of the sociological work relating to power has been concerned with the problem of definitions. Much more time and effort has been expended in attempting to measure power and map its distribution across individuals in society. Here, it might be thought, the matter of what power is would absolutely have to be addressed; but it is not so. Almost universally the problem of measuring power has been equated with that of finding and processing measurable 'indicators' of power. Very often these 'indicators' are postulated *effects* of the use of power, so that the measurement process makes us look away from power itself much as current definitions do. And in just about every case where 'indicators' are used there is no adequate discussion of how the 'indicator' may be known reliably to 'indicate' power itself: there is no attempt to 'find' power and use it to validate or calibrate that which is being used as an 'indicator' of it. In sociological research of this kind, power continues to be the wind that one keeps at one's back.

There is nothing wrong with the use of indicators, whether in the social sciences or any other context. It may be sensible to look at the switch on the electric iron instead of feeling the plate. But the use of indicators is only straightforward when they are known to be reliable signs of that which they indicate. Only when we know that the switch position of the iron correlates with the temperature of the plate can we use the former as a straightforward indicator of the latter. Less straightforwardly, we may use indicators as legitimate means of ascertaining the state of invisible theoretical entities. The chemist has dozens of indicators which tell him how things are with atoms and molecules: he has no independent access to them but like a good realist he infers their condition from indicators. The chemist's indicators, however, are in striking agreement one with another, so that the reliability of any one may plausibly be checked against the 'consensus' provided by all the many others, and that 'consensus' of indicators may reasonably be accounted the consequence of the existence of what is indicated, atoms and molecules themselves. In contrast, the continuing problem with the use of indicators of power is that no method currently exists of assessing their reliability, and the criticism that can properly be advanced against those who have used indicators of power in their research is that they have taken very little interest in developing any such method.

Two very different kinds of indicators have been used in sociological studies. One approach has been to use attributions of power made by members as reliable indicators of where power really lies in their community. Members are asked to name the most powerful individuals in their community, and perhaps to rank-order these individuals according to the 'amount' of power they possess. All the individual responses are then combined and processed to produce a map of 'the' power structure of the community. This is commonly called the *reputational* approach to the measurement of power, precisely because it assumes that those reputed to be powerful in a community will indeed be powerful therein.[6]

The rationale for the reputational approach is that members know their own communities more thoroughly and intimately than any outsider could hope to, and hence are the most trustworthy sources of knowledge concerning those communities. A member of a community is perfectly

capable of recognizing possessors of power, and will accordingly build
up, over a long period of time, a reasonably accurate map of power in
that community. By combining many such reasonably accurate maps an
even better indicator of the true distribution of power may be obtained –
an indicator which, whatever its deficiencies, may be claimed to be as
reliable as any available.

There are, however, strong arguments against this rationale and its
trust in second-hand reporting. For all that members ought to know their
own community well, even the most rudimentary surveys suggest that
their knowledge of it is superficial, incomplete and variable. Reputationalists themselves acknowledge that different individuals in the same
community commonly provide massively divergent accounts of the distribution of power within it. So a question mark exists against the
reputational approach, even if one refrains from asking how everyday
actors can be expected to identify power when professional social
scientists appear themselves to have no idea what it looks like.

Certainly many sociologists have been averse to using an indicator of
power that relies upon second-hand reporting, and appears to make
sociological findings no more reliable and trustworthy than everyday
opinions. They have rejected reputationalism as scientifically unsound
and methodologically inadequate, and have favoured an alternative
approach which measures power in terms of its directly observable
effects. This is the *event* approach to the measurement of power, which
originated in the immensely impressive work of Dahl (1961).[7] For Dahl
the only convincing indicator of the existence of power was an instance
of its successful use. Essentially, Dahl was a behaviourist: not so extreme
a behaviourist as to deny the existence of power as a capacity, but
enough of one to reject all attributions of power that did not rest directly
upon observed behaviour. Dahl studied the attempts of individuals to
influence the outcomes of specific political decisions. Successful inter-
vention in decision-taking processes was an indicator of the power of the
intervener: those individuals whose interventions were most frequently
successful could be considered the most powerful. Here was an indicator
which was not dependent upon unreliable second-hand reporting, and
which could be employed in what were considered to be properly scientific,
methodologically adequate studies.

This new indicator did, however, have some unsatisfactory features
when judged in intuitive common-sense terms. It failed, for example, to
distinguish between individuals who influenced decisions out of inclination
and those who did so because they were told or expected to do so: Dahl
did not consider the possibility of individuals' forming long chains of
power relations. Similarly, the indicator failed to discriminate powerless
persons from powerful persons who never used their power. Advocates

of the reputationalist approach were quick to emphasize this last point, but amongst Dahl's supporters, with their behaviourist predispositions, the notion of power which never found employment was itself problematic, and the inability of their methods to identify *that* sort of power scarcely seemed a disadvantage at all. The event approach blossomed into a method of measurement as widely used, or more widely used, than reputationalism; and controversy between the different approaches duly got under way.[8]

Earlier I spoke of scientific reputability and moral utility as the two factors that have most to do with the acceptability of current definitions of power. The same factors appear to underpin the credibility of the various methods of measuring power. Here, concern with their perceived moral and evaluative implications seems to have been of considerable importance in dividing opinion upon the relative merits of the event and reputational approaches. If one maps power in American communities in terms of events there is a tendency for it to emerge as widely distributed, fragmented and available to serve a considerable diversity of distinct and often conflicting interests. The event approach and methodology reveal a *pluralist* society. Reputationalist methods of measurement, on the other hand, tend to reveal power as being relatively concentrated, monolithic and coherent. They point to the existence of an *elitist* society. Since many people have prior inclinations either to defend or to criticize the existing state of society, and since, in the context of the debate, it is easier to defend a pluralist society and easier to criticize an elitist one, there is a natural temptation to select the method of measuring power that produces the result one prefers. For the critic this is the reputational method, yielding an elitist society to denounce and decry; for the defender it is the event method, yielding a pluralist society with its modest benefits.

Everyone would agree, nonetheless, that where there are two indicators of power and hence two distinct methods of measuring its distribution, and where the two methods give widely divergent results, both cannot be right. This is why there has been controversy between the advocates of the reputational and the event approaches: one approach must be better than the other and there is a need to ascertain which. Such an ascertainment, however, cannot look merely at the internal consistency, the technical details, the precision of the alternatives. It must appraise them in terms of their *validity as measures of power*, which means relating them in some way to that which they 'indicate' – power 'itself'. If this is not a possibility then it is pointless to term the alternatives 'indicators' at all: the reputational and event approaches are then nothing more than conflicting methods of myth-creation to be chosen between according to taste.[9] What is curious about the controversy concerning the measurement of power is that participants have treated it as a genuine controversy wherein at least one position is simply incorrect, and yet studiously avoided the only route to a resolution of the controversy as so conceived – an attempt at an analysis of the nature of power itself. Even the pressures of debate and disputation have failed to deflect participants from their exclusive concern with the effects of power, and to overcome their dogged lack of interest in the causes of those effects.

In summary, then, the mainstream tradition of sociological research and analysis clearly indicates the importance of obtaining an understanding of the nature of power in society, but it contributes nothing to the generation of such an understanding. It has much to say about the consequences of power, but nothing to say about power. Thus, in so far as the purposes of this book are concerned, the mainstream of research has little to offer. Common sense accounts of power are more suggestive than careful sociological definitions. Common sense means of identifying power are more interesting than systematic sociological methods of measurement. Sociological refinement threatens actually to refine away the guts of the common sense concept.

1.3   A THEORY OF POWER

Although attempts to define and to measure power have generally managed to avoid analysis of what it is and what its basis is, these questions have not been entirely ignored. Theorists in many different traditions have contributed invaluable insights which advance our understanding of the nature of power in society (Lukes, 1986). Such insights, however, remain fragmentary. There has been no sustained, systematic, concerted attempt to elucidate the nature of power. Thus the brief account sketched by Talcott Parsons in the 1960s remains one of the most important sources for sociologists with an interest in the subject.[10] It will be worthwhile to spend some time looking at Parsons's ideas. This will help us to identify some of the general features which any theory of power must possess, and to understand how a theory of power must itself be based on a more general theory of the nature of social order. There are, in addition, a number of specific insights in Parsons's account that have their own intrinsic interest.[11]

Parsons's concern is with the nature of power, not at all with its effects. Hence, he is unwilling to treat power as *anything* that produces compliance, or as *anything* that increases the probability of compliance, whatever its basis. He proceeds on the assumption that social power is just one specific kind of thing, which must be identified and described. Other things may occasionally have the same effects as social power, but sameness of effect does not mean sameness of nature, and such things should be distinguished from social power itself. This change in orientation is rather like that which occurs in medicine when a disease originally defined by symptoms (effects) becomes redefined in terms of its nature (the causes of the effects). Thus, a fever, originally considered as a grossly overheated state with quickened pulse and bodily agitation, became redefined as an *infection* which gave rise to overheating, quickened pulse and agitation. Such a redefinition represented a more developed theoretical understanding of the nature of fevers (involving theoretical entities and processes: bacteria, viruses, infection, contagion and so forth), but it also required some 'feverish' conditions to be set aside and considered separately. Sunstroke and heat-stroke, for example, originally authentic fevers when fevers were defined in terms of symptoms, could no longer be considered fevers when fevers were redefined as conditions caused by infections. It was then necessary to say that fevers were infections, and that the symptoms of infection could sometimes be produced by other kinds of things, like the sun. Different kinds of things, stroke and fever, could have the same symptoms.

For Parsons, then, power is a kind of thing, not anything at all with a specific kind of effect. Parsons's conception of power is much narrower than either the common sense conception or the sociological conceptions so far discussed. He seeks to 'treat power as a *specific* mechanism operating to bring about changes in the action of other units, individual or collective, in the processes of social interaction' (1967, p. 299). He assumes that this 'specific mechanism' operates, in modern societies, predominantly in the 'political sub-system': it is the mechanism that sustains *political power*, and generates those phenomena conventionally associated with political power. To put it another way, most of the phenomena that we conventionally regard as manifestations of political power are, according to Parsons, generated by one 'specific mechanism' operating within the political subsystem of society. Obtaining an understanding of the nature of political power is very largely a matter of identifying and describing the nature of this mechanism.

This is a very well conceived line of thought. If such a mechanism could be described it would add greatly to our understanding of social processes, just as the identification of a mechanism underlying most fevers added greatly to our understanding of bodily processes. The comparison with medicine illustrates very effectively the potential value of such a speculative, theoretically oriented way of thinking. But it must be remembered too that such thinking is very difficult to appraise in terms of its implications at the level of visible phenomena. One cannot expect to see a mechanism generating manifestations of power, just as one could not expect to see bacteria generating calories when the infection theory of fevers developed. The comparison suggests that one should be tolerant when appraising speculations about underlying mechanisms, whilst at the same time retaining a healthy scepticism about their status: slow to believe yet slow to reject would seem to be the best kind of evaluative strategy.

Power and money

How then does Parsons actually seek to understand political power? What is his theory of its underlying nature? Parsons proceeds by analogy. Power exists in the political system, he says, like *money* exists in the economic system. Just as money is a circulating medium that facilitates economic transactions, so power is a circulating medium that facilitates political transactions. Just as the possession of money gives one a generalized capacity to secure any of great numbers and kinds of goods and services, so the possession of power gives one a generalized capacity to secure the performance of any of great numbers and kinds of political obligations. Indeed, for Parsons, power *is* a generalized capacity to secure the performance of political obligations:

> Power then is generalised capacity to secure the performance of binding obligations by units in a system of collective organisation when the obligations are legitimised with reference to their bearing on collective goals, and where in case of recalcitrance there is a presumption of enforcement by negative situational sanctions – whatever the actual agency of that enforcement. (1967, p. 308)[12]

Again, Parsons's approach is well conceived. By treating power as analogous to money he relates the puzzling realm of political phenomena to what he regards as the much less puzzling realm of economic phenomena. He uses a familiar and reasonably well understood system, the economy, as a model in terms of which to explain the operation of a much less well understood system, the polity. This is precisely what successful attempts at systematic theoretical explanation do: they subsume the puzzling and opaque to the familiar and well understood by a process of modelling (Hesse, 1974). The familiar system provides a pattern which is projected upon the puzzling system, and used to order it and make it intelligible as structured and organized. If the pattern proves useful in the new context, then it will continue in use. The puzzling system will be described and indeed perceived in a new way, and may be considered to be 'explained' or 'understood' by virtue of the new description and perception. Let us see then how far Parsons is able to make phenomena associated with power less puzzling and better understood by analogy with familiar patterns of monetary exchange.[13]

Consider first the origins of money. Initially monetary metal is used as a medium of exchange. Such metal has its own real value as a commodity; there is general confidence in that value and monetary transactions accordingly have much of the nature of barter, wherein one intrinsically valuable good is exchanged for another. But eventually money extends beyond monetary metal, which merely acts as an underlying reserve for paper promissory notes worthless in themselves. Great amounts of paper money may be circulated, backed by but a small quantity of metal. It is indeed conceivable that at a certain point the reassurance of monetary metal may be dispensed with altogether, and the currency made wholly of paper, wholly without intrinsic worth. Such a paper currency makes an extraordinarily effective and sophisticated economic instrument, capable of lubricating highly elaborate transactions between large numbers of parties. But as such currency lacks intrinsic worth and any worth actually imputed to it is purely symbolic or conventional, the functioning of the currency must necessarily depend upon the existence of institutionalized confidence in the monetary system. Without such confidence a purely symbolic medium of exchange cannot continue to function.

Now imagine a political system wherein there exist generalized means of enforcing compliance – means of coercion involving the use of physical violence and brute force. Such means may be thought of as the analogues of monetary metal. They represent a real capacity to apply negative sanctions to others to secure the performance of obligations, and may hence rightly be trusted and treated as valuable sources of power. But power is readily extended beyond those directly in possession of coercive resources, which resources merely become a reserve, a last resort, available to all those much larger numbers of people symbolically designated as power-holders. Great amounts of symbolic power may be underpinned with but a small quantity of coercive resources. Such symbolic power may serve as a sophisticated political instrument lubricating elaborate political transactions, just as paper money lubricates economic transactions. But being purely symbolic the utility of such power depends wholly upon institutionalized confidence in the power system and this, says Parsons, depends upon its being imbued with legitimacy. Legitimacy in the political system is a strict analogue of confidence in the monetary system, and legitimacy is therefore to be considered an *essential* aspect of the possession of social power.

Already we can feel the rich suggestiveness of Parsons's analogy. Intuitively, we recognize the complexity of systems of power. Parsons points out how such complexity requires a symbolic ordering, shows how such an ordering may stand upon a much simpler and cruder system of coercion, and notes how the ordering must command confidence, or, as he puts it, be invested with legitimacy, if it is to continue to exist. The analogy immediately prompts us to ask what happens if confidence is forfeited. And a possible answer is immediately suggested: just as loss of confidence forces economies back upon gold and monetary metal, so it forces a polity back upon the expedient of direct coercion and the use of violence.

If we turn now from the origins of money to the manner of its routine use a whole range of further analogies suggest themselves. Think of the way that money simplifies and increases the efficiency of economic transactions. Every economy, whether it possesses money or not, can be said to involve a supply of goods and a demand for goods from consumers. But without money demand may express itself very ineffectively, with potential consumers and potential suppliers unable to find ready partners for profitable barter exchanges. Money permits exchange to be organized efficiently, so efficiently that its existence may transform by an order of magnitude the actual benefits gained from a given supply of goods, even before it stimulates increases in productivity and the formulation of new wants and needs. Similarly, every polity may be thought of as seeking to further the interests of various groups and alliances within itself, and as possessing, in the form of members' obligations to the collectivity, a supply of resources available for the task. Here power permits members' obligations to be organized and coupled efficiently to the furtherance of interests, and thereby greatly increases the effectiveness of the polity in fulfilling goals and objectives. Ordered groups of decision-makers in possession of power – the generalized capacity to call upon obligations and secure their performance – may greatly increase the efficiency of political action in comparison with what could be achieved by so many autonomous individuals.

Perhaps the most striking of all the analogies developed by Parsons is that of the 'power bank'. Consider first how the banking system in a modern economy operates to increase the supply of credit. A depositor may place a sum of money in a bank and retain the right to withdraw it upon demand. But despite accepting this binding commitment to the depositor the bank will nonetheless lend on the money at interest, making it available to be used by a borrower over a given period of time. Effectively, over this period of time, the money is possessed by two persons and facilitates the actions of both. The initial depositor may spend in the knowledge that he possesses his deposit, available on demand. The borrower may spend the borrowed money to meet a need. Thus, in an economy with an excess supply of goods the excess may be taken up; in an equilibrated economy a demand-led expansion of the supply of goods may be secured. The bank, by over-committing itself, compensates for under-commitment in the use of money on the part of its depositors. The depositors' caution is compensated by the bank's daring. The bank makes itself notionally insolvent to make money work harder, but that notional insolvency rarely becomes actual because its depositors very rarely systematically abandon their disposition to under-use their money: there is rarely a concerted run on the bank.[14] Thus, in its normal routine operation, the bank may be said to serve the interests of all participants; depositors, borrowers and shareholders in the bank itself. Its existence leads to the production of extra economic output which more than covers the costs of its operation and its dividends: it does not take a cut of the economic cake but a cut of an increment which it adds to the economic cake.

How can power be banked in the way that money is banked? Parsons imagines power being banked with political leaders. When leaders are elected, people deposit power with them for a time. Leaders find themselves able to invoke a wide range of political obligations, and able to enforce them, should it be necessary, by means of coercion. This power can be used, or 'loaned on', in the furtherance of objectives decided by the leadership. The leadership will seek to further the interests of those groups which supported it and to which it made promises and commitments, but it will also be able, on occasion, to further additional interests, perhaps for the very long-term common good, perhaps in response to short-term unforeseen developments during its period of office. Certainly, in a collectivity with an excess supply of political resources, imaginative political leaders may deploy a deposit of power so that all of that excess supply is taken up and put to use. In an efficient political system new political interests may be encouraged, and then furthered by an expansion in the supply of political resources. Thus, provided there is continued confidence in the political leadership, analogous to the confidence necessary for the operation of a nominally insolvent bank, the leadership may operate in a way that is in everyone's interests, using power that represents a drain on the resources of no one. The leadership may increase in power simply by expanding the range of obligations it is able to draw upon, and in this way it may allow a collectivity to do more, to achieve more of its ends and objectives in the political sphere, without any corresponding sacrifices or restraints being necessary elsewhere.

This represents a particularly insightful and significant suggestion on Parsons's part, since it is usual to think that an increase in the power of one person must necessarily be obtained at the expense of another. To the extent that one person gains power, we tend to think, another or others must lose it. But Parsons shows that this 'zero-sum' conception of power is far from being the only means of understanding the distribution of power in society, and indeed is unlikely to prove an adequate means in modern societies with differentiated political systems.

Enough has now been said, I think, to indicate the many positive merits and advantages of Parsons's theory, but what of its shortcomings and limitations? It is actually extremely difficult to offer a systematic technical criticism of such a very general and vaguely sketched analogy. It is the kind of suggestion which best reveals its defects, along with its advantages, as it is used and developed by a group of people over a long period. Only in this way could important differences between monetary and political phenomena be expected to emerge; and only in this way could the implications of such differences be properly assessed – whether they were of a kind which required abandonment of the analogy, or merely restrictions in the way it was used. Parsons's analogy has not been developed in this way, so it is only possible to appraise it in very general terms, commenting on the overall implications of the use of the analogy and any fundamental problems that might be involved therein.

Much the most common general criticism of this kind charges Parsons with offering a one-sided and systematically biased vision of power in society. Commentators point to the deliberately restricted scope of Parsons's theory, and relate the restrictions to political concerns and objectives. It is suggested that a broadly conservative political stance leads Parsons to ignore cases of the illegitimate use of power and cases where its legitimate use has adverse consequences. The suggestion is perfectly plausible. Parsons initially developed his views in reaction to those of the radical sociologist C. Wright Mills (1956), and he stressed the legitimacy and the generally beneficial consequences of systems of power as a corrective to Mills's tendency to treat power merely as a source of oppression and exploitation. Just as alternative definitions of power and alternative methods of measuring power have been sustained by opposed political convictions and objectives, so too have alternative theories of power. In the study of power, as in practically every other area of study, sociologists have been unable to differentiate technical explanatory concerns from polemical and propagandist objectives. None of this, however, amounts to significant criticism of Parsons's theory as such.[15] For sociological purposes, its origins, the basis of its present credibility, indeed all factors other than its technical merits, are beside the point. I have already noted the good technical grounds for the deliberately restricted scope of Parsons's theory. These grounds are adequate as a defence against charges of undue narrowness. Anyone who considers that important social phenomena exist beyond the scope of Parsons's account may, after all, move beyond that account and turn their attention to the phenomena in question: nothing in Parsons's account precludes such a move.[16]

Money is part of the problem

A more interesting fundamental criticism of Parsons's analogy concerns the familiar, well understood system which serves as the model for an understanding of power. The monetary system is indeed familiar, but are we entitled to think of it as well understood? Do we really have an adequate understanding of the nature and basis of monetary transactions and of what underpins and sustains money as a circulating medium of exchange? The answer must surely be that we do not. It may well be that our understanding of money exceeds our understanding of political power, and to that extent Parsons's analogy may prove to be richly rewarding to pursue. But it would be a serious mistake to imagine that an account which successfully pressed home that analogy would thereby provide a full understanding and explanation of the nature and basis of power. Money itself is a profoundly puzzling set of phenomena, and everything that is puzzling with regard to money would be puzzling with regard to power after the analogy had been made. Money is not the ideal basis for an explanatory analogy because money itself is something the operation of which has not been satisfactorily explained.

It is easy to overlook the fact that money is something not yet properly understood, because at the everyday level its operation seems obvious and straightforward. But once we think about our everyday operations with money we quickly realize that we carry them out without full awareness of the basis of our actions. Why are we willing to work, or to pass over goods, in return for money? How is it that monetary transactions and exchanges pass off so smoothly, with the parties involved being in perfect agreement on nearly every occasion? What is the basis of the agreement concerning the relationship of different forms of money – not just pounds and dollars, but pounds and pence? These may seem very simple questions, but the answers to them are far from straightforward, and if money is to be used as a basis for the understanding of power, then the answers to these questions will have implications for parallel questions concerning power. Why do we tend to obey powerful agents? Why do transactions in power hierarchies tend to pass off smoothly? How do we recognize different manifestations of power and relate them to one another?

There are further questions to be asked, that concern not just the nature and mode of use of money but the context in which it is used. As Parsons himself rightly emphasizes, money is an array of generalized rights, and circulates in a context of particular narrowly specified rights.

Money represents a generalized capacity to secure goods and services, and serves as an exchange medium in a system of specific capacities to secure goods and services – the rights of property. By analogy, power also represents generalized rights, and circulates in a context of narrowly specified rights. Power is a generalized capacity to secure the performance of political obligations, and serves as an exchange medium in a system of specific capacities to secure the performance of political obligations. Parsons identifies these specific capacities as the rights exercisable by authorities: he treats the existence of authority in the political context as analogous to the existence of property in the economic context.[17]

If we are to understand the use of money, and by analogy the use of power, we must become clear what a right consists in, and why it is that people will respect a right and act more in support of it than against it. But to say that we must understand what a right consists in is tantamount to saying that we must understand the nature of social order itself. Whether we talk of rights and obligations, or of roles and institutions, or of patterned social relationships, the import is much the same: we are talking of a presumed structure and orderliness in social activity, and a need to understand the nature and the basis of such structure and orderliness is implied. Parsons's discussions of the parallels between money and power presume a background of pre-existing social order and serve well to show how a satisfactory understanding of power (and of money) requires a satisfactory understanding of social order. Parsons was perfectly well aware of this but it posed no problem for him. He was in possession of a developed general theory of social order, his own, and throughout his discussion of power he would constantly refer back to this general theory and use it to underpin his more specific claims: he was able to sit his specific theoretical account of power on top of his more general theory of society and social order. For us, however, the problem of social order cannot be solved so simply. We cannot take Parsons's own solution to the problem for granted; it has to be considered and appraised along with alternatives in the light of existing knowledge. This will be the task of the next chapter.

2

SOCIAL ORDER

2.1 HOBBES'S PROBLEM

If power exists in a system of institutions and social relationships, then to understand power we must seek to understand institutions and social relationships, and in particular what it is that makes them to some extent stable and enduring. The problem of the basis of power can only be solved after we have a solution to the more fundamental problem of the basis of order and stability in society. Talcott Parsons's early work seeks to provide precisely this: in his study of *The Structure of Social Action* (1937) he identifies the central problem for sociology as that formulated by Thomas Hobbes in *Leviathan* (1651). Hobbes asked how it could be that people obliged to live in proximity to each other, each involved in the pursuit of their own specific ends and interests, did not rapidly fall into a state of strife, a war of all against all. Parsons attempts to show how in European sociological writings from the late nineteenth century onwards, and notably in the work of Durkheim and Weber, a viable solution to this problem gradually emerged.

Hobbes's problem is not the most fundamental problem that can be posed about social order. It speaks of linguistically competent, knowledgeable individuals: it presumes the existence of meaningful, mutually intelligible interaction and asks why such interaction should be co-operative rather than conflict-ridden, and its forms and patterns persistent rather than transient. One could ask how it is that mutually intelligible interaction is possible in the first place, but Parsons does not regard this more fundamental question as a question about society. People engaged in mutually intelligible exchanges as they randomly rob, rape and murder each other are not engaging in his idea of genuine social behaviour. Societies, for Parsons, are constituted of stable co-operative interactions. Hence, for him, Hobbes's problem is not the small problem of why social life is a little less vicious and nasty than one might expect. It is the large problem of why life is less vicious and nasty than it might be, to the extent that it is worth calling social life. For Parsons, societies are sets of individuals living at artificially low levels of strife compared to what would appertain in a 'state of nature'; and the central problem of sociology is to explain how these levels are achieved. Let us accept for the moment that the problem is a genuine one. Its precise formulation may be open to question but the tendency of people to engage in persisting co-operative interactions does nonetheless demand analysis, and, if possible, explanation.

The failure of individualism

Parsons's first move in *The Structure of Social Action* is to reject individualistic theories of social order. Like Durkheim, indeed through Durkheim, Parsons criticizes the individualistic economic theories of society which had become so widely accepted in the nineteenth century, and seeks to expose them as fundamentally misconceived. Nineteenth-century economists and utilitarians thought of society simply as an aggregate of independent, rational, self-interested individuals. Social interactions between these individuals were so many separate transactions, whereby goods or services were freely exchanged to the mutual benefit of the parties involved. Each party entered a transaction seeking individual gain, that is, in the expectation that an individual end would be secured or an individual objective furthered. Interactions persisted simply because they were rational and profitable, and thus, by definition, society persisted for the same reason.

Parsons makes a number of formal criticisms of this account, and he stresses its empirical inadequacy as a description of social relationships in actual, existing societies. No actual societies are constituted simply as isolated individual transactions, least of all our own. Economic exchange within our society occurs within a legal framework. The validity of a transaction is not merely a matter for the parties involved. In every case it is dependent upon wider considerations: parties must be adult, sane, sober; goods must be legitimate merchandise and so on. Here Parsons makes use of Durkheim's celebrated analysis of the non-contractual element in contracts to highlight how even the simplest of our economic transactions cannot be understood solely by reference to the ends and the rationality of the individuals involved (Durkheim, 1933, ch. 7).

Nor is it merely ourselves and our society which are unintelligible in terms of individualism. No society can be so intelligible. If individual self-interest is to sustain social interaction then individual interests must interlock in a way that encourages co-operative exchange, but any such interlock must be a 'brittle thing which comparatively slight alterations of conditions can shatter at vital points' (Parsons, 1937, p. 404).[1] Happy congruences of self-interest are fortuitous and unstable, and in a society of self-interested individuals they cannot be stabilized by rewards and sanctions:

> The ultimate source of the power behind sanctions is the common sense of moral attachment to norms – and the weaker that becomes, the larger the minority who do not share it, the more precarious is the order in question. . . . A social order resting on interlocking of interests alone, and thus ultimately on sanctions is hence hardly empirically possible . . . the greater the need for sanctions, the weaker the ultimate force behind them. (Parsons, 1937, p. 404)

This remained Parsons's view when he came to write on power many years later and began by explicitly repudiating 'the idea that any political system that rests *entirely* on self-interest, force, or a combination of them, can be stable over any considerable period of time' (Parsons, 1967, p. 265). It is actually because of this fundamental conviction, rather than on empirical grounds, that Parsons rejects individualistic accounts of society and develops his own profoundly sociological analysis of social order.

Unquestionably, Parsons's rejection of all wholly individualistic conceptions of social interaction is correct. Individual exchange transactions are possible, after all, only with goods and rights which are *owned*, and individualism has no account of the institution of *ownership* and the basis of its stability.[2] In individualistic, 'economic' accounts of society, ownership is treated as a given, almost as a natural phenomenon, whereas it is actually a profoundly puzzling and problematic aspect of social order itself. Because of their unreflective dependence on the notion of ownership, 'economic' individualistic accounts of society offer no insights into Hobbes's problem. They proceed at too superficial a level. Far from penetrating to the basis of social order, they merely describe some of the activities which the existence of that order makes possible, and often do so in a way that systematically obscures the nature and the basis of that order.[3]

Individualistic, utilitarian accounts of social life have an initial plausibility. The freely decided, mutually profitable exchanges they describe do have their analogues in our everyday experience. But such exchanges do not and cannot occur against a background provided by 'nature' and nothing more. They can only occur in a world wherein every object has a label attached, a label which states 'This object is the property of . . .'. Individualism offers no account of the provenance of these labels or of the recognition accorded to them. It is as if the labels are tied by the hands of God, and their credibility is sustained by divine power. A fully satisfactory account of the basis of social order must provide a more adequate understanding of the provenance and credibility of these labels.[4]

Norms as explanations

Parsons's own attack upon the social order problem presupposes that a society of independent, self-interested agents would rapidly degenerate into chaos and strife. Some additional constraint upon human action is required, in addition to individual calculations of interest, if harmonious social interactions are to persist. Of the infinite number of ways of acting which a heap of individuals might manifest there is a subset, still infinite but bounded, of ways which are recognizably and persistently patterned and orderly. When a heap comes to act in one of these ways it may be described in Parsons's terminology as a 'functioning social system'. Functioning social systems exist as empirical phenomena. But actions in functioning social systems are not the actions that individuals would perform out of natural inclination. It is necessary to identify what it is which ensures that such actions actually are performed. This is Hobbes's problem in Parsons's formulation.[5]

His solution to the problem is based upon the presumed amenability of individuals to socialization, and on a particular theory of the nature of socialization. In the course of socialization, values, rules and norms are imparted: certain human ends may be specified as right and proper; certain means to ends may be specified as appropriate and legitimate. Suppose that values, rules and norms defining stable harmonious inter-action are *internalized* or *introjected*. Suppose that they become part of the very self of the socialized agent, so that he acts out of inclination along lines that are normatively indicated, to obtain individual desires which are normatively desirable. If this indeed happens, then natural inclinations and individual calculative reasoning may be outweighed by normatively specified inclinations and normatively constrained modes of inference. Human nature may be reconstructed from without, so that the clashing natural proclivities of isolated egoistic individuals cease to be a cause of anxiety.

If this conception of socialization is correct then Hobbes's problem is almost solved. It only remains to ask how the norms that agents internalize actually come to be strife-reducing norms that encourage persisting orderly activity. Here we can think in terms of historical development and long-term evolutionary change. Where norms actually enjoin strife, disruption and chaos, the norms themselves will disappear in the chaos; but where they enjoin stable, self-reproducing activity the norms themselves will persist with that activity. Thus, even if functioning social systems appear in the flux of action but rarely and unpredictably, once in existence they will tend to remain in existence as self-perpetuating entities. Hence the flux of action, over time, crystallizes into functioning social systems and every extant society stands as a crystal of persisting patterned action, a distinct solution to Hobbes's problem, a particular normative order.

Needless to say, Parsons's treatment of societies as normative orders and socialization as the introjection of norms has been immensely influential. It has inspired study after study wherein specific social actions are explained by reference to specific norms and overall social stability is explained by reference to the coherence of the whole system of norms. There is much of value and interest in this literature, but also a certain amount to regret. Increasingly, writers came to apply 'normative determinism' with inadequate care and sophistication. For some it became little more than a catch-all, sense-making system, routinely applicable in any and all circumstances, a sedative for curiosity and a substitute for thought: where patterns of action were stable it was said to be because 'the norms' were stable; where they were changing it was said to be because 'the norms' were changing; where they were lapsing into chaos and disorder it was said to be because 'the norms' were breaking down. The functionalist sociology inspired by Parsons consequently failed to sustain a genuine curiosity about the nature of social norms and their status as explanations of action. And the aspect of his work of immediate concern to us here – Parsons's fascinating and original conception of power as normatively defined and normatively underpinned – was never adequately explored, criticized and developed from a theoretical point of view.

Let us recall and reflect upon Parsons's theory of power. In describing power he describes aspects of a larger system of norms. Normatively specified holders of power apply or threaten to apply sanctions as norms allow, to mobilize binding obligations they are normatively entitled to call upon in normatively appropriate circumstances. The ultimate point of reference in seeking to understand whatever is legitimately being done, and why people are doing it, is 'the norms'. The basis of social power is the same as the basis of social order generally; its exercise is underpinned by what underpins every legitimately exercised right – the system of norms. Powers are specified in terms of particular norms and accepted because they are so specified. The explanation of their acceptance is a socialization process wherein particular norms are internalized and become determinants of actions. The explanation of the existence of these norms, amongst all the various norms which are internalized, is the contribution that they make to the overall normative order as the basis of a functioning social system.

The failure of normative determinism

Clearly, if Parsons had been correct in his account of how norms are internalized and how they thereby come to determine action, then the basis and nature of power would have been revealed and established: the fundamental questions addressed by this book would have found their answer. Unfortunately, Parsons was not correct. Over the years it has become increasingly clear that although norms may rightly be claimed to exist in all societies, and all societies may indeed plausibly be described as normative orders, it is nonetheless untenable to *explain* social order by reference to *internalized* norms and the psychological constraints they impose upon the socialized individual. If norms are to *determine* actions in this way, so that social order emerges primarily from the activity of so many internally constrained individuals, then first of all every genuinely social action must be constrained or conditioned by norms, and may count as *social* action only to the extent that it is so constrained or conditioned. Secondly, norms and values, in order to constrain or condition action, must be implanted securely within the individual mind. Finally, norms and values must have clear and unambiguous implications for action: norms must press individuals to specific, clear-cut forms of action, and press separate individuals alike to the same forms of action. These are the minimum requirements if a normative determinism of the kind advocated by Parsons is to be viable, and they cannot be met.

The unrealistic nature of the first requirement has long been recognized. It is implicit in one of the oldest criticisms of Parsons – that he fails to account for deviance and for social change. The criticism here is not, of course, that Parsons overlooks deviation from norms or fails to state why such deviance occurs. On the contrary, he recognizes that deviance is ubiquitous, and actually requires it as a part of his theory. Parsons is a critic of the view that actions simply flow or emanate from norms. He is not an idealist. He recognizes that an internalized norm is not a *sufficient* cause of conforming actions, but merely produces an inclination to conformity. Such an inclination may not result in actual conformity: actual conformity may be technically impossible, or the individual may be subject to conflicting inclinations, including egoistic desires and interests. Because individuals may be inclined to depart from the norms they have internalized, and also because in all societies there are individuals who have failed to internalize the norms, socialization has to be reinforced by a system of sanctions and rewards serving as a supplementary source of pressure to conformity.[6] A moderately successful but necessarily incomplete socialization process plus a supplementary system of social control is considered enough of an offset to individual interest and natural inclination to solve Hobbes's problem, but not enough to produce so many socialized automata.

The real trouble with Parsons's account is that it fails to account for deviance and social change as the systematically ordered, patterned and persistent forms of authentically social activity which they manifestly are. The social, even the socially ordered, is demarcated too narrowly. Whole classes of social actions are incorrectly consigned to the residual category of 'egoism'. Patterned harmonious social interactions, merely because they are innovative or deviant, are set outside the domain of the theory which is supposed to explain such interactions. Consequently, social order is constantly springing into being beyond the pale of Parsons's sociology.

The undue restrictiveness of Parsons's conception of 'the social' has unfortunate consequences throughout his work and does not merely vitiate his treatment of deviance and change. Even his basic exposition of standard, routine social interaction is undermined. Think of the complexity and the rich detail of social interaction as it actually exists around us. Clearly every last detail of every last action cannot be specified by norm or rule. The rule-books would overstock any library and take more than a lifetime to read. Yet, on the other hand, it is difficult to accept that a normative order merely sets rough-and-ready limits on actions and leaves vast areas within those limits to be decided by egoistic rational calculation or by random individual eccentricity. Think of a string quartet giving a polished interpretation of a standard work.[7] Every nuance of every part will be crafted to blend with every other in some inimitable way that makes the style of the quartet recognizable, its total effect an overall pleasure and a source of insight. Here is a paradigm of co-operative *social* action, beyond dispute. But where are the norms for the nuances? Conceivably such norms might exist on the night of a concert, the *product* of earlier co-operation; but where were they at the first rehearsal? Even if they are considered actually to exist, can it really be held that they specify the whole of the social component of the performance? Social interaction here demands to be understood in ways which go quite beyond the citation of norms: it is created and maintained without normative determination. But this must mean at the very least that Parsons's conception of the social is insufficient, even if we should not yet wish to say that it is altogether incorrect.

Let us now consider the second requirement for normative determinism. Whatever else, if Parsons's account is to stand, norms and values must have some degree of fixity once they are internalized, some amount of resistance to removal or dissolution, some tendency to stick in the head. Socialized agents must lack some degree of discretion in relation to their norms and values: if these could be taken up and cast away at whim, if agents could pick and choose whether to follow them and how, without any inner constraint, then the explanatory role of norms would cease to exist as Parsons understands it.

Once again the sociological tradition has long contained findings and arguments which can be set against this requirement. In particular, the empirical studies of symbolic interactionist sociologists have revealed the comparative ease with which individuals may be 'resocialized', the willingness with which they will transfer not just from one set of routine practices to another but from one set of professed norms and values to another, if circumstances encourage it. Howard Becker, an outstanding exponent of the symbolic interactionist approach, argues that the apparent existence of a visibly stable distribution of norms and values in society is the product of stable *contexts* of action, not of stable individual value-orientations or personalities (Becker, 1964). As individuals move from one context to another, says Becker, they may be observed shedding old values and adopting new, more situationally appropriate ones. The conversion is rarely difficult. On entering prison, first offenders orientate themselves to prison values, quite the opposite of the fundamental values enjoined and accepted in the wider society. As their release date nears, a swing back to the values of the outside world begins. Adolescents, similarly, enter deviant subcultures celebrating values blatantly opposed to those of the social mainstream. But they easily reassimilate into that mainstream at the appropriate time. Members of the learned professions are trained to conform to lofty ideals and demanding standards of good work, but rapidly adjust to the mundane realities of actual practice once they are qualified, and to a normative order and general ethos that reflects those mundane realities.

Given the extent of human ingenuity it would be unwise to claim that there is no way of reconciling normative determinism with materials of this kind. But it is nonetheless hard to understand how norms may serve as contributory causes of action through the internal constraint they exert upon the individual, and yet be internalized so superficially that they may readily be set aside or replaced at every level.

In recent years criticism of normative determinism has moved to the problem of how 'implications' can be derived from norms. The whole idea that a norm or a value may of itself specify or imply a particular action in a particular context has been called into question, and this is precisely the third requirement for normative determinism.

Consider a norm or a value existing entirely separately of all of the particular actions which, allegedly, it implies.[8] What does such a 'separated' norm or value look like? How is it internalized? Presumably it can only exist, and only be introjected into the mind, as a verbal formulation, a maxim, or a principle, or an aphorism. But how can particular implications be drawn out of such a formulation? The answer is that they cannot be. There is no 'inside' out of which to draw implications. Nor does such a formulation come like an electrical appliance, with an instruction book attached indicating how it is properly to be used. In isolation, the verbal formulation of a norm or a value is a mere jumble of meaningless symbols, an uninterpreted formalism awaiting interpretation. It is devoid of implications of any kind.[9]

To have content a norm must be learned in conjunction with actual examples of its application.[10] It must be learned as a stream of such examples. Then conformity to the norm is a matter of acting in proper analogy with previous actions which are accepted examples of conformity to the norm. Not even in the case of a well-exemplified norm, however, is it possible to speak of its 'logical' implications. No set of examples of a norm, however extensive, however carefully selected, however clear-cut, can serve logically to determine the import of the norm for the next case. Human experience and human activity is richly detailed, endlessly complex, elaborately embedded into a similarly rich and complex context. Every example of a norm both resembles yet differs from every other; every next case resembles yet differs in some way from every previous case. It is always possible, in a given case, to assimilate a new instance to a rule or norm by analogy with existing examples, but equally it is always possible to resist such assimilation by emphasizing its uniqueness and citing differences between it and existing examples. At the level of logic and explicit interpretation, 'No course of action could be determined by a rule because every course of action can be made to accord with the rule' (Wittgenstein, 1968, 201, p. 81). In a strictly logical sense norms cannot have implications.[11]

Most of the time, of course, people do find themselves able, routinely, and in agreement with each other, to identify cases of conformity and deviance from norms, cases where rules are being followed and cases where they are not. Children taught to add by rote and example may continue to add, solving entirely new problems involving previously unseen numbers, routinely, without hesitation, and in perfect agreement one with another: what is to count as proper addition may be clear and agreed by all; the difference between fair financial transactions and short-changing may be similarly agreed in all actual cases. Similarly, people may learn by example to distinguish males and females: such distinctions may then be made routinely, without hesitation, time after time, with everyone in perfect concord with everyone else, with no problems ever, as a matter of fact, arising.[12]

Cases where the blind, unreflective following of rules or norms produces agreement in practice in a community encourage the notion that norms have logical implications. Accordingly it is important to

remember other cases where the following of norms engenders disagreement. Learned judges interpret laws in terms of precedents, long series of
specific examples of particular applications of the laws. But learned
judges are liable to disagree on the next case and to be forced into
majority verdicts.[13] Nor, in the main run of such cases, can divided
opinion be attributed to the incipient senility of some of the individuals
involved, although of course many particular cases may well be intelligible
in these terms. Ministers of the Crown refer extensively to precedent and
example in seeking to ascertain what they may legitimately decide
independently and what requires legislation. But precedent is frequently
unclear and its 'implications' may be fiercely contested before an agreed
or a dominant interpretation is eventually established.

When the members of a society follow a norm they act in concert to
sustain and extend an analogy. Further actions designed to conform to a
norm are modelled on existing actions recognized already as conforming
to the norm. Existing practice guides future practice. But 'guidance' here
is not 'logical determination'. Existing practice *suggests* future practice:
that is all. If existing practice in following a norm suggests a different
future practice to different individual members of society, to the extent
that individuals develop analogies in systematically different directions,
then society ceases to be sustained. If existing practice moves members
alike, if most individuals extend analogies in practical agreement with
each other, then society may persist. In this case it is the actual, manifest
agreement in practice that is turned to, in order to define 'what the norm
really implies', what counts as following it *correctly*. In this sense, the
norm is necessarily and irreducibly a *public* entity not a *private* one; it
exists as agreement in practice not as an instruction in an individual
mind.[14]

When an individual seeks to follow a norm, 'the norm itself' cannot
tell him what to do. Suppose that the individual experiences an 'inner
voice', an internal prompting coming from 'the norm'. He still cannot
know that his voice speaks truly, that the action it recommends is the
'correct' one. Only the response of other people will establish whether or
not he acts correctly in relation to the norm.

To follow a norm is not to follow instructions in the manner of a pro-
grammed automaton. Nor is it to yield to some inner feeling or urge or
emotional disturbance emanating, as it were, from the norm.[15] It is to
continue with existing public practice. At times, what counts as
continuing that practice will initially be perceived differently by different
individuals: their immediate, blind, unhesitating moves will not be the
same; their first spontaneous attempts to follow a norm will clash. At
such a time, if individuals were constrained internally by whatever
happened to strike them as 'the' implication of a norm, there would be

chaos in cognition and conflict at the level of action. Far from a war of everyone against everyone being prevented, it would be instigated. The reason that such wars do not break out (when they do not) is precisely that people are *not* constrained internally by norms, and are able to adjust their judgements and their actions into closer alignment if they choose.[16] Social stability requires that the normative order is *not* internalized, so that continuing active mutual adjustment and development of norms may occur. The existence of social stability is a pointer of the *essentially public* nature of norms.

Norms as objects of cognition

In summary then, none of the three fundamental requirements for normative determinism is fulfilled by the actual empirical characteristics of social action itself. Social action is not coextensive with normatively contrained action; it extends beyond it. Norms and values are not implanted stably in individual minds; they persist in the public realm not the private, the social context not the individual psyche. Norms and values have no inherent implications which enforce and sustain a social order; on the contrary they are provided with implications by interacting human beings, so that what norms imply can in no sense explain how people interact. Accordingly, we can conclude, without equivocation or qualification, that normative determinism fails. And with its failure Parsons's theory of power, for all its deep interest and its embodiment of so many of the desirable features of a good theory, must be recognized as a failure too, for the theory of power rests upon and relies upon the more fundamental Parsonian theory of social order and stands or falls with it.

Needless to say the formal failure of a theory does not make it value-less. Both Parsons's specific theory of power and his general account of social order continue to be richly suggestive. In particular, he rightly emphasizes the central importance of norms and rules in the context of social life. Only the priority given to the process of internalization or introjection is fundamentally misconceived, and the consequent inference that individuals are internally constrained by norms. It remains legitimate, when this fundamental mistake is set on one side, to continue to refer to normative order. People in all societies do, as a matter of fact, understand some actions to be in accord with norms or rules and others to be in conflict with them, and they do this, much of the time, in substantial agreement with each other.[17] They may not be internally coerced by norms, but they reveal an awareness of norms and a readiness to take account of norms. In all societies members have knowledge of a normative order. Indeed if we remove the coercive, internalized element from a normative order we leave it precisely as an aspect of members' knowledge. The normative order becomes a *distribution of knowledge*, and it continues as a distribution of knowledge so long as members remain in agreement on what norms routinely imply. This is agreement at the level of *understanding*, agreement in how we initially, unreflectively, automatically, make connections between norms and specific actions.

Unfortunately, agreement at the level of understanding does not directly imply harmony and stability at every level of action: for this it seems that something more must be needed. If individuals are simply *aware* of norms rather than *bound* by them, they may choose to conform with the practice of others, true, but equally they may choose to deviate from that practice, or oppose it, or ignore it. Only a degree of conformity at the level of action solves Hobbes's problem and the fact that there is a shared awareness of norms, that norms exist as a part of members' knowledge, does not on the face of it explain persisting conformity. This is precisely why Parsons asserts that internalization is necessary and imbues norms themselves, as it were, with the power to constrain action.

Since Parsons is incorrect here, and since there is no alternative account of comparable generality, there is a widely recognized need for a theory of social order that does not rely upon internalization, a theory which solves or dissolves Hobbes's problem by an analysis of systems of reflectively aware human action. In what follows I try to show that there is every chance, eventually, of meeting this need. I argue that social order is constituted of calculative action and that all we need to refer to in order to make it intelligible is the basic characteristics of human beings generally and the knowledge carried by those human beings who constitute the order. Needless to say, I do not claim to make the case conclusively in what follows, but I hope to make it sufficiently well to justify an analysis of power which attaches no fundamental significance to internal normative constraint.

2.2 SOCIAL ORDER AS COGNITIVE ORDER

Social interaction cannot be explained solely by reference to the interests and the reasoning-power of independent individuals, and the natural environment in which they exist. But Parsons moved altogether too quickly from this valid conclusion into a search for internal constraints upon the egoism of individuals.[18] He did not dwell long enough upon the public context wherein action and interaction occurs, or upon the inherited knowledge and culture which everyone learns and which thereby becomes the collective possession of all members of a given society. In his reformulation of Hobbes's problem he presumed the existence of shared knowledge and aligned understandings and passed on immediately to consider the problem of order in terms of actions. But shared knowledge and aligned understandings are themselves social phenomena generated by social processes, and the fact that they are achieved and sustained in itself constitutes a problem of social order. It will not do to treat learning and 'socialization' as mere preliminaries to social action; they must be looked at as authentic social activities in their own right.

Reformulating the social order problem

Parsons's account of child socialization involves the social being, as it were, injected into the individual. Enter baby; and the rush is on to get him socialized before he is big enough and strong enough to embark upon a career of pillage, rapine and murder. Unfortunate egoistic tendencies have to be subordinated to social rules and standards. But, from the start, baby gives clear evidence of being far more than a mass of seething egoism. He is a voracious learner, and in learning is trusting, co-operative, sensitive to signs of approval and disapproval, and as keen on the one as he is averse to the other. These characteristics are not mere products of socialization; they are exploited from the beginning in teaching the child, and are of particular importance in the process of language acquisition, well before the child is able to interpret norms and rules as verbal formulations.

No doubt innate competences and propensities are implicated in the acquisition of language: there is a good deal of evidence to suggest that the child is preprogrammed for language-learning (Richards, 1974). Nonetheless, we should not think of the process simply and solely as an automatic operation, carried out by special circuitry somewhere deep in the brain. The initial process of language-learning is invariably also a process of becoming a member of some collectivity and becoming recognized by others as a member. No first language is ever learned save as part of the business of becoming such a member; linguistic competence is always first developed as part of the routine competence necessary to perform as a member of some social unit. Learning the language involves trusting members of the social unit, participating in the activities of the unit, and actually taking successful participation as a criterion of successful language-use. Learning the language is becoming involved in collective life: continuing to learn the language is accepting and valuing the implied involvement in collective life. From the very start therefore, we tend to orientate ourselves as a part of a larger unit and to seek and value participation in the routine practices of such a unit (Vygotsky, 1962).

What is true of language-learning is true of the initial learning of knowledge and competence generally. Trust and co-operation are manifest, and the quest for standing as a competent member in the relevant context. In the acquisition of language and in the acquisition of knowledge, the child reveals an inherent sociability. This sociability is essential; verbally mediated learning would be impossible in its absence. The interactions that constitute learning are *social* interactions: social interaction exists prior to 'socialization' and is not the pure product of it. Interaction is social from the start.

From the start, also, in the learning of language and the acquisition of knowledge and competence, there is an inherent tendency to habituation of response and routinization of perception, and a corresponding tendency to presume similar habituation and routinization in the responses and perceptions of others. Without these tendencies being present from the very start it would be impossible for the individual terms or signifiers of a language to be learned, and the acquisition of practically applicable bodies of knowledge would be prevented. 'Social-ized', competent individuals can and do turn upon habituated, routinized responses, evaluate them, override them, discard them; but a prior tendency to habituation and routinization is nonetheless essential.

In the first instance, the child learns language trustingly and co-operatively; his linguistic responses become habituated and routinized in the ways already established in the community of which he is becoming a member.[19] He learns the everyday verbally formulated knowledge of the community in the same way, with corresponding habituation and routi-nization of inference and perception. He acquires technical skills and competences in the same way with corresponding habituation and routi-nization of behaviour. In the first instance, the child seeks to imitate and emulate what goes on around him, and in particular the routine com-petences and ways of acting of those individuals who constitute an enduring presence in his environment and upon whom he is accustomed to rely. It must surely be unsound to assume that all these prior tendencies suddenly switch off at some point, when childhood ceases, so that people abruptly become unrestrained egoists and a social order problem suddenly looms.

Clearly it is a mistake to ask what must be added to human nature to transform people from calculative egoists to conforming social actors. People can only *become* calculative, knowledgeable individuals, capable of formulating their own ends and planning their own fate, as they become members with a place in a social unit. If individual ends and interests threaten social order, therefore, they do so only as emergent features of the social order itself.[20] Social forms are prior to any and all egoistically oriented reflection upon them. The routine activities of social life are the setting within which individuation occurs and concern with self finds expression, to whatever extent it does find expression. The question is whether and why routines persist as those who execute them become aware of them, and of themselves in relation to them.

This is the social order problem satisfactorily formulated. We only need to ask what keeps the actions of calculative individuals from becoming intolerably at variance with an existing routine practice in existing social situations wherein they have standing. Given that people often have something to lose by deviance or innovation in such pre-structured situations, that their attempts to advance self may adversely affect others and call forth retaliation from others, that the existing situation may itself be precious to the individual and a source of continuing satisfaction, there is no shortage of resources available to account for calculative conformity and no evident need to appeal to internalization and the inner prompting of norms.

A sketch of a solution

An individual may be knowledgeable and calculative, yet the knowledge he possesses and the scheme of calculation he employs will be those of his society, and the calculations he makes will be social actions, the actions of someone who accepts and trusts a given system of routines. Such calculation itself represents a kind of conformity, and is simply unintelligible as the outcome of a purely egoistic orientation. The knowledgeable individual chooses between socially available actions according to a socially shaped judgement. He trusts socially accepted knowledge and employs socially recommended competences in identifying the courses of action which best serve his ends or interests. Even his individual ends and interests are conceptualized in socially defined ways, and are possessed by the individual only by virtue of his standing as a member with rights in a social order. There is no reason to suppose that any 'interlock' of ends and interests of this kind, constituted by interdependent calculations all based upon a single shared body of knowledge, must necessarily always be 'a brittle thing'.

Complete individuation probably never occurs empirically: individuals never become entirely devoted to self-interest and fully reflectively aware, self-monitoring and consciously calculative at every instant as they go about furthering it. But let us assume this very thing as a worst-case scenario. Could systems of routine persist in circumstances of this kind? Might the routine course of action still more often than not be the preferred course of action, so that routine is reconstituted in action and the system of routines persists? If so, then the social order problem is always soluble in principle without internalization.

What does persistence of this kind entail? First of all, it is necessary that every involved individual who considers his own actions in isolation should usually find routine actions to be his preferred actions: given his knowledge of what others are doing and of how others will routinely respond to what he does, he must, more often than not, decide in favour of routine. Secondly, and more problematically, there should be no obvious, readily negotiated, concerted variation from routine by just a very few individuals which would profit those individuals more than routine itself: if such a possibility existed then no doubt it would be exploited and the situation would be seen to change. This is a less clearcut requirement than the first, since one is led to ask how many individuals are a few and what kind of variation is readily negotiable. Let us leave these questions hanging for the moment. Roughly speaking, we can say that the more difficult variant activity is to organize, and the more individuals are involved, the greater must be the perceived gain and the more secure the calculations that indicate its existence, if variation is to occur. Beyond a certain point, organized variation from routine and reliable calculation of its consequences very rapidly become massively difficult: if there is no obvious advantage in simple variation by just small numbers of individuals, then a situation will have at least some short-term tendency to persist – which is enough. There is no need to show how situations might persist for ever, since they never do.

One happy consequence of approaching the social order problem in this way is that language and cognition may be put on a par with action. Routine speech-acts and acts of inference and calculation may be treated as typical social actions, and the question of their stability and persistence may be raised. What happens when linguistic routines become objects of reflective awareness? Is there a threat of chaos and disorder at the level of language, of Babel supplanting ordered communication? The very suggestion is ludicrous; it stimulates amusement more than curiosity. But why is this? The question concerns a genuine empirical possibility: why do we intuitively recognize it as unrealistic and implausible? Presumably it is because all that people seek from language is effective communication and benefits which derive from effective communication. The interests of the community and of the single individual in the community are furthered by the routine and the habitual at the level of language, and by no more than concerted, slow change to the pattern of habit and routine. People have no incentive to move far away from habit in the direction of linguistic disorder. The concerted collective development and modification of language to facilitate shared activities and further shared interests is ubiquitous: even concerted, systematic linguistic deviance is commonplace, as a correlate of collective deviant activity. But Babel profits nobody and hence is nowhere found. The move to linguistic disorder, if indeed we can conceptualize and properly refer to such a move, must always be a cost, never a benefit. All the diverse ends and interests within a community, whether public or private, serve to press members actually to strengthen and buttress whatever shared practices exist amongst them at the level of language, to reinforce their existing agreement in the language they use.

Such intuitions are consistent with what is found empirically. Linguistic routine does indeed persist without any reinforcement from internalization or inner fixations as is evident when deviation from routine occurs. Poetry is not an immoral activity. We expect poets to kick against semantics, even syntax, and at times to change and develop it, and we think of that activity itself as a good. It is an activity in which we ourselves indulge all the time, if less self-consciously and systematically: nor is our constant development and modification of the routines of language-use attended by much in the way of guilt and anxiety.

The social order problem is soluble in relation to speech-acts and language-use without need for any reference to internalization in Parsons's sense. Knowledgeable individuals will continue with linguistic habits and routines, mutual intelligibility will be sustained, despite variation in the ends and interests of those individuals. At the level of the intelligibility of language, interests converge. Linguistic order is sustained as the solution to a *co-ordination problem*. Conformity to the routines of language-use profits the individual most of the time if most other people also so conform most of the time. Every individual has an incentive to a high level of conformity so long as all other individuals manifest a high level of conformity (Schelling, 1960; Lewis, 1969).

Much of what has been said of the routine use of language can also be said of the routine use of knowledge. Just as every community possesses and passes on a language, so do they possess and pass on a body of knowledge. Just as there can be no communication without shared language, so there can be none without shared knowledge. Indeed, as phenomena, the possession of language and the possession of knowledge are indistinguishable, and so are the transmission of language and the transmission of knowledge. Like a language, a body of knowledge is the possession of a specific community and sustained in its practical activity.[21] Knowledge does not arise out of individual observation of reality and continue in existence because direct experience sustains and validates it. There are any number of versions of experience compatible with that experience, and only one of them is normally sustained by any given community and transmitted to new members as authoritative. Conformity in the common use of one version of experience results from tendencies to routinization causally sustained by shared interests in communication and intelligibility and opposed by no significant countervailing interests. People have no cause to move into conditions of *fundamental* cognitive disorder, just as they have no cause to move into conditions of fundamental linguistic disorder. Disorder, whether for the individual or the whole community, is a cost, not a benefit. Most of the ends and objectives of individuals, whether shared or not, actually press them to strengthen whatever agreement exists amongst them in the way of shared knowledge and belief. Thus, the problem of social order may be solved at the level of knowledge and cognition, just as it is solved at the level of language, without reference to processes of internalization. It will similarly be clear empirically that the conventions embedded in bodies of knowledge are not in general internalized: the innovations of scientists are no more immoral than those of poets.[22]

It only remains to be asked whether individuals who are able to agree in the language they use and the knowledge they share might also be able to agree in their practice overall, that is, in what they actually do. Might individuals co-ordinate their practical activity so that nobody has an incentive to depart from routine, given that most other people are conforming? Might a single routinized system represent something close to a local maximum of desirability for every individual participant therein?

Talcott Parsons is uncompromising in his rejection of this possibility. Practical activity cannot be co-ordinated calculatively, he insists, but only by shared, non-rational, moral commitments to values and norms. If self-interest and egoism are not constrained by such commitments they will act as causes of deviance sufficiently strong to disrupt and destroy any given system of routines. It is in the course of practical activity that people actually move to secure the means of achieving their objectives and interests. But these means are limited, demand exceeds supply, so that calculative individuals must necessarily come into competition and conflict in their attempts to secure them. Unavoidably, once reflective awareness emerges and individual ends are recognized and formulated, incompatible individual plans and projects will be designed, and agents will struggle against each other in their attempts to carry them out. No system of routines can persist in these conditions. Every conceivable system of routines will be unstable under reflective awareness: some individuals at least will always be impelled by their egoistic desires to reject it, whatever the constituent routines may be. Only the internalization of the norms of such a system could save it from disintegration. Sanctions would be insufficient, if indeed it was in anyone's interest to apply them; for sanctions in such a situation, where egoism was significant, would have constantly to be applied, and under such heavy pressure any system of sanctions would be bound to collapse.

This has been a widely accepted form of argument, but it has been accepted altogether too readily. The basic claim that conflicting ends imply conflicting actions has no inherent plausibility. Whyever should a single stable pattern of action not emerge and persist, sustained by conflicting individual ends? Why should a clash of human ends necessarily lead to a clash of human actions, when every little baboon learns to leave the coconut for the big baboon? The answer surely is that stable patterns of human action *may* be sustained alongside conflicting human ends, that the slave may no more recognize the moral propriety of his position than the little baboon, that Parsons is simply wrong. Patterns of social interaction may emerge amongst individuals with conflicting ends, such that nobody will find it expedient to deviate from the patterns, whatever his ends.

Patterns of this kind will generally involve sanctions. The existence of sanctions will play a crucial role in co-ordinating action, in making the same actions the 'best' actions for both of two parties with opposed ends. The master and the slave with their opposed aims will agree in their practice, just as the big and the little baboon will agree in the matter of the coconut, because there are sanctions to be taken into account. But simply because sanctions are essential in the co-ordination of calculative action there is no reason to assume that they must be applied frequently, and that the sanctioning system must face pressures which render it liable to collapse. The mere threat of sanctions may maintain a given pattern of action as the pattern best favouring the conflicting aims of all parties – the pattern that represents an equilibrium from which no party wishes to depart. This will mean that little deviance actually occurs, and hence that no pressure is actually put upon the sanctioning system. Informed, calculative action, taking account of a sanctioning system, may actually be less likely to put pressure upon that system than 'non-rational' action devoid of calculation and reflective awareness.

Sufficiently stable systems of calculative action

An extermination camp is a setting where resources for coercion and explicit violence are essential to the maintenance of routine. Inmate behaviour in such a camp is to a great extent structured by the use of coercion, scarcely at all by acceptance of the 'legitimate authority' of those in formal control. Nor, in this context, is control through coercion and sanctioning particularly easy, since inmates have very little indeed to lose in such a nightmare situation. Nonetheless, from what we know empirically, it is evident that extermination camps can be sustained effectively with quite small immediately available coercive resources. A few guards can control a very much greater number of inmates, and sustain social order. The imposed routinized systems of such camps tend to persist under reflective awareness: inmates see deviance as inexpedient, since it leads to immediate death or brutalization instead of deferred death. And this seems, in practice, to be sufficient to allow control with very little pressure on the sanctioning system. Only a few individuals need to be shot out of hand, or offered lesser violence, in a given period of time, for the necessary impact to be made upon inmate knowledge and for social order to be maintained. Evidently, a system heavily reliant upon coercion can continue without difficulty for an indefinite period, without undue stress being placed upon the apparatus of coercion itself. Parsons's assertion that 'The greater the need for sanctions, the weaker the ultimate force behind them' is palpably false. The need for sanctions may be absolute and impelling, yet the cost and difficulty of supplying the need may remain small.

Parsons accepts explicitly that a system of sanctions is a necessity in all ordered social systems, but denies equally explicitly that such a system could exist without internalized norms. In the case of an extermination camp he could rightly point out that there is a need to explain the ordered actions of the sanctioners themselves, the guards. But, again from what we know empirically, it does not seem that a moral commitment to exterminating had to be the predominant factor in accounting for their ordered harmonious activities. Nor is it at all clear that if we were to look at those who controlled the guards, and then at those who controlled those controllers, and so on, we should in the end arrive at an internalized norm.

Parsons simply presupposes the primacy of internalized norms. Even in discussing the monetary system, generally taken as a system of calculative action *par excellence*, he proceeds from this presupposition. Yet where is the difficulty in understanding monetary exchange in terms of routines, public norms and sanctioning activity? The alignment of aims in monetary transactions ensures that every individual is policed by others, most of the time: in a faulty exchange one agent's gain is another's loss, most of the time. An effective system of sanctions is thus sustained more or less automatically. Any given individual knows that if he gives short change, or fudges the books, or fails to keep contracts, other individuals will find it in their interests to call him to account. Reflectively aware calculation indicates the expediency of conforming action most of the time. There are, of course, some situations wherein control by opposition of aims is attenuated or even absent, wherein deviance is profitable, but in such situations graft rapidly becomes ubiquitous. Everywhere in the monetary system, from supermarket check-outs to Lloyd's of London, weak control means the growth of rackets, even entire racketeering subcultures with their own moral orders – subcultures the routines of which are stable under reflective awareness. The monetary system is a vast body of custom and convention which participants must recognize and take into account, but there is no clear reason for holding that its norms must, of necessity, be internalized.

Systems of monetary transactions may be constituted and reconstituted by the calculative activities of participants just as the systematic interactions of the extermination camp are constituted and reconstituted: in this respect the two systems are alike. Note how in both cases persistence under reflective awareness is emphatically not the same as desirability to a reflecting individual. The point is obvious in the case of an extermination camp, but is worth making explicit in relation to a monetary system. Most participants may regard a monetary system as iniquitous or inequitable, and particular monetary transactions therein as unfair and exploitative, and may yet participate in the transactions and sustain the system. Participants may evaluate the system negatively, and yet, given the knowledge they possess and the calculative procedures they employ, still see their own individual conforming actions within the system as the best possible.

Both in the extermination camp and in the context of the monetary system individual agents calculate that the immediate consequences of their own actions are maximally beneficial when those actions conform to routine practice. We might expect that any system wherein this is the case would tend to persist under reflective awareness. But in any system where sanctions surround actions and make their performance expedient this is indeed the case. Why then should not any such system persist solely and simply as a self-reconstituting system of calculative action? Why not indeed? Any given individual in such a system, would, if he were to detach himself from ongoing routine and reflect upon it, have a strong tendency to fall back into routine as the most profitable course of action. And this very course of action would then be part of what comprised the system itself, as it appeared to other reflective participants within it. The routinized system could thus exist as the product of a continuing socially ordered self-fulfilling prophecy. Calculation that routine action was the best thing in the given system would produce the routine action that constituted the given system. Every individual's calculations would lead to actions which, in total, were the calculative frame for everyone else. The result would be a self-referring and self-sustaining system of calculation. Such a system would carry itself along by its own bootstraps (Barnes, 1983).

Clearly, a system of this kind has very strong tendencies to self-sustain, even when all participants are very highly reflective, self-conscious and calculative. But in fact individuals are never fully reflective and consciously calculative at every single instant: they are well able to calculate that such a strategy is less than optimal. Typically, they operate much more efficiently, remaining most of the time in a habituated, routinized mode, switching out of that mode when special circumstances arise, or occasionally to review and take stock of the situation, promptly switching back in again as the special circumstances pass by, or the situation proves satisfactory. This tendency to habituation and routinization, which ensures that consciously calculative action occurs against a continuing background of routine action, vastly reinforces the overall system and enhances its capacity to self-sustain and self-reproduce. Imagine that the individuals of a society act routinely most of the time, nine times out of ten, and tend to monitor their actions, reflect upon them, evaluate their effectiveness, only occasionally – say, ten per cent of the time. In these circumstances the routinized system could take on a monolithic stability. Every individual would tend to see it as having much of the solidity and externality of a material physical object, and the totality of individuals perceiving it in this way, and acting upon their perceptions, would thereupon constitute a system with the properties that they perceived.

Parsons's rejection of calculative action as a basis for social order is unjustified and probably incorrect, but it is in line with sociological orthodoxy. Ever since Durkheim made a fundamental distinction between the sacred and the profane, sociologists have tended to assume that rational individual calculations must be overridden by some non-rational 'social' factor if a stable collective life is to be sustained. Calculation has been perceived as the activity of the independent individual, as part of 'egoism', and thus as at the opposite pole to genuine social activity. But this is simply incorrect. Calculation depends on knowledge. Knowledge transcends the individual and is carried collectively by the interactions of a society. Calculation is therefore itself social action, a part of social life, a symbol of the individual's attachment to a specific culture.[23]

Concerted deviance

If social action is basically calculative action, lacking inner normative constraint, then the normative order cannot be sustained by the individual conscience and must be a product of the public realm. The normative order must reflect not internal pressures within the psyche but the pressures people exert upon each other. The normative order must arise from calculative conformity and the calculative sanctioning of others into conformity. Such an externally sustained normative order may be stable to the reflective awareness of an isolated individual, but unlike an internalized normative order it cannot be unconditionally stable to the reflective awareness of an unlimited number of individuals, and unconditionally secure against concerted deviance or concerted innovation on their part. Parsons's internalized normative order can constrain every separate individual in a society and thereby prevent concerted deviance as readily as individual deviance: 'the norms' may be considered as separate entities that have effects on people. But an externally sustained normative order is nothing more than people themselves, holding each other into some degree of conformity in practice: there is nothing independent of the actions of people themselves to sustain conformity in those actions. It follows almost as a logical point that any externally sustained normative order is vulnerable to concerted deviance.

Curiously, however, this apparent theoretical weakness is in truth a strength. There is no warrant for granting a normative order immunity to concerted deviance. We should accept instead that all normative orders are indeed inherently unstable in the face of concerted deviant action. Such action may be inhibited to some extent by various contingencies, problems of communication and organization for example, but its chances of occurring cannot be reduced to zero and at times it will happen. Actual societies are merely routinized systems where such concerted action has not happened since the last time it happened.

Think again of an extermination camp. Thousands of inmates are controlled by but a few armed guards: a mass attack upon the guards would almost certainly succeed, even if at the cost of several casualties. Most individuals would benefit from such a concerted action, whether one thinks in terms of the hard-nosed criterion of life-expectancy or of more tenuous, difficult-to-define notions of dignity and self-respect. All individuals should find the risks inherent in such concerted action worth taking. Thus, an extermination camp, of the kind with which historians have made us familiar, exists in a vulnerable condition. It is vulnerable to the concerted action of inmates, and the possibility of its disruption is always there. Yet it exists – that is to say such camps have existed over long periods without potential disruption becoming actual. Here is a metaphor on the basis of which to understand social stability generally.

Why is it that in so many cases the potential for concerted disruption never becomes actual? It is because to act in concert requires communication, shared routines, organization, direction, control, and such things are often both technically difficult and risky to establish. Where, as in an extermination camp, large numbers of disorganized individuals face even just a small amount of ordered, routinized repression, the problems of a successful concerted resistance may be truly formidable. To establish communication amongst large numbers of initially unrelated people, to order their actions and responses, to weld those actions and responses into concerted action, may take time, too much time, and intense effort in the face of constant danger. There is also the problem that, in a disorganized mass, crystals of order and organization may appear independently at different points and subsequently clash: there may be no single

pattern of organization that naturally suggests itself as the proper
response to organized repression, only alternatives which may conflict
with and undermine each other. Finally, and perhaps most daunting of
all, there is the problem of developing the means to deter opportunism.
Before the initiation of concerted action, everyone may be tempted to
spill the beans. When concerted action begins, everyone may want to be
in the second row. If there are no strong disincentives to yield to such
temptations then concerted deviance is likely to fail. Thus, it may be that
routinized systems of action are always vulnerable in the abstract to
concerted action by subsets of participants, and yet that they continue to
exist because concerted action does not materialize. Routines may persist
without internalization because they can be destabilized only by large-
scale concerted activities which have a low probability of emerging
within any given time.

Individuals have a sense of living in ordered social situations so long as
activity in those situations is routinized, and stays routinized to the
extent that it can be described as conforming to publicly recognized
norms. I have said that such activity must persist under the reflective
awareness of the individuals who enact it. Perhaps it would be better still
to say that such activity persists *because* of such awareness. Routines
persist not of themselves, but by being continually reconstituted in the
course of calculative action. It is calculation itself which carries and
sustains routine: routine action is a form of calculative action. We have
to think of individuals who know the routines, who calculate on the basis
of what they know, who consequently act routinely most of the time, and
who thereby collectively reconstitute the objects of their knowledge and
confirm what they know.[24] Such individuals will have a sense of living
in an ordered social context, a context not merely intelligible and
describable but one that manifests some degree of pattern and predictability at the level of action. For any given individual that context will
be other individuals, appropriately conceptualized. And the order and
stability generally perceived in the context will be the achievement of all
the individuals who together constitute it.

2.3 SOCIETY AS A DISTRIBUTION OF KNOWLEDGE

Where people are interacting in ways that constitute and take account of
norms or rules, we are inclined to speak of the existence of a society.
Society exists where normative order exists. Sometimes a society is said
to be a normative order. Perhaps we should not say this; perhaps it
encourages selective perception and over-simplification. But at the
moment there is a need for simplicity, so let us hold that a society at least

includes a normative order and that to understand society involves understanding the nature of normative order.[25]

Parsons regards norms as entities embedded within individuals. A normative order is essentially a single set of norms embedded in a number of individuals. The norms constrain what the individuals do, and their existence is thus revealed by their effects upon action. We have seen how this view is inadequate, how norms must be defined and enforced from without not from within, how they are sustained in the public realm. This may encourage a social-behaviourist view of norms as regularities in practice, and of normative order as nothing other than the pattern and order observable in social life itself. However, a strictly behaviourist view of normative order turns it into a wholly inexplicable phenomenon, a disconnected series of regularities with no underlying rationale. There is no way of refuting a strict behaviourism of this kind, provided its practitioners stay within the limits it imposes upon them. But in practice those limits are rarely, if at all, conformed to, even by behaviourists themselves, and the advantages of going beyond them and speculating about the characteristics of the agents who behave are widely recognized. I accept the need for speculation of this kind throughout this book, and assume at every point that individual members of societies have a range of dispositions and capacities which are relevant to understanding how they act: I refer to such dispositions and capacities when I speak of people knowing, memorizing, reflecting, inferring, calculating.

If people do indeed possess capacities and dispositions of this kind, then they cannot remain unaffected by the pattern of their own lives and a developing awareness of the public norms that surround them. They must inevitably take account of the existence of such norms as they learn, memorize, reflect, infer, calculate. Hence I am bound to presume that where there is a normative order, a system of routine practice, actions resulting in its continuation must be found expedient by the calculative individuals who constitute it: given what they know they must generally be disposed to persist with routine.

If human beings act calculatively on the basis of what they know then we may characterize a society as a persisting distribution of knowledge instead of as a persisting set of routine practices.[26] The one characterization is as good as the other. Individuals know what the routines are. They know how such norms and rules and regularities emerge from the calculative, knowledgeable actions of other people. They have, accordingly, a systematic and sophisticated knowledge of the normative order. And this knowledge, along with everything else they know, leads them to act so that the normative order continues, so that their actions figure amongst the phenomena through which others know the normative order and are themselves able to act in ways which take account of its existence. Evidently, if people are presumed to possess the capabilities and dispositional characteristics of knowledgeable, calculative agents, then shared knowledge suffices to solve Hobbes's problem after all. A society is a distribution of knowledge. There are some distributions of knowledge over individuals that prompt individuals to act in ways which confirm and reconstitute the original distribution.

How people act depends upon what they know. Anything that is known may affect how people act. Therefore, everything that people know is constitutive of their existence as a society. To the extent that they are differentiated, knowledge of society and knowledge of nature both constitute society. Considered as knowledge, a society is everything its members know, just as, considered as practice, a society is everything its members do. It is profoundly mistaken to imagine that natural knowledge is not a part of the social order, just as it is mistaken to imagine that technical and material practices are not a part of the social order.[27]

Self-reference and self-validation

A society is everything its members know, including everything they know about each other, and each others' knowledge of each other and so on. Such a body of knowledge will be used by its possessors to make reference to each other, and to make reference to each other as possessors of knowledge. What is known will be something that is referred to in using the knowledge itself: the use of knowledge will involve the specification of the content of the knowledge, its basis and its distribution as referents. The knowledge that constitutes society is *self-referring*.

Whatever the members of a society know may be referred to by members within the framework of what they know. If a society is a distribution of knowledge then it is a self-referring distribution of knowledge. To learn such knowledge is to do two things. It is to become *informed* about whatever the knowledge is used to refer to, and it is to be *constituted* or reconstituted as a referent, an entity that may be referred to by others, or indeed oneself, using that very same knowledge. It is easy to overlook the constitutive or performative dimension of learning when a single individual is concerned, but if we think of the entire membership of a society at once this dimension becomes vividly apparent. In learning what a society knows the members as a whole thereby constitute the society itself as a distribution of knowledge, much of which knowledge will be *about* the society itself, and hence valid and 'consonant with social experience' only when it has been learned. Where knowledge is self-referring it must also be self-validating. A membership must learn it in order to become what it correctly describes.

Neither epistemologists and philosophers of science nor sociologists of knowledge have given much detailed consideration to systems of knowledge that involve self-reference. Yet if social action is indeed generated by knowledgeable human beings, acting calculatively and reflectively, this is a topic of great importance. Even in the present context it is worthwhile to pause whilst it is given some extended consideration. The fact that society and knowledge of society are not fully separable independent entities is of some importance when we seek to identify the basis of power.

Let us begin on familiar ground by considering our knowledge of everyday material objects (see figure 2.1). We know that the billiard-ball is spherical. On one side, there we are, with our knowledge, or, if preferred, our shared belief. On the other side is the billiard-ball, completely separate from us. To check whether our belief is or is not correct we move to the ball, observe it, measure it, rotate it. The shape of the ball remains unaffected by what we do to it or what we believe about it: it is there to be investigated as an external phenomenon. If the shape is indeed found to be that of a sphere, this shows that our belief is correct, that we were indeed properly informed about the nature of the billiard-ball (2.1.a).

This is perhaps our commonest paradigm of knowing. We have a shared belief about some separate, distinct, independently identifiable thing, and if the nature of that thing is as we believe it to be then our belief is correct. But not all our beliefs about the objects in our physical environment are like this. Suppose we believe that this rock is the summit of the mountain. Once again there we are, with our knowledge; and there, separate from us, is a thing or object that can be pointed out, the summit. But now it is no longer the nature of the object itself that makes it a proper referent of our belief: now it is the relationship of the object with things outside itself. Suppose that some vandal hammers the top from the Matterhorn and makes off with it. Should the headlines read 'Vandal steals Matterhorn summit!' or 'Vandal lowers Matterhorn summit!'? The newspapers may take their choice, but what is certain is that the Matterhorn would not subsequently be known as a mountain without a summit. The weather may indeed have scraped an inch or two from the Matterhorn over the last century or so, without depriving it of its summit. A summit is that part of a mountain which exists in a certain relationship with all its other parts. To check that something is a summit is not the same kind of process as checking that it is a sphere: with the latter one looks to the nature of the thing itself – one looks at or inside the thing; whereas with the former one looks outside the thing itself, to its relationship with its context. Our belief that what we are pointing to is a summit is valid only if what we are pointing to relates to its context in a

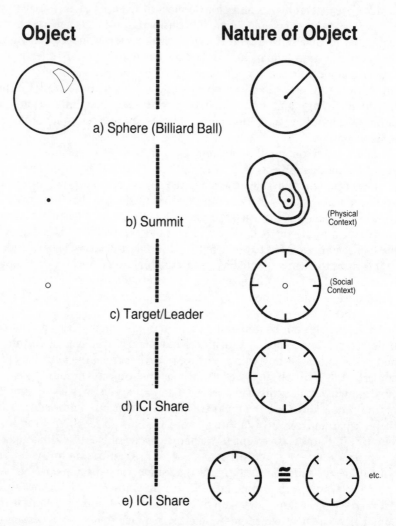

Figure 2.1 Objects and their natures

specific way. Indeed we cannot even understand what summits are as we understand what spherical objects are, by looking at them in isolation and noting their properties.

Summits are physical objects, quite separate from us, but objects which are what they are only because of circumstances outside themselves (2.1.b). There are other physical objects just like summits, but objects of a nature defined not by a context of physical circumstances, but by a context of human activity. The list of such objects is endless: auguries and omens, cups and reliquaries, jewellery; more mundanely, pets, pollutions, rubbish; at a yet more practical level, reagents and solvents, targets and weapons, vermin and weeds. All these are independent entities which can be pointed to and identified, picked up and examined, described and measured; yet they are only what they are because of how we act in relation to them.

With objects of this kind it is no longer a matter of us and our belief here, and the object and its nature there. It is no longer even a matter of us here, and object in context there. We now *are* the context which makes the object what it is. The target is the target because we believe it to be the target, and hence treat it as the target. Physical object though it is, the target is a target only to the extent that it is believed to be such and treated as such. In ceasing to believe that an object is a target, we dissolve away its nature as a target. In coming to believe that an object is a target, we constitute the context that makes it a target, and hence we constitute it as a target. Our believing self-validates: we validate what we believe by referring to what we believe (2.1.c).

Here at last is a simple stereotypical example that captures something of the nature of our knowledge of society, (which is the most intensely self-referring component of the knowledge that is society). Social objects, if we may call them that, are often very much like the objects we call targets. They are identifiable as objects, as substantial bounded entities, but their nature is constituted by our beliefs about them: our beliefs constitute the context that makes them what they are. John is the leader of the gang. He is the leader because the members know him to be the leader, and act routinely on the basis of what they know. Whoever the leader is, he is the leader, in just the way that whatever is the target is the target. Both the physical and the social object are the objects that they are because of the context of belief and action that rings them about (2.1.c).

Most, indeed probably all terms denoting a social status or position are analogous to the terms 'target' and 'leader' in this respect. Status terms denote objects the natures of which are constituted by the surrounding context of belief and action. Beliefs about the status of individuals in society are accordingly not fully independent of that to which they refer. To come to believe something about the status of an individual is to do two things at once: it is to accept a *claim about* his status and at the same time to contribute to the *constitution of* his status.

Given that the nature of a social object is constituted by what rings it about, the actual physical manifestation of the object itself may actually be dispensed with. Only the hollow ring of belief and action is actually necessary. Consider shares in Imperial Chemical Industries (ICI), or the value of a share in ICI, or the voting power of a share. Here are three hollow rings of belief and action: neither the share, nor its value, nor its power, exist or are manifested as tangible objects. It is only our general familiarity with objects and how to treat them, and their mnemonic convenience, that induces us occasionally to set marker-objects at the centre of such hollow rings; and then it is important not to confuse the marker with what is marked, the share certificate with what is certified, the paper banknotes with the value of the share (2.1.d).

The invisibility of self-reference

When a social object is designated one quickly looks out from the object to check the correctness of the designation, and, in practice, to acquire a sense of its point and significance. What one looks toward is the generally accepted designation of the object, and the generally accepted way of acting in relation to it. An object is designated validly if that is how it is designated generally, and/or if action in relation to it is action routinely associated with that designation. A social object is constituted as a social object to the extent that it is generally believed to be such an object.[28] Analogously, if a social structure is an array of social objects, then it too is constituted by being believed to exist. Social structure is the product of those who live in it; they encounter it through the actions that flow from their belief in its existence. But if this is the case, why are we not more aware of a fundamental and profound contrast between natural and social knowledge?[29]

It is very important to recognize that even where a society makes a strong and explicit divide between its conceptions of natural and social order, the discernible differences between the two kinds of order are very slight. Natural order is an ordering constructed by people and used to make sense of nature, not an ordering insisted upon by nature and imposed upon people by nature. Natural order is just as much a system of conventions as social order. Conversely, the objects classified into a social order may be just as material and tangible as those classified into a natural order: John the gang-leader is just as substantial as the spherical billiard-ball, and once designated he is identified and reidentified by his physical characteristics just like the billiard-ball – indeed, recognition of John's physical form is crucially important in the continuing routine treatment of him in terms of his social status as gang-leader.

Natural order and social order are not just similar conventional orderings. They are orderings which are taught and transmitted in just the same way. In particular, in both cases, specific objects and processes are pointed out and displayed directly as examples of terms: natural and social order are both transmitted by *ostension*. The ball is pointed out as a spherical ball; John is pointed out as the leader of the gang. Thus, learning about nature and learning about society are the same kind of process: they feel the same; they can be run together; indeed they are the same. Just the competences and procedures which allow us to learn about our physical environment and respond appropriately to it also allow us to learn about society, respond appropriately to it, and thereby keep it in existence as something we have learned about and know how to respond to. There is a marvellous economy of explanation here: people have to be assigned learning capabilities in order to account for how they cope as organisms in a physical environment, and those very same learning capabilities may be what is necessary both to account for how people cope as agents in a social environment and how they constitute that environment in the course of coping with it.

The small difference between knowledge of physical nature and knowledge of society only becomes evident when we take an interest in the grounds for accepting the knowledge, the features that make it valid. At this point, with our knowledge of nature, we often find ourselves giving closer and closer attention to the independent referents of the knowledge, whereas with our knowledge of our own society we usually find ourselves referring back to our own collective action, our own practice, as the focus of our reflection. Even at this point, the distinction between the social and the natural may be exceedingly slight and difficult to discern for the isolated individual. Durkheim says that, like material objects, social facts are external to the individual – and so they are, almost. Every individual in John's gang observes John to be the leader by noting the actions and inferring the beliefs of the other members. Every individual, when reflecting upon John's putative leadership, looks outward at a near-complete ring of confirming action, action confirming and thus constituting John's social position as leader.

That all these slightly different contexts around the social position may be brought together as perceptions of essentially 'the same' context allows an agreed social order to be created and sustained. The 'error' in individual perception involved here is so extremely small as to be for all practical purposes no error at all. The individual who accepts the 'external' social fact of John's leadership will be making no mistake, even though a tiny part of what constitutes John's leadership is not 'external' to that individual at all but internal to him, being nothing more nor less than his own belief in John's leadership. For most practical purposes the individual may neglect his own contribution to the social reality in which he believes. The gang-member may take the leader as externally given, provided the gang is not too small; the share-seller may take the share-price as externally fixed, provided his holding is not too large (2.1.e).

The ubiquity of self-reference

The contribution of any given individual to the constitution of a social object may be minute, but however minute it is the nature of that object will nonetheless be *wholly and entirely* constituted by the totality of the individuals in the relevant society: its crucial characteristics, its nature as a social object, are the surrounding activities of all these individuals. However 'external' to any individual a social object may be, it is completely 'internal' to his community. The gang-leader is constituted as such by gang-members' actions. The share-price is constituted by market transactions. However many the individual pieces into which the hollow ring of belief and action around a social object is broken, it remains a ring of belief and action, nothing more. As with social objects, so it is with knowledge of society generally. Whereas knowledge of nature refers in the last analysis to entities and processes beyond itself, knowledge of society refers in the last analysis to knowledge, and hence precisely to itself. Whereas knowledge of nature may be confirmed or disconfirmed by processes involving reference to states of affairs that exist independently of the knowledge, knowledge of society must be confirmed or disconfirmed by processes involving reference to states of affairs that exist only because the knowledge is generally presumed to be true. If we step back from all these ongoing processes, and focus on knowledge of society as a core constituent of society itself as a distribution of knowledge, then society is revealed as a sublime, monumental, self-fulfilling prophesy.[30]

Knowledge of society self-refers. There are no objects beyond its existing domain of application waiting to be discovered, nor any existing social objects with features other than those they are already known to possess. Yet individuals may nonetheless rightly feel dissatisfaction with the accuracy or the extent of their knowledge of their society, and may rightly seek to correct mistakes therein or to add to it and extend its scope. For individuals may be systematically incorrect in their beliefs about each other, or ignorant of pattern and order in their own beliefs. Consider the cyclic character of fashion in clothing. A few people, opinion-leaders, at the top of the social hierarchy, may seek to dress distinctively, differently from everyone else. The rest of the society may seek to dress like those just above them in the hierarchy. If at a given time the opinion-leaders know what is generally being worn, then they will set in motion a wave of activity which will eventually invalidate that knowledge. They will dress at variance with the norm, whereupon their new mode of dress will pass down the society and become a new norm. As they correct their increasingly inadequate knowledge, so they will increasingly tend to vary their dress yet again, inaugurating new waves of change, so that the familiar cyclic pattern in fashionable dressing is established and sustained. A recurring oscillation in social practice is established, associated with a continuing small degree of inadequacy in social knowledge. Note too that once it is established the oscillation itself becomes a complex social object, available for examination and reflection. A new layer of knowledge may be built up, as it were, by scanning what exists already. And the new knowledge may inspire new practice: explicitly formulated knowledge of the cyclic tendencies in dress-routines does indeed inspire a significant range of economic activities in our society.

Knowledge of society is therefore open to correction, modification and development. People can learn more about their society just as they can learn more about their physical environment. But there is a crucial difference between the two kinds of learning. Ideally, to learn about the physical environment is to take account of more information about an independent realm, which realm remains unchanged by the learning process. We may proceed, confident that the acquisition of knowledge makes no difference to that which is known. But to learn about our own society may be to change that society, since in learning we change ourselves and we are part of our own society. An act of learning in this case may both take account of the nature of society and change the nature of society. The act alters knowledge of society and at the same time alters the referents of that knowledge. It is both an act of learning and an act of reconstitution of the phenomena being learned about. It is at once cognitive and performative. Learning involves the adjustment of belief, but society just is constituted of rings of belief and action, so that the performative role of learning is indeed immediately and straight-forwardly intelligible.[31]

This is a key point to keep in mind in what follows. Society is a distribution of knowledge. Power, as will shortly be argued, is an aspect of that distribution. But the knowledge in question is self-referring, and to acquire it or forget it has not just a cognitive but also a performative significance. We shall not be able to treat power as independent of knowledge of power, or the distribution of power as independent of knowledge of that distribution. Many difficulties will have to be faced because of this.

On the other hand, the difficulties should not be exaggerated. It may be that as members we cannot learn about society without changing society. But that does not mean that learning must necessarily invalidate itself. Knowledge and referent may change together, and yet the knowledge may remain valid throughout – satisfactorily related to its referents throughout. More and more people may learn that Bob Geldof is a celebrity. Such learning changes the society wherein it occurs, and indeed alters the ring of belief and action around Geldof which constitutes his celebrity in the society. But such learning does not invalidate what is learned or in any way lessen the celebrity of Geldof: on the contrary. The fact that learning about society changes what is learned about should therefore in no way discourage such learning, but it should be taken into account when learning, and when making use of the knowledge generated by such learning. In particular, it should not prohibit or even discourage sociological enquiry, but it does need to be taken into account in the course of such enquiry.

The point being made here is indeed a trivially obvious one. New members, after all, learn what their society knows, including what it knows of itself. Thereby they change the distribution of knowledge that is their society. But far from invalidating the knowledge they learn, their learning is actually what allows that knowledge to persist as valid knowledge: their learning reproduces and reconstitutes the society they are learning about; in learning they become confirming instances of what they learn. Everything changes; and everything stays the same.[32]

3

THE NATURE OF POWER

3.1 SOCIAL POWER

Imagine a society asleep. It remains a society. Everything necessary is there in the slumbering individuals: society does not need a night-shift. Later the society will awaken into its particular familiar environment, partly its own artefacts, partly the given of nature, and it will carry on. For the most part it will carry on routinely, along the old familiar paths.

Why is this? What is it about all the sleeping individuals that makes them a society? A society, I have said, is a specific distribution of knowledge. Social action in a society is intelligible, and to some extent predictable, simply because of the specific things its members know and the general human characteristics its members possess.

Every society possesses a shared body of technical, manipulation-related knowledge, knowledge of nature, and a shared body of social knowledge, knowledge of a normative order.[1] In any society accepted knowledge is used to make sense of familiar experience and is, for the most part, found to make sense of it. In any society also, calculative action taken upon the basis of accepted knowledge suffices to reproduce the experience with which members are familiar.[2] All the many actual stable distributions of knowledge meet these requirements in their given environments of operation, as indeed would innumerable conceivable alternatives.[3]

The knowledge of nature established in a given society is just one of innumerable alternative viable ways of acting upon and making sense of the natural order. Consequently its credibility is the credibility of convention and custom. It is an established way of acting and speaking, sustained by a given society as a part of its culture and tradition. It is received from the ancestors on trust and is sustained by sanctions and social controls. Nonetheless, natural knowledge is always learned in conjunction with the operations of manipulating and controlling material objects and physical processes, and its terms are used to refer to such objects and processes in specific situations. There is a genuine sense in which natural knowledge can be said to have external referents.[4]

If norms are internalized they too can be referred to like objects are referred to. Knowledge of society can then refer to something external to itself: it can refer to 'the norms'. Internalized norms are like physical afflictions: they exist as independent entities, the nature and effects of which may be known or unknown to members, just as the nature and effects of traumas and pathologies may be known or unknown. But non-internalized norms are not like this. With such norms the evidence that they exist and the evidence that they are known to exist is the same. In each case the evidence is that members take account of the norms. Thus there are no longer 'the norms' on the one hand, and knowledge referring to 'the norms' on the other hand. A member's knowledge of the normative order is knowledge of what members generally know. Members' knowledge of the normative order is the normative order.

Through a variety of means ranging from explicit instruction to direct independent observation new members of society acquire knowledge of what is generally done, what is generally sanctioned, what is generally advocated, and so forth. They build up a map of the normative order. But what makes this map valid to the extent that it is valid? It is nothing more nor less than the general acceptance of the map itself. I know that red means stop at the traffic-light. I have knowledge of a norm. But what is my knowledge of and to what do I look in order to check it? My knowledge is knowledge of what others know, and I check it by observing what others do and inferring to what they know. To the extent that others do not know that red means stop, my knowledge that red means stop becomes less and less sustainable. My knowledge of that part of the normative order which has red meaning stop is knowledge of what my community knows. My community's knowledge that red means stop refers to itself and is implicated in its own validation.

In a stable normative order knowledge that an action is normal and routinely done encourages the performance of the action, so that the general dissemination of the knowledge suffices to validate it in practice. I drive up to a red light. I am free to stop or go, but I know that it is normal to stop. I stop: it is, I believe, in my interest to stop. Others in my community share my knowledge and are disposed to act upon it as I do. Hence my knowledge, and theirs, is validated. Should the others in my community disagree with me concerning the truth of this knowledge of mine, should they stop at green and go at red, then by that very fact my knowledge would be incorrect and I should find it rapidly and trauma-tically disconfirmed. Were I to live the necessary ten minutes or so I should rapidly adjust my knowledge. I should come to believe that green means stop, or that it is normal to stop at green. I should make my knowledge knowledge of what everyone else knows and hence valid. I should make my knowledge what it ought to be according to everyone else's knowledge, and hence a confirmation and validation of what everyone else knows.

Power redescribed

A society is a distribution of knowledge, part of which knowledge is self-referring knowledge of the nature of the society itself: the self-referring knowledge of the society includes the normative order of the society. Power, therefore, that is to say social power, must be an aspect or a characteristic of a distribution of knowledge, and indeed this is precisely how I propose to define it and conceive of it. Any specific distribution of knowledge confers a generalized capacity for action upon those individuals who carry and constitute it, and that capacity for action is their social power, the power of the society they constitute by bearing and sharing the knowledge in question. Social power is the added capacity for action that accrues to individuals through their constituting a distribution of knowledge and thereby a society.

Consider an isolated individual in a given environment. Such an individual possesses general capacities for action and can thus be said to possess power, the power to act that resides in his own body. It is not easy to specify what such power amounts to, but it is easy enough to notice losses and gains therein: loss of strength involves loss of power; gain of skill involves gain of power; and so on. Similarly, in a collection of isolated individuals in a given environment, all possess general capacities for action, and hence all possess power separately. The totality of the power possessed separately is roughly the sum of all the separate capacities for action of the different individuals, although there is little point in referring to such a total capacity for action since it is never exercised coherently.

Consider now a genuine society of individuals, who carry and constitute a distribution of knowledge and act and interact coherently on the basis of it. The total power available is considerably increased; overall capacity for action is larger and wider ranging than that of so many isolated individuals: things are now possible that were not possible before; other things may be done more quickly and with less effort. A shared distribution of knowledge confers a capacity to carry out routines and execute projects in concert, which is an added capacity for action, which is social power.

Much more power resides in a genuine society than resides in so many isolated individuals. But the additional power is never available equally to all the individuals of the society. As action becomes routinized and coherently ordered, so discretion in its direction tends to concentrate. Most individuals cease actively to exercise discretion over many of the actions of their own bodies, and a few acquire effective discretion over those actions. Those who gain discretion in the direction of the capacity for action of a society, discretion in the use of power, are those who in conventional usage are called 'powerful' individuals: in what follows I often refer to them as 'powers' or 'power-holders'. Although, in theory, an increase in the power of a society need not be accompanied by such a concentration of discretion in the use of that power, in practice the one thing is accompanied by the other. The elaboration of systems of concerted, routinized interaction tends to occur in association with a concentration of discretion in the use and direction of such systems and hence an unevenness in what is conventionally called the distribution of power.[5] Typically, some individuals constitute a set of routines and others direct it. As often as not some individuals predominate in constituting the entire social system of routines and other individuals predominate in directing its operations. The capacity for action in the society is made available to some much more than others. Routine social actions are directed predominantly at the discretion of a subset of members.

Social power *is* the capacity for action in a society, and hence is predominantly but not wholly identifiable as that which is routinely possible therein. Social power is *possessed* by those with discretion in the direction of social action, and hence predominantly by those with discretion in the use of routines. A routine may be thought of as a potential or capacity, to be set in operation or not, pointed this way or that, combined with other routines or kept apart, at the discretion of a controlling agent. Such an agent possesses social power. The possession of power is the possession of discretion: to gain power is to gain such discretion; to lose power is to lose such discretion. Such gains and losses are effectively gains and losses in the agent's capacity to act through the bodies of others. (In contrast, if an entire society is said to gain or lose power the implication is that it has gained or lost competences and capabilities, parts of its general capacity for action.)

We have here a very simple, embryonic account of power and its distribution. Later, it will have to be elaborated and modified, but it will do for the moment. Note that the account raises no new fundamental problems of the kind discussed in chapter 2. Successfully to exercise discretion in the direction of social actions is usually to exercise a known and recognized right. To accept direction in the performance of social actions is usually to take account of the existence of a right, and may involve recognition of the existence of sanctions in support of the right.

The social order problems associated with the possession and use of power are the problems of the stability of calculative action under reflective awareness already considered. The problem of why a power is obeyed is no deeper than that of why a traffic-light is obeyed.

Consequences of the redescription

How does this account compare with the common sense conceptions of power, and the sociological definitions and methods of measurement outlined in chapter 1? It is actually very close indeed to common sense. As common sense requires, power is a potential or capacity which may or may not be used. Again as common sense requires, power is possessed, and its possessors have something real at their disposal. Where the present account goes beyond common sense is in specifying what that 'something real' actually is. Social power is the capacity for action embedded in the society, the capacity implicit in the existence of a shared distribution of knowledge, the capacity largely known to members as their own routine practices and competences. In equating the possession of power with the possession of discretion in the direction of these practices and competences the present account points to the source of the ability to get things done characteristic of powerful agents.

The present account also accords with some of the features of the most widely accepted sociological definitions of power. As it stands at the moment it treats discretion in the use of power as something attributable to an individual, and power itself as embedded in the social relationships surrounding that individual. Where the present account may represent an advance upon sociological orthodoxy is in its allowing power to be characterized independently of any particular effects it may have. Nor is this virtue bought at the price of empirical irrelevance. There are many empirical methods of identifying a capacity for action which do not need to refer to the effects of its use.

As far as the systematic identification and measurement of power via indicators is concerned, the present conception is incompatible with the 'event' approach. It asserts that power exists independently of particular acts of use and can be identified independently of its use. It is willing to assume, for example, despite the paucity of confirming events, that there is probably a person or persons with discretion to use our nuclear weapons. This discretion exists, indeed is exercised, all the time, but it will be manifested in an event only when a change in the mode or extent of use of the capacity is ordained.

There is no similar fundamental clash with the reputational approach to the measurement of power, since reputationalists accept that power is a capacity and seek to map its distribution by drawing upon members' beliefs about that distribution. There is indeed a close affinity between reputationalism and the present approach, although the two are not identical. Reputationalism takes the overall distribution of belief about power in a society as an *indicator* of the distribution of power itself. The present conception takes a distribution of knowledge in society to *define* the distribution of power itself. On the present conception a system of routines and an associated distribution of discretion in the use of those routines exist as a distribution of knowledge, simply that. To possess power an agent must be known to possess it.[6] That distribution of knowledge which makes the discretionary activities of the agent possible is not an indicator of the power he possesses but the very embodiment of that power: the capacity of the agent to generate action inheres in the relevant structure of knowledge, just as the capacity of the car engine to generate motion inheres in the structure of the engine.

On the face of it, this may seem to indicate the clear superiority of the reputational approach; for if the powerful are merely those who are believed to be powerful, then it must be impossible for an individual to be mistaken with regard to who has power, and this is counter-intuitive. It is, however, perfectly possible for individuals to be mistaken about power within the framework advocated here. Social power is identified as a distribution of *knowledge*, not of mere individual *belief*. Knowledge is accepted belief, generally held belief, belief routinely implicated in social action.[7] Recall how a society may know that red means stop at the traffic light. An individual may nonetheless believe that red means go, and only come to realize his mistake as he realizes what everyone else knows. Similarly, an agent may believe someone to be powerful and only realize his mistake as he realizes what everyone else knows.[8] Every individual in a society may be in error about some aspect of social power in this way, so that none of them truly knows where power lies overall, and yet power will lie, necessarily, by its nature, where it is known to lie.

Social power is not the simple product of individual beliefs. Reputationalists are entirely justified in taking such beliefs, even massive samples of such beliefs, as nothing more than indicators; for social power is constituted as a distribution of knowledge. Because power resides in a patterned distribution of knowledge over many people, it appears to any given individual as being external to himself. To a very good approximation that is a correct perception. But the perception is often rationalized by the claim that power is really there, independent not just of belief but of knowledge. Norms, institutions and social structures are often accorded a 'fully objective' reality in much the same way. The problem stems from an impoverished way of thinking, which allows attributes, characteristics and capacities to manifest a real and genuine existence if they reside within the individual or within external nature, but not if they reside within a number of interacting individuals. This impoverished conception allows for the subjective (that with a basis within the single individual), and for the objective (that with a basis in the natural external order), but fails to recognize that which is largely external to any individual yet wholly internal to the set of interacting individuals.[9] It fails to recognize intersubjective phenomena, and often ends up by mistreating them as analogues of fully 'external' natural phenomena.

Social power is precisely a feature of a set of interacting individuals. It is their general capacity for action, and exists as a distribution of knowledge which they carry and sustain. There is nothing obscure or opaque about such a conception; indeed it makes power visible and accessible in a way which other conceptions fail to do. It makes it clear, for example, why a society with a highly developed technology is, on the whole, more powerful than a similarly sized society which lacks one. It is curious how few sociological accounts of power are able to deal straightforwardly with this simple contrast.

Power is embedded in society as a whole. But discretion in its use is usually distributed more selectively. Power structures or distributions of power are actually, in my view of the matter, distributions of discretion in the use of power. The possession of power is the possession of discretion in the use of that power. When one person is said to have more power than another it is a matter of the one having discretion over a greater capacity for action than the other. Nonetheless, it is cumbersome to refer always to discretion in the use of power when a reference simply to power will do, and I shall adopt the latter usage as a kind of shorthand much of the time. Indeed, I have occasionally lapsed into this idiom already, and referred to power when to be precise I should have referred to discretion in its use.

A power-holder holds power that actually resides in the capacity for action of others. He is like a driver who has at his disposal the 100 b.h.p. of his motor car. The power is in the car; it resides in the nature of the engine and so forth; but the driver has it at his disposal and may be said to possess it. Strictly analogously, the powerful agent possesses power in a sense, but the power he possesses resides in the social context and outside its possessor.

Perhaps all this will seem obvious, and the explicit discussion of it pedantic. Nonetheless, there is no harm in labouring the point. We are far too prone to think of power inhering in the individual who possesses it. Even when we explicitly recognize it as erroneous we are still liable to lapse back into this mode of thought in unguarded moments and to make mistaken inferences in consequence. Perhaps we should blame our history for the difficulty. In Europe, since feudal times or earlier we have made a fetish of hierarchy and assumed that all of value is concentrated at the 'top' of society. Power has radiated from heroic figures; they have glowed with it and illuminated everyone else. There could be no question that they might actually need anyone else. The lower orders were the dross through which the mythical knight cut swathes, *en route* to a true knightly opponent: all power was in the knight and his opponent; none in the hundreds who fell as he cut his path. Later, idealist doctrines conceived of spirit emanating from God into the higher realms of His Church and His society, animating human clay and forcing it into motion: brute matter was inert and incapable of independent action, becoming active only as spiritual power suffused into it, spiritual power mediated by God's agents and deputies at the head of society, spiritual power which radiated from above to activate and direct the clay below. Thus was initiated many centuries of controversy between a dominant idealism and materialism, and thus was defined and established the enduring ideological dimension of this controversy.[10]

Our very language and linguistic idiom are structured around this emanationist conception. Dominant figures are 'powerful', as if jugs of power have been poured down their throats. They 'possess' power, like the finery they wear and the silver in their dining-rooms. Power is 'divided' or 'distributed' amongst them like the spoils of war or the food at a banquet. Custom being what it is, one must needs employ this emanationist idiom, at least to some extent. But it remains the case that power, capacity for action, is actually right down there amongst the supposedly powerless, and that it is only discretion in use which is strongly concentrated at the higher levels of society.

The deposition of the Shah in 1979 marked the onset of revolutionary change in Iran. Many Western politicians and their advisors found it surprising. Many social scientists and political theorists found their ideas in need of revision. The Shah, after all, 'had' vast oil revenues; immense stocks of armaments and advanced weapons; formidable resources for coercion including the notorious secret police force Savak; a developed state apparatus and goodness knows what else. The clerics who engineered the Revolution 'had' very little. How then could the latter overwhelm the former? The problem, of course, is formulated wrongly. No doubt cartoonists were entitled to draw the Shah with bombs protruding from his hip-pocket and fighter-planes from his attaché case, but nobody should have thought in that way. What the Shah 'had' was a certain degree of discretion established in an overall distribution of knowledge. The fighter-planes and bombs were elsewhere. What had to be done was to shift the structure of discretion, a difficult enough task no doubt but much easier than to destroy the entire capacity for action embedded in an entire society. The Revolution shifted discretion and succeeded: this is all that successful revolutions ever have to do. We need to ensure that we have broken completely free of the residue of an emanationist view of power, and explicitly to recognize that power lies outside and beyond the power-holder is as good a way as any of doing this.[11]

Difficulties

The present conception of power, even in an embryonic and undeveloped state, clearly has interesting implications and raises some deep issues. Merely to assert that the power of a society is its capacity for action, and that it is discretion in the use of power which powerful agents 'possess', is to take a useful step forward. Nonetheless, this simple statement glosses over a host of difficulties and complications. It is a possible starting-point for thought, not a culmination. Hidden by its central terms is an endless tangle of problems, conceptual ambiguities, obscurities and issues in need of prolonged empirical investigation. Let me conclude this section by briefly making mention of some of these problems and hinting at how much is left unspecified by the simple account given so far.

To state that power is the general capacity for action in a society immediately raises fundamental problems, since it means that power is quite beyond precise description. A society is capable of innumerable possible forms of action in any given situation, and those possibilities themselves change from one situation to another. The best we can do here is to accept a fact which is as true of the power of an engine as of the power of a society and console ourselves with the knowledge that in both cases it may still be very useful for practical purposes to talk about power. We say that one army is more powerful than another, thinking in terms of general capacity to act; or we say that a new tank will add to the power of an army, again thinking in terms of general capacity for action; and statements of this kind make sense and have practical utility. We calculate on the basis of them; we have to do so, and although we always find our calculations less than adequate, we generally find them better than nothing.

Our thought about power as capacity generally moves at the ordinal level. We are generally content with our ability to note changes which add to or subtract from power as capacity. With a little more caution we may compare two blocs of power and decide which is the greater. But we are notably and rightly reluctant to state precisely how much power is here or there, or by how much one accumulation of power exceeds another. Social power is simply not a metrically measurable quantity and any attempt to impose a metric upon it, far from improving the precision and predictive power of our knowledge, would merely divert attention from the way in which capacity to act varies with situation. Even ordinal comparisons of power can mislead. Britain, so it is said, is a major naval power, and Iceland a minor one; yet in their 'cod war', in the 1970s, the British navy lacked the requisite capacity for effective action and went down to defeat. A similar moral can be drawn from the Vietnam War. [12]

I have said that social power is largely embedded in routines and organized interaction. For the most part I think that this is correct, but as well as being a qualified statement it is one that should not be interpreted too strictly. A formation of aircraft attacking in perfect order is a manifestation of power. So too is a riot. Whoever is able to direct the aircraft at discretion possesses power. Whoever can start the riot and point it roughly in the right direction possesses power. Similarly with mobs, strikes, mutinies, commotions: however chaotic, they are manifestations of power, or so I choose to regard them. No doubt as rioters, strikers and similar groups become more organized, and their activities more skilled and co-ordinated, their power, their capacity for action, increases. And no doubt a power-holder finds very highly ordered routinized actions more reliable instruments to use at discretion than disordered confused masses of action. Nonetheless, even weak trends and tendencies in collective action make it an instrument of a sort: if the rocks or the petrol-bombs tend to land in some sort of a pattern, then their source may perhaps be directed purposefully and profitably.

Where power is exercised with the active support of subordinates it might be thought that the routinization and prior organization of action is so much less important, since willing underlings will bear the objectives of the power-holder in mind and improvise and creatively adapt their actions on the spot to further those objectives. This, however, is to make a false contrast. Creative, improvisatory, collective activity is generated most readily out of organization and routinized activity. When an army needs improvisation and on-the-spot judgement it sends in its most highly trained personnel. When a government seeks to fill a sensitive diplomatic post it seeks experience. The spontaneity of chamber music requires a more secure technique, a more developed command of routines, than is needed to meet the more predictable demands of the orchestra's conductor.

Power is predominantly, if not totally, embedded in or based upon routines and organized actions. But it is discretion in using the routines and the organization that is involved in *possessing* power. What, then, is this discretion? It is nothing more than the ability of an agent to act or to give a sign, which act or sign is followed by an appropriate change in the routine in question. If signs from an agent stop, start, redirect, or reorder a routine as he intends, then he has discretion over that routine. (Perhaps we should say that if there is a probability of the signs having the intended effects, then discretion exists. Or perhaps we should say that the higher this probability, the greater the discretion. This aspect of the notion can be adjusted to taste, since nothing fundamental is involved.)

An agent has discretion over a routine, and hence has power, to the extent that the routine is responsive to his direction. Thus, Atahualpa was as powerful after his captivity as before, or almost, and Mahatma Gandhi was as powerful in prison as in freedom, if not more so. Merely making the actions of powerful agents *costly* does not diminish their power. Routines have, on occasion, been directed by hunger-strikes, or moves in and out of captivity. These are costly procedures not to be employed too frequently, but those employing such procedures have nonetheless possessed power: routines have been at their disposal and have been directed and controlled as they decided.

A strange anomaly is created by use of this notion of discretion. Consider a soldier in an army. His actions are at his discretion: his limbs respond to his direction; they move as he decides. Consider now the soldier's commanding officer. The soldier's actions are available at the discretion of the commanding officer: the soldier's limbs respond to the officer's direction; they move as he decides. It would appear that two agents have discretion over the same action(s), which is counter-intuitive. Yet it would be pointless to deny the control of the officer if complete compliance is actually observed, and it would be incorrect to deny the control of the soldier himself, acting voluntarily, perhaps to avoid the firing-squad, not involuntarily, without calculation and conscious control.[13] Hence the counter-intuitive formulation, if less than ideal, is perhaps the best. When we map a distribution of discretion in the use of power, we may find the same capacities assigned more than once, 'possessed' by different agents. So long as those agents never clash in how they employ their discretion there is no difficulty: should they clash, then knowledge ceases to guide action and routine may break down. Sometimes power-holders pre-empt such difficulties by making it known that the commands or directions of one have *priority* over those of another. This is a key technique in the creation and maintenance of hierarchies, wherein priorities are generally widely known and sustained by sanctions.

Finally, there is the matter of the agent who exercises discretion, the power-holder, the possessor of power. So far I have treated the power-holder as a specific individual, but it need not be so. Power may also be held by a 'collective actor', to use the customary term. Any persisting and persistently recognizable set of interactions from which clear directions emanate may replace an individual as a power-holder. Nothing prevents recognition of a board of a company, or a central committee, or an army council, as a substitute individual. Nothing prevents such an entity developing procedures and practices which produce a single coherent output of accepted judgements and decisions, analogous to individual judgements and decisions yet identifiable with no individual. Nothing prevents such an entity carrying through processes of calculation and inference in the way that an individual might. Technical differences may exist between an individual and a collective actor in the way that various tasks are accomplished, or in the ease with which they are accomplished, or in the conditions for the stability of the actor itself, but none of these differences are fundamental. A collective actor may possess power in just the way that an individual does, with that power being independent of and unattributable to any lesser part of the actor, since it is known to be that of the whole actor. There is nothing problematic about this: consider the power to fire a nuclear weapon possessed by its two key-holders, or the power to legislate possessed by a majority of representatives.

Power may be possessed by an individual or by a collective actor. It may also be associated with an office. Discretion may be delegated to an individual or to an office according to the judgement of those who delegate. Discretion may be presented as that of an individual or that of an office-holder. There is no fundamental problem here.

There are, however, some fascinating technical problems, which stem from the fact that the individual acting *ex officio* and the individual *per se* are indistinguishable as visible phenomena, and are often differentiated incompletely in practice. Some people may initially see a leader as an office-holder; others may see an individual commanding personal loyalty; others again may fail to distinguish the two alternatives. And as members act toward a leader on these diverse grounds, and come to know that this is how they act, everybody comes to recognize the 'personal' component of the leader's power, even those who initially discounted it, and everybody comes to recognize the power of the leader's office, even those who initially gave no thought to it. Such a leader never quite becomes a 'normal' agent on retirement from office: even if all official appearances have been in uniform, the face has been a part of the uniform and remains a part of the individual. Similarly, the successor to such a leader never quite becomes the same leader with the same power. And indeed there is no need to speak of 'such a leader' here, for this is something which is true, to a greater or lesser extent, with all leaders and all successors.

It is told of General Franco that late in his life he became seriously ill, and not being expected to live laid down his office and passed it on to his successor. Spain could hope to enjoy political continuity, whilst Franco, now an ordinary citizen, received the last rites and passed away. But Franco's illness took an unexpected turn, and eventually, after many days, he regained his health. His return to power was apparently a simple matter. One day he arrived at the office of the head of state. 'I am recovered, Arias', he said, and walked in.[14] Franco was known to have a 'personal' following.

3.2 DELEGATION

In section 3.1 power was defined as capacity for action and the possession of power as the possession of discretion in the use of capacity for action. Both power and its possession were then characterized as features of a distribution of knowledge and hence as properties of societies as a whole and not of independent individuals. To discover what powers an individual possessed required examination of the context: it depended on what others knew, including what others knew that others knew and so on. Nonetheless, the discussion remained unduly individualistic in its concentration on the individual power-holder. It is now necessary to recognize that power is distributed over many power-holders who engage in interaction with each other. We need to consider how systems of powers may be developed and stabilized so that they persist as features of the distribution of knowledge, and how all the myriad interactions in the society, based upon and informed by the distribution of knowledge, somehow serve to keep something close to that distribution in existence. We must not look for anything like a properly adequate understanding here: given the inordinate complexity of all actual societies that would be Utopian. What we can do, however, is to look at some of the social processes involved in the generation and development of extensive systems of power relations, and hope thereby to understand a little of the conditions which make for their stability and the conditions that undermine them.[15]

Let us first look at processes wherein power is *delegated*. A power-holder may make over to another the direction of those routines which are initially under his control. Since the power-holder has discretion over how such routines should operate, he may use that discretion to set them under the control of a delegate. He may make it generally known that powers have been assigned, and thereby assign them. This is simply one way of exercising discretion in the use of power. If we understand how a power-holder is able to exercise power, then we also have a basic understanding, *ipso facto*, of how he is able to delegate it. But if the possibility of delegation raises no deep issues, the details of the process are nonetheless worth extended consideration, since by delegation simple systems of personal control may metamorphose into complex tiered hierarchies, and the further development and elaboration of such hierarchies may frequently involve the extension, or alternatively the curtailment, of the delegation of power.

'Upward' delegation

Consider first the 'upward' delegation of power, whereby individuals make over some of whatever routines they control, perhaps merely the routine actions of their own bodies, to be used at the discretion of someone with a greater available capacity for action than any delegating individual.[16] The incentive to delegation of this kind is the logistical gains that come from organization and the ability to act in concert with others. A delegate may be endowed with the capacity for action of a great number of individuals, in the hope that he will use it to produce gains beyond the reach of those individuals acting independently. Such a delegate may be supported and obeyed willingly, either because what he is doing is seen to be beneficial or because whatever he does is trusted to be beneficial. The delegating individual may accept some loss or alienation of power as the necessary price for gains which are only obtainable through organized action. The disincentive to such delegation is the risk that delegated power may be turned back upon its origins, that a delegate may metamorphose into a ruler and an oppressive ruler at that. The individual who enters an organization to further his interests, and makes over some of his capacity for action to others thereby, must beware that he does not become a part of a human machine, serving those who originally promised to serve him.[17]

We are on familiar ground here. The horns of this dilemma have been extensively explored by sociologists, building on the initial statements of Max Weber, Roberto Michels and others. In particular, Michels's (1915) analysis of political parties, thorough and richly illustrated as it is, continues to serve as a model exposition of the dangers of upward delegation. The delegate to a political party becomes involved in a bureaucratic and administrative structure, a structure which is a technical necessity if political ends are actively to be pursued and fought for. The delegate accordingly develops technical and administrative skills, deep experience of the organization and its operation, familiarity with committees and their procedures, and he becomes a part of the organization of the party, a link in many vital chains of communication, a component of decision-taking systems. On both counts he gains power. Crucial routines would break down without him; laboriously acquired capacity for action would be dissipated, coherence lost. He is no longer a mere delegate. He is a permanent fixture. Even if he is nominally subject to frequent re-election, he is effectively safe: far from facing removal from office, he may actually threaten to resign it in order to enforce his

will: 'In the German Empire the average official life of a minister of state
is four years and three months. In the leadership . . . of the socialist
party we see the same persons occupying the same posts for forty years in
succession' (Michels, 1915, p. 106). Such persons, securely ensconced
over long periods of time, are ideally placed to accumulate further
powers: the control of party finances will fall into their hands, and the
power of appointment of lesser officials and functionaries, which
patronage may guarantee them the unswerving support of numerous
toadies and lackeys. The eventual result of all this must be oligarchical
control, even of what initially was a democratically ordered party. An
active minority will decide the policies for which the majority will merely
provide the resources, and the policies decided upon by the active
minority will increasingly reflect their interests, as distinct from those of
the majority they supposedly represent. They will be policies tinged with
the conservatism of the bureaucrat and administrator, suffused with the
compromise and hesitancy of those well placed in the existing order of
things, weakened by the venality that is so much more readily exploited
in the few than in the many.[18] They will be policies reflecting the vested
interests of the delegated, not of those who delegate. 'The party is
created as a means to an end. Having, however, become an end in itself,
endowed with aims and interests of its own, it undergoes detachment,
from the teleological point of view, from the class which it represents'
(ibid., pp. 405–6). This leads Michels to his final and most deeply
pessimistic conclusion of all, with regard to the case in which his interest
is deepest: 'The socialists might conquer, but not socialism' (ibid.,
p. 408).

It is hard not to be impressed by Michels's 'iron law of oligarchy'. Not
quite iron, perhaps, it is nonetheless as hard and metallic as these things
ever get in the social sciences. The efficient pursuit of collective goals in
the face of resistance does indeed require organization and the concentration of discretion as 'a matter of technical and practical necessity'
(ibid., p. 40). Coherent collective action requires direction by a few, and
direction by a few just is oligarchy. Michels's law is nearly, if not
completely, a tautology. But if the law is thus, in a certain sense,
acceptable, the overall pessimistic vision of its proponent is not. The
unremitting gloom of Michels's study is not entirely justified and needs
some correction. The 'detachment' of representatives from those whom
they represent occurs neither so readily nor so completely as Michels is
ready to believe. Indeed, he himself recognizes that 'oligarchy' is one
thing and 'detachment' another, that 'The democratic party, even when
subjected to oligarchical control, can doubtless act upon the state in the
democratic sense' (ibid., p. 381). What prevents him from exploring
possible positive aspects of oligarchy seems to be a lofty contempt for

any one or any group willing to submit to oligarchical direction, a high disdain for the majority which 'is really delighted to find persons who will take the trouble to look after its affairs' (ibid., p. 58). Like many intellectuals, Michels finds it undignified to be 'looked after', particularly when the mental rather than the physical realm is involved, and he is unwilling sympathetically to consider the position of those who 'experience a profound need to prostrate themselves not simply before great ideals, but also before the individuals who in their eyes incorporate such ideals' (ibid., p. 73).[19]

Let us, however, focus for a moment upon these individuals and the extent of their 'detachment' from those they represent. It is true no doubt that such individuals develop distinct interests and objectives, and it is also true that they acquire powers which give them some autonomy, and lessen their dependence upon their initial supporters. But they still have to rely upon the resources provided by the great mass of supporters, and they have no ready means of enforcing the provision of these resources and turning active support into compelled obedience: strong sanctions, comprehensive surveillance, means for sustaining insulated and fragmented forms of social experience, all the essential tools of systematic coercion are lacking. The supporter of a party is normally in a position to walk away from it. Even if he has to pay some small exiting costs, he may leave – and what can safely be left may safely be created.[20]

Those who delegate power upwards must expect, to some extent, to be betrayed. The leaders they create will invariably represent them less effectively than might be wished, and almost invariably divert some of their enriched capacity for action to feathering their own nests. But so long as leaders need the resources provided by those they represent, and so long as these resources may be withdrawn, some return must be made for their provision. Leaders and followers are thrown into a bargaining relation. Together they possess organized resources which may yield a return. The leaders are in a position to disrupt the organization; the followers are in a position to withdraw the resources. A trade-off is to be expected. Those who dominate the party machine and those who pay for it will both benefit, even if the former, in practice, benefit far more than 'in theory' they should.[21] The real danger to those who delegate only arises when their ability to withdraw, to retire beyond the ambit of the system, is restricted. As boundary fences are built, as exit costs become intolerably great, sanctions, surveillance and social control may be extended and intensified and the many may stand in danger of coercion by the powerful few. Only in closed contexts can a complete 'detachment' of delegates or representatives occur; only in these contexts does Michels's full pessimistic vision carry credibility.[22] Perhaps we should say that only as the party comes close to becoming the state can it become a serious threat to the majority of its own members and supporters.

'Downward' delegation: empowering and authorizing

Let us turn now to the 'downward' delegation of power. When an existing power-holder delegates some of his capacity for action to a subordinate, he may still remain more powerful than that subordinate and hope to exert a continuing control over him. Nonetheless, downward delegation gives rise to dilemmas similar to those already discussed. As before, logistical gains are the incentive. The power-holder may simplify his controlling activities and increase their efficiency; he may save time and so hope to direct more and more routines; he may obtain more benefits from a given effort in the use of power. But also as before, to delegate power is to risk the loss of power. The delegate may metamorphose into a rival; alienated powers may react back upon their origin; discretion once handed over may prove impossible to recover. With downward delegation, however, the situation is complicated by the existence of alternative forms of delegation. The power-holder may delegate in different ways as he attempts to resolve the standard dilemmas. It is worth considering two extreme, contrasted forms of downward delegation. I shall call them 'empowering' and 'authorizing': the former, I shall say, confers genuine power upon subordinates, whereas the latter confers mere authority.[23]

When an agent is empowered, discretion in the direction of a body of routine activity is transferred to him. It is made known that he possesses delegated discretion, which results in his indeed possessing it. He may be 'given' an army for a campaign, an army unit for a siege, a fleet for exploration or for piracy, a laboratory and a budget for company-relevant research, or a cheque for an advertising campaign. The empowered agent is expected to further the objectives of the power-holder, but enjoys discretion in the use of power in order to further those objectives. He formulates his own on-the-spot plans, and puts them into action independently. He is, in effect, an authentic power-holder in his own right, even if in some cases the delegator continues to make use of the delegated powers directly, overriding his delegate whenever he so chooses.

Empowering is a simple and adaptable method of mobilizing a capacity for action and keeping it operative. But the power-holder must ensure that he can recover the discretion he has foregone at an appropriate time. A dictator may place a part of his army at the disposal of a subordinate, perhaps for the execution of a specific task. He cannot be sure that his subordinate will act as desired, and refrain from using his armed force against the dictatorship itself. The dictator must therefore assess the loyalty of the force and of his subordinate, and the capacity for independent action of the force if loyalty should prove to be lacking. Where an army has an independent capacity for action, and is not liable to immediate paralysis by withdrawal of external support, it would be a foolish policy to delegate control of any great proportion of it to a single subordinate for any length of time, although given the number of *coups d'états* engineered by army chiefs of staff in recent times this would seem to be a principle honoured as much in the breach as the observance. Nonetheless, the empowering of subordinates is a commonplace practice, and the subsequent recovery of power is often routine and unproblematic. Even the greater part of an individual's power may be delegated to others without danger in suitable circumstances. Emperors from Augustus to Napoleon used family and close kin as trustworthy repositories of delegated power. At their apogee, European monarchs employed officials of mean birth within their realms, and adventurers of equally inauspicious origins to glean the wealth of far-off lands, secure in the knowledge that no threat was thereby posed to their position. Indeed, like despots the world over, they were able almost casually to send even the greatest of such figures off to execution, as personal whim or political expediency dictated.[24]

There is much to be said for empowering. It relieves the power-holder of much of the burden of control. It allows the subordinate on the spot to respond creatively to the realities of a situation and to whatever unforeseen circumstances arise therein. And the risks and dangers involved can often be reduced to manageable proportions, whether by the tried and trusted methods of despots and totalitarian regimes, or by more refined and complicated means. The most sophisticated method of empowering is probably the subsidy or subvention, which can be turned on or off, reduced or increased, with great rapidity, so that an unusual degree of dependence can be hoped for on the part of the subordinate power. This is a method of long standing still much favoured in current international relations.

Nonetheless, at whatever level of sophistication, empowering involves a loss of discretion. The power-holder becomes dependent upon the future decisions and judgements of others, and may lose the ability to direct his resources according to a coherent, detailed and harmonious plan of action. It may be that the power-holder is unwilling to pay this price. He may seek to keep all the levers of power under his own hands, whilst recognizing nonetheless that delegation of some kind is essential to solve the logistical problems of control. In these circumstances he may attempt to proceed by delegating *authority* to subordinates, not power, so that actions are directed by them, but not as they choose. He may make it known that delegates are to be obeyed only in so far as they transmit instructions from 'above'.

The routinized activities of a society do not carry on automatically, like a vast non-stop assembly line. They must be directed according to circumstances. I have described those who direct routine activities at discretion, those who start or stop them, point them this way or that, combine them or disassemble them as they see fit, as the powers in a society. But routines may also be directed routinely. Control may be routinized just as much as the action that is controlled. The controller may respond to signs and signals just as those he controls respond to him. Whole systems of nested routines may be built up wherein controllers in one layer are themselves closely controlled and directed by instructions from the layer above.

Subordinate controllers in this position I wish to call 'authorities'. Whereas powers direct routines and organized actions with discretion, authorities are expected to direct them as if without discretion. Authorities may be considered, in the first instance, as mere relays in developed systems of control. They direct routines in response to external signs or instructions. Perhaps they always throw a switch when a light comes on, or perhaps they have an instruction book and consult the book to ascertain how they must act in response to a given signal. The immediate source of such external signals may be a power, or another authority acting routinely, or even an instrument or a mechanical device. But the ultimate source of such signals, the end-point of the chain of control, will always be a power. An authority, therefore, may be characterized as the passive agent of a power.

The difference here being drawn between a power and an authority will, I hope, be reasonably clear intuitively, and recognizably related to some aspects of the everyday usage of the two terms. When a stockbroker has the use of a client's money to deal as he decides he is empowered; when he is given a specific detailed buying-order he is then merely possessed of the authority to carry it out. When a plenipotentiary is sent to negotiate he is empowered; when he sets forth to the subsequent signing ceremony he is merely authorized. An interesting case is raised by the position of the British monarch, who signs Acts of Parliament into law. The monarch's signature switches on the provisions of an Act. This is uncontroversial. But it is debatable whether or not this stands as part of the power of the monarch, and when the point is discussed and argued in common-sense terms the distinction of power and authority set out above is liable to emerge. If the monarch is considered to retain real power, of which the Assent is a part, then it is likely to be said that the monarch has some recognized discretion, whether to withhold it or to give it. If it is denied that the Assent affords power to the monarch, then it is likely that the monarch's authority will be acknowledged, but that the existence of any recognized discretion in its use will be denied: any properly constituted Act, it will probably be said, simply must be given the Assent.

Evidently my distinction between power and authority has some basis in common usage. I would not claim, however, that it is fully vindicated by common usage, or even that it derives from the predominant tendency of common usage. Much of the time, in everyday discourse, 'power' and 'authority' are used interchangeably, and where a distinction is drawn between the one and the other there are a number of alternative ways of doing so. Should a police officer, without a warrant, break down the door and put his underlings to turning our dwelling upside-down, smashing the furniture and ripping out the fittings, in a search for something or other, it would be evidence of realism, as well as of regard for the niceties of common usage, to protest his lack of *authority*, not his lack of power. This seems to suggest that authority is something *more* than power, not something less as I have claimed. In the above example authority seems to be thought of as something like 'power plus the right to use it'.

This notion of authority as power *plus* has carried over into the literature of sociological theory. There is something like a consensus that authority is power plus an additional ingredient, which ingredient greatly enhances the effectiveness of the original substance and makes it much easier to use. It is commonly asserted that power-holders should convert their power into authority as soon as they may, if they wish to enjoy a secure, long-term predominance in their society. How, though, is the conversion to be achieved? What precisely is the necessary additional ingredient? Many writers refer to processes of routinization here, and think of authority as power institutionalized. Others speak of a need for legitimacy, and take authority to be power accepted and recognized by those over whom it is exercised. These are not the only ways of treating authority in the literature but they are the major ones, and many alternative formulations are actually very close in substance to one or the other. Accepted wisdom, therefore, may be fairly summarized thus: either authority is power plus institutionalization, or it is power plus legitimacy.[25]

In contrast, I have defined authority as power *minus* – power minus recognized independent discretion. If I were obliged to defend this view I should insist that power and authority are indistinguishable by reference to institutionalization. Power, that is, social power, just is a capacity for action produced by institutionalization and routinization: dissolve institutions and routines from a power structure and the power goes too. Hence it must be incorrect to treat power as something prior to institutionalization, something that is capable of being institutionalized but so far is not: power and authority *both* involve institutionalization. Conversely, I should say that *neither* power nor authority necessarily involve legitimacy. What a police officer is authorized to do, and is generally known to be authorized to do, may produce just as much outrage and just as much dissension as what he does without authorization: the South Africa of the 1980s offers many examples. Analogously, concentration camp inmates may speak of what some particular guard has the authority to do, and what not, without any question of legitimacy arising in either case. Indeed particular guards, with residual inclinations to normal human behaviour, may use their *powers* to help inmates, passing them food perhaps, or fuel, in contravention of an *authority* which derives from superiors, not from those below them. Finally, I should suggest that even when we employ everyday language to condemn the illegitimate actions of authorities, we often recognize that authority has the character of a constraint upon power rather than an addition to it or support for it. To return to the intrusive police officer: does not an assertion of his lack of authority remind him, not of the illegitimacy of his actions in the eyes of those suffering from them, but of their incompatibility, or possible incompatibility, with the expectations of his superiors? Is it not that he has *exceeded* his authority? And does not this acknowledge that the officer is no longer constrained by restrictions from 'above', that he is acting as a power and not as a mere authority, that he possesses a discretion he can freely exercise over subordinates who have 'forgotten' the limits upon how he is supposed to act?

All these, however, are arguments which I should advance only if pressed, in order to show that my chosen nomenclature is viable and sensible, and that it makes a secure connection with common usage along which useful intuitions can flow. I do not wish to criticize alternative conceptions of 'power' and 'authority', or even to discourage their further development.

Why authorities never quite are

Let me return to the task of describing authority and authorization as I conceive of them. When a power-holder delegates authority rather than power, when he authorizes, he again faces the problem of retaining control over his subordinate(s). Part of the problem is that of retaining sanctions in his own hands, or at least of having a sufficiency thereof quickly available. Just as it is unwise to delegate too much power to a single agent, so it is unwise to delegate too much authority, since authority may metamorphose into power and react back upon the original power-holder. The power-holder will attempt to make his subordinate authorities known as authorities, recognized as authorities and nothing more, but *their* subordinates may nonetheless tend to 'mistake' them for powers, or find it expedient to treat them as power-holders in their own right. Hence authorities will constantly be tempted to abandon their simulation of passive agents and to act as independent powers in their own right, and to the extent that they succeed in doing this they become powers in their own right and correspondingly diminish the powers of those 'above'.

Authorities will constantly be tempted to exercise their own independent discretion. If this temptation is to be overcome authorities must remain vulnerable to the powers of which they are the agents. Powers must be able to make it costly for authorities to exercise an autonomous discretion, whether by removing rewards or by applying sanctions. Only this will force an authority, who is after all an active, calculative, knowledgeable agent, to operate reliably, even against his own immediate inclination. Hence authorities will be given subordinates by whom they are disliked or with whom they share few interests, and power-holders will delegate to a number of authorities, so that any one may be coerced or overawed by the mobilization of others, and every part of the system of authority is at once sustained by threat and a source of threat. Authority will often be structured with a mind to the principles of divide and rule, just like delegated power.

There is, however, a further problem of control which arises when authority and not power is delegated. In this case it is necessary to give detailed instructions to the subordinate; otherwise the operation of his independent judgement is actually necessary. Large amounts of information have reliably to be transmitted: precise specifications of actions and of the circumstances surrounding actions have to be codified, and what is codified must be accurately decoded and understood. A shared signalling system is therefore essential, a system that employs signs and symbols interpreted everywhere in the same way, in other words a shared language.[26] Thus it is necessary to appreciate some of the general features of language and linguistic representation in order to grasp the nature of authority and the problems involved in establishing and sustaining it.

All languages allow speakers to construct innumerable practically useful specific verbal formulations from but a few thousand generally understood terms. This enormous versatility is to a great extent a product of the *generality of reference* of the empirically significant terms of a language. A natural-kind term, 'cat' for example, may be routinely used to refer to a vast number of distinct specific entities, even though innumerable other such entities may be ruled out as likely referents when the term is used. By speaking of cats we narrow down the likely referents of our speech, but we do not fix a specific referent. Consequently, it is possible to obey the command 'Fetch a cat' in innumerable different ways, if only because any number of cats exist to be fetched. Analogously, terms that refer to actions refer to innumerable possible behaviours, so that a command that requires an action may be obeyed in any number of ways by choosing between alternative behaviours. Where the command is 'Fetch the cat', and there is but one cat plausibly available, there are nonetheless innumerable methods of doing the fetching. Hence no command can ever be said to fix precisely what is done by way of obedience to it. A command may, at best, define a class of possible obedient actions from which the subordinate is able to choose. No elaboration of instructions or proliferation of verbal output can serve to alter this basic condition. 'Fetch the cat in a box', or 'Fetch the cat in a box carried in the right hand', or other developed forms of the initial command, may narrow the range of acceptable obedient responses, but they leave the basic relationship between language and what language specifies untouched: innumerable ways of meeting the linguistically formulated specifications always remain.

It follows that no individual may ever be made to operate as the completely passive agent of a power. There can be no perfect authority. The very business of obeying instructions, of acting as directed, will always involve one way of obeying being preferred to another as a matter of the individual judgement of the subordinate. The most that the power-holder can do is to specify which of two alternative classes of actions the subordinate is obliged to draw from, as it were, for the particular action he performs. The subordinate remains able to select at discretion from the particular class so specified.

Discretion of this kind may, however, detract scarcely at all from the effective control of the power-holder. On the one hand, the power-holder may be indifferent between all the possible acts of obedience which fall into a specific general class: any of them may do equally well as far as his practical purposes are concerned. On the other hand, the power-holder may not be indifferent, but in this case he may always develop further the linguistic specification of what he wants his subordinate to do, until finally a class is specified of actions between which he is indifferent. One way or the other the power-holder should be able to specify the actions he requires to an extent sufficient to serve all his practical purposes. The generality of reference of terms or concepts may mean that obedient actions are never *ipso facto* fully determined actions, but they may nonetheless be sufficiently determined as far as the power-holder with his specific interests and objectives is concerned.

More serious for the power-holder is the *indefiniteness* of reference of terms or concepts.[27] A body of empirically significant concepts cannot be acquired simply by familiarity with verbal rules for their proper use; it is necessary to be given *instances* of such proper use, actual cases, paradigm examples: there is, for example, no verbal rule in use amongst us for what is red and what is not; we learn 'red' by familiarity with particular instances of correct use. Such instances do not fix a definite boundary between what is red and what is not; rather, they serve as an *analogy* for the further development of proper usage. We encounter new instances of 'red' which, notwithstanding the fact that they are non-identical with existing instances, strike us as like existing instances, and hence are spoken of as 'red' also. Or rather, they may be so spoken of, or they may not; for an analogy can only suggest; it cannot compel. The correct use of language does not exist ahead of what members of society actually say or state: members do not discover it or perceive it set out ahead of them; they lay it down as they go along. As they travel along the road from their paradigms of 'red', toward 'pink', in the direction of 'white', different competent individuals may cease to speak of 'red' at different points, each equally plausible as the place up to which to take the analogy, each equally plausible as the place at which to abandon it. This is as good an image as any of the relationship between existing correct usage and later correct usage. Existing usage guides later usage; it serves as a resource in the development of later usage; it generates individual inclinations for or against specific kinds of later usage; but it does not and cannot determine later usage: later usage is open-ended, and underdetermined by existing usage.

Because reference is indefinite and the future use of terms is open-ended, the reliable communications essential to the delegation of authority are not ensured merely by the existence of 'language' or putative shared rules of language use. 'Language' and linguistic rules do not constitute a system of communication independent of the people who participate in it. Reliable communication is actually constituted by people themselves: it occurs, to the extent that it occurs, when people respond alike to signs and symbols, act alike on the basis of rules and instructions. Reliable communication is a matter of common responses and common actions permeating a set of agents, not a matter of a set of verbal rules and meanings determining the behaviour of those agents. The problem of achieving reliable communication is therefore not that of establishing a specific formal system of rules and meanings. Linguistic and symbolic constructions do not embody and transmit information through their alleged intrinsic significances and implications, but through their empirical, behavioural consequences as they are used by some and impinge upon others in specific sets of people. The problem of reliable communication is therefore that of generating uniform responses to linguistic constructs within a given set of people.

More precisely, the problem is that of achieving acceptably uniform *initial* responses throughout a given set of people within a given situation. A linguistically formulated command like 'Switch on the light' may serve as a clear instruction for members in many situations, and hence serve to connect power and authority in such situations. No matter that the sense of the instruction is specific to the situation, and that in other situations it may be given other senses. No matter that outsiders may interpret the formulation differently from members. No matter that members themselves, by taking thought, may produce any number of plausible interpretations of the formulation. So long as the formulation elicits what for practical purposes is just one *immediate* response, then it may serve as the basis of reliable communication. The immediate, unhesitating, unreflective, matter-of-course response may be fastened upon and talked up, *ex post facto*, as the implied response, the correct response, and thereby may be standardized for the practical purposes of communication and information exchange. The immediate response is the 'prominent solution' to the problem of what the power-holder's instruction means.

How though is the essential uniformity of initial response to be generated? How is the requisite conformity in understanding to be achieved? No fully satisfactory answers to these questions can be given, but some tentative steps can be taken in the right direction. Conformity at the level of understanding is characteristic of those who share, not superficial verbal formulations of rules, but whole ways of living, common practices, a specific form of life. To participate competently and successfully in a form of life requires a profound and comprehensive training at the level of practice, and where the form of life is highly standardized and uniform the associated training must be highly ordered, intense and systematic. It must be full of rote, repetitions, drills carried out, ideally, in an environment that is itself highly ordered and designed to provide shared perceptions and shared experiences.

We may conjecture then that the conditions for the successful delegation of authority are demanding ones. The reliable sustained communication which must pass between the power-holder and his 'passive' agents can only be established in the context of an ongoing form of life, ideally a form of life of unprecedented uniformity and homogeneity. To create and sustain such a context is no small task. It must be a global enterprise: it requires a willingness to monitor and manipulate every aspect of the world of social experience, and indeed of the world of physical experience as well.[28] The flat hard surface of the parade-ground plays its part in generating uniformity of response in recruits to the army. The ingenious arrangement of the materials of the traffic-light plays its part in sustaining uniformity of response amongst motorists and other road-users. Social order is not independent of natural order.

Needless to say, a global enterprise of this kind must always be to some extent a failure. An operative system of pure and perfect authority relationships is impossible to produce. Such a system can exist only as an ideal toward which power-holders may, in some circumstances, seek to move. In practice, power-holders will always find their commands blighted by imperfect communication, and their capacity to direct action impaired. In practice too, authorities will always possess some leeway to use their own unconstrained discretion, even against power-holders, whilst remaining in some sort of plausible conformity with their instructions from those very power-holders. No doubt in many circumstances power-holders find themselves engaged in a continuing struggle to direct their supposedly passive agents, and to limit the ever-present tendency of these 'authorities' to metamorphose into powers. Conversely we may assume that authorities often resist the pressures upon them, and strive to activate their own independent discretion within the very system of communication and control that is designed as a constraint upon it. Eventually, resistance of this kind may induce power-holders explicitly to allow independent discretionary action on the part of subordinates, and to revert to a policy of empowering.

By delegating the direction of action a power-holder may create subordinate powers, or (ideally) authorities, or something between the two. He may hand over discretion without strings, or discretion with strings attached; and he may add more and more strings in the attempt to create a puppet, even though in this he can never fully succeed. This limit on what is possible by means of delegation is also a limit on the possible extent of subordination itself, however it comes about. Whether it is established by delegation from above, or attachment from below, through fear or inducement, in the visible present or the obscure past, any relation of dominance and subordination will have its limits. The subordinate may be massively restricted in his direction of action, but in practice he will always retain some autonomy, the ability to make some choices free of extrinsic costs, and hence he will never have the status of a completely passive agent. This conclusion can be extended as a matter of course to the very bottom of any tiered hierarchy, and applied to that final layer of subordinates which carries out commands and instructions but does not itself issue them. The control of the powerful over the powerless must necessarily be imperfect and incomplete. Those who perform actions at the behest of others will always retain a residue of unrestricted discretion and autonomy. Indeed, this layer of 'powerless' agents at the bottom of a tiered hierarchy may be considered as a final layer of authority, engaged in the business of direct bodily control, the movement of limbs, the contraction of muscles. Like every other layer of authority in the hierarchy, this final layer will be irreducible to complete passivity. Discretion in the use of social power may be massively concentrated into the hands of a few, but never ever wholly concentrated into those hands.

3.3 DELOCALIZATION

Delegation is an instance of a social process whereby access to power, the ability to use power, is *delocalized*. A power-holder retains the right and ability to use the power he delegates, yet he cannot in practice prevent his subordinate also making independent use of it. Delegation helps a power-holder to enlarge his power as we have seen, but it also enlarges the power of his subordinate. Overall, power *increases*. It increases because capacity for action originally established as the power of one agent becomes established as the power of two, and may indeed be used by both provided only that they do not conflict or interfere with each other in what they do. Note also that in delegating capacities a power-holder both creates the time to direct other capacities and adds to the variety of capacities available to his subordinate: the powers of both agents are *generalized* and cover a greater range of routines than previously was the case.

An act of delegation, then, not only delocalizes access to power, it increases both individual and overall powers and it generalizes the powers available to specific agents. In this it is typical of actions which involve delocalization: the attractiveness of such actions precisely derives from the consequent increase in power and its generalization.

Trade in powers

Another important kind of social process that results in delocalization involves the exchange or trade of powers. Where a power-holder possesses a specific capacity for action and is only able to make use of that capacity some of the time, he may find it profitable to make his spare capacity available to another power-holder on the basis of reciprocity. By acting as another power-holder requires, he may hope to gain a commensurate control over the capacity for action of that other power-holder, and thus convert an over-capacity of one kind into a useful capacity of another kind. Consider one power-holder with capacity for action C_1, and another with C_2. Through reciprocal interaction both may become able to use capacity $(C_1 + C_2)$ for some of the time, instead of C_1 or C_2 all the time. Given that C_1 and C_2 are specific, under-utilized capacities, this may represent an effective increase in the power of both parties and a generalization of the power of both parties, as well as a delocalization of access to power.

Trading in power requires trust, and will thrive where trust can thrive. Trust between individuals may grow if they are obliged to interact with each other frequently and over long periods of time: then each may learn inductively to rely upon the other, and each may reckon on the possibility of future retribution where breaches of trust occur (Axelrod, 1984). It is said plausibly that where one may sanction there one may trust, and our stereotypical images of power-holders wheeling and dealing in smoke-filled rooms, of power being traded and deployed by informal cliques and coteries, fit nicely with this maxim. But trust does not have to be based upon recurrent interpersonal interactions, and the delocalization of powers does not have to be confined to the small numbers constituting cliques or elite groups. There is no reason in principle why a complete and fully generalized trade in powers should not be established throughout a society, analogous to trade in goods and commodities, based on a similar generalized system of trust.

To see that this is so we have only to follow Talcott Parsons's lead and take up the connection between money and power once more. To own property is to possess specific localized sets of rights. But in a monetary economy the owner of a given amount of property has access to a vast range of other rights, through exchange lubricated by money. His possession of property may also be counted as the possession of so much wealth, the monetary equivalent of the property, which serves as a measure of his rights in the whole economic system. The economic rights of the individual are effectively generalized. He may even choose to acquire goods or rights for which he has no desire, which he never sees and never uses, simply to store his rights in general, only taking care that his 'investments' consist of what others most and most consistently desire so that his chances of loss are minimized.

In a monetary economy, access to any given set of goods and services is spread and delocalized; what a given individual has access to is generalized; the overall ability to make use of goods and services increases both at the individual and the collective level. Parsons would wish to claim that as money delocalizes access to 'economic' goods so power delocalizes access to 'political' goods, basing his case on the extent of the analogy between power and money. Having defined power somewhat differently I am able to make the simpler claim that where monetary transactions are routinely established power is correspondingly delocalized. Access to goods and services *is* access to power. Having property rights, financial rights, 'economic' rights generally, *is* having power. When we speak of 'purchasing-power' it is no metaphor. Our purchasing-power is a generalized measure of the associated capacity for action available to us, where the range of available capacity comprises whatever can be bought.

Monetary economies of great size exist. Therefore the delocalization of powers across great numbers is possible. Precisely how it is accomplished may perhaps remain an open question, but that it is accomplished is indubitable. Presumably, access to power is delocalized and generalized successfully because trust itself is delocalized and generalized successfully. In an 'economic' exchange, the receiver of a good, the user of a power, hands a token to its donor. The donor must still await the 'real' recompense for what he has provided: he must still trust others to provide that recompense. But at the point when the token is received trust shifts from its specific source to the entire society wherein the token is recognized. Before reception of the token there is an individual requiring trust, perhaps a stranger or an outsider, idiosyncratic, liable to default, or move, or die. After reception there is an entire society in the habit of accepting the token; and an entire society must therefore transform its habits if the value of the token is altogether to be lost. Value is immune to individual eccentricity, individual duplicity, every kind of individual variability. Societies take a long time to change their gross characteristics, time enough to use a token. Every monetary token, every coin, is in this sense a microcosm of the entire social order within which it circulates: its value is stabilized by the stability of the whole order, and crumbles away only as the order itself crumbles away.[29] Vast routinized orders do not crumble overnight: calculative agents may trust them to last until the next transaction; and in trusting them so long they constitute them for longer.

Systems of monetary exchange are, of course, extremely difficult to establish and institutionalize, and have to develop in long historical processes. But it would be a mistake to think that the restricted scope of monetary exchange in modern societies in any way follows from this difficulty, as though there are areas of interaction where we have not got around, so far, to routinizing the use of money. With monetary exchange the difficulty of institutionalization is all at the beginning. The process feeds upon itself. Half-way is all the way: once a significant number of things have a price, everything has a price. The existing system can be extended to anything at all practically effortlessly: banana-juice futures, sexual services, assassinations, higher degrees – a market could be made in any or all at the drop of a hat. Nor is the use of money in the exchange of powers at all a recent development, or in any way less important than the use of money in the exchange of goods. A key development in the establishment of modern monetary economies was of course that whereby powers became commodities, and the capacity for action of wage labour became purchasable in the market like any other good. Since this point there has been little to gain from making a strong distinction between political and economic power. Wealth now provides generalized capacity for 'political' action; political power provides generalized capacity for 'economic' action; the same generalized medium of exchange is operative and employed routinely in both cases.

In a developed monetary economy trading of any kind is easy to establish at the technical level. The delocalization of access to power is easy to accomplish by these means. Nor does delocalization necessarily act against established interests. Delocalization of access to power is not redistribution of power. Indeed, delocalization will generally most favour those who predominate in any existing status quo. Those with the largest capacity for action have proportionately even more spare capacity to trade. They may look for proportionately more benefits from exchange – organization of powers, economies of scale in the use of power and so forth – all further securing their predominance. In addition, they may hope to monopolize even more securely the long-term transformative capacities for action in their society, since these capacities will become more and more marketable, and like very long-term investments of all kinds will be purchased predominantly by those at the top end of the market. Delocalization will increase and generalize the powers of everyone, and probably increase the powers of the 'powers that be' in the greatest proportion. It seems reasonable to suggest therefore that where delocalization by exchange does not occur in a monetary economy it is because it is being actively curtailed and restricted for quite specific reasons. Where the market has limits, systematic constraining activity must be assumed to be at work, and since the scope of the market remains massively limited even in developed modern economies, it is important to understand why such constraints exist.

Restraint of trade

Restrictions upon the exchange of powers may be inspired by many things, but just a few basic themes stand out. Generalized exchange may be rejected in some circumstances because it actually fails to increase power and proves to be 'economically' inefficient. In other circumstances it may be efficient 'economically', and may be rejected for that very reason. There are times, too, when 'economic' factors are secondary and exchange is restricted precisely in order to sustain a strong separation of powers. Finally, there are kinds of exchanges which would threaten the definition and integration of exchanging units themselves, and which appear to be prohibited for that very reason.

Free trade in goods or powers may often be economically or instrumentally inefficient, and be shunned for no other reason. Market inefficiencies of this kind, which are of particular interest because of their relationship to some current simplistic economic and political ideologies, have been surveyed and assessed by Williamson (1975). His approach is that of the institutional economist: he simply surveys the conditions under which market transactions are likely to be unduly costly.

Given that every market transaction involves its own intrinsic cost, the cost of its own execution in time and effort and so forth, it follows first of all that a move away from the market may be efficient, and hence supported, if it reduces the number of transactions. Thus a move to payment by job classification and collective wage-bargaining, which implies a movement away from market exchange to hierarchical orderings, is economically efficient because of the massive reduction in transactions it accomplishes, and is favoured in consequence both by employers and workers in modern industry. Similarly, part of the cost of a market transaction is information cost, and information costs may be lessened if transactions are localized, standardized and brought under the proximate control of a hierarchical organization. It is difficult to set out in general terms precisely how markets and hierarchies compare in terms of information costs,[30] but there are clearly many circumstances wherein vast savings in information processing and distribution can be effected if transactions are withdrawn from the market and ordered within a hierarchy. Finally, market transactions involve costs resulting from the imperfection of the market mechanism itself and its vulnerability to opportunistic distortions, particularly when monopoly or near monopoly conditions arise. By ceasing to rely upon market exchange and producing a good or maintaining a power within a hierarchy, protection is possible against such uncertainties.

Thus Williamson explains why within the mainstream of 'the economy' itself there should be such grotesque distortions of free market exchange as those represented by the existence of the corporation and the industrial organization. *Laissez-faire* and the free market are in many respects economically inefficient; it is better on instrumental grounds to depart from unrestricted exchange and to accept the existence of entities like Unilever and ICI.[31]

The inefficiencies of free market trading are sources of concern where one's own capacities for action are at issue. The very efficiency of the market may engender similar concern when the capacity for action of others is involved. Maintaining hierarchy and relative placing may be regarded as more important than maximizing powers, so that a loss of power through restrictions on exchange may be accepted provided that others thereby lose proportionately more. Many of the restrictions upon access to information or to specialized competences within hierarchical organizations may be understood in this way (Collins, 1979). So may the institution of potlatch wherein societies systematically destroy accumulated spare capacity for action. Consider too the way that restraints on trade tend to fall particularly heavily upon those with a low capacity for action in the first place, so that the distinctive competences and goods of minorities and deviant groups are prohibited from the market and the increase and generalization of the powers of such groups is selectively discouraged.

Perhaps restrictions that sustain a strong division of powers should simply count as cases of the kind just discussed, but they are nonetheless worth specific mention. Consider the restraints placed on trade in votes. No doubt an economist could make an excellent case not just for a market in votes but for traded options and a futures exchange as well. But money is a pollution in the context of the voting system: it is ritually excluded as a celebration of the separation of economic and political powers. Voting by wealth is the norm at company meetings not at general elections; one share, one vote, reflects powers based in wealth: one person, one vote, reflects powers based in numbers and equally distributed rights of citizenship. These two systems of powers permeate our entire society and continue in a curiously stable coexistence, separate yet intertwined. It is their existence which makes meaningful many of our standard contrasts between 'economic' and 'political' aspects of society. Most widely distributed rights sit wholly within one or the other system so that the rights of every individual are made up basically of two kinds, those which are readily exchangeable and unequally distributed, and those which are non-exchangeable and equally distributed. Much of the political discourse of our time concerns which rights should fall into which system, and the tension between the goals of maximizing powers and equalizing powers is fully recognized in this discourse.

Where restrictions on trade serve to maintain a separation of powers they may actually be definitive of the natures of powerful agents themselves, and thus effectively mark out the bounds of instrumentality in a given context. Agreed conceptions of what are to count as exchanging agents may be established by the specification of *inalienable* powers: some powers are agents' utilities whereas others are agents themselves, and the two must be distinguished and kept separate in the course of calculative action. Thus, at one extreme we have the state as agent, possessed of inalienable powers, ringed around with restrictions upon exchange, supported by armed forces wherein the role of monetary inducements and trade in powers is explicitly minimized. At the other extreme is the individual agent, with inalienable rights over his own body (although some societies have managed to make markets in blood and hair), his own life and his own individual vote. Between these extremes are innumerable ordered social formations which may be treated to a greater or lesser extent as active agents of intrinsic worth, rather than as mere instruments for other agents.

One of the intriguing features of the growth of modern industrial societies is the way in which everything in between the sovereign state and the individual has increasingly become conceived of as mere instrumentality and denied inalienable attributes.[32] In particular, in striking contrast to nearly all earlier economic units, the modern firm or company, the dominant form in which economic activity is currently carried out, is stereotypically conceived of as being of no intrinsic worth or value whatsoever: it is nothing more than a hunk of instrumentality. Needless to say, the company is often regarded as of intrinsic worth by those who work within it, particularly those who manage it and are thereby able to make it the basis for a rich and satisfying overall way of life. This is clear enough from the howls of outrage which often emerge from the boardroom when an asset-stripper ventures to treat a company as a mere purchasable commodity. Faced with such a sacrilege, 'economic rationality' tends to be set aside and tribal warfare is apt to ensue. But in the war the sacrilege itself cannot be mentioned: although what is truly appalling is the treatment of a company as a purchasable commodity at all, its defenders are generally obliged to direct their fire at the alleged inadequacy of the purchase price. The separation of the ultimate ownership and the everyday control of that capacity for action which is a company produces a corresponding division between instrumental and intrinsic evaluations; and the continuing predominance of owners over managers likewise produces an order wherein generalized instrumentality predominates.[33]

To summarize, powers are not difficult to market in modern societies and hence access to them could be extensively delocalized through trade; but in practice such delocalization never occurs. Nothing like a free market in powers has ever existed or will exist. Important pressures against delocalization exist. On the other hand there are always major incentives to delocalize power, whether by trade or delegation or otherwise, and some degree of delocalization will always be found. Were this not to be so, calculative action would operate to make it so. A distribution of knowledge of localized powers would be unstable and fail to reconstitute itself in practice. Actual societies will tend to operate close to the point where tendencies to specify and divide powers counterbalance tendencies to generalization and delocalization. This is not a point of 'functional equilibrium' where the 'needs' of 'society' or even of its members are optimally fulfilled; it is merely the point of partial delocalization, moves away from which always provoke an increased level of countervailing calculative action.

Trust and interpersonal interaction

Where powers are not fully delocalized through the use of a generalized currency they are likely to be delocalized to some extent through interpersonal interactions.[34] Recurrent interactions allow the growth of trust, and where there is trust access to powers may advantageously be delocalized. It is a plausible conjecture that, within all strongly interacting small groups or communities without exception, powers are delocalized to a significant degree, so that the capacities for action of any given member become to some extent available to all. Informal exchange of powers in such contexts cannot be subjected to any elaborate system of bookkeeping and will normally settle into a pattern of generalized reciprocity, wherein the spare capacity for action of any individual is presumed to be at the call of others for any use which does not cause loss to its actual possessor. Probably this is relevant to an understanding of the elaborate stratification of social life characteristic of modern societies, wherein relations based on equity and reciprocity seem only to be established with others of closely comparable resources. Neighbourhoods and local communities are to a considerable extent defined by income brackets. Informal reciprocity in bureaucracies and hierarchical organizations is established predominantly between those on the same level, whether in the same hierarchies or different hierarchies.[35] Representatives in assemblies and legislatures trade powers which in theory are perfectly equivalent. In all these situations and many others the individual makes his powers available to others in the knowledge that he thereby gains access to powers of equivalent magnitude. This is the unspoken principle which underlies the ordering of a great deal of friendly and neighbourly interaction: the rich and powerful, if they are to stay rich and powerful, must fraternize only with each other.[36] Stratification of powers is invariably associated with differentiation and stratification of communities and ways of living.

Where a relatively small number of major power-holders interact intensely together, perhaps in isolation from others, perhaps as possessors of distinct and specialized powers best exploited in combination, a very high level of delocalization of powers will frequently result. In these circumstances it may make good sense for others in the relevant society to abandon individualistic perceptions altogether, and to refer instead to the overall power possessed by the entire set, recognizing that every routine at the disposal of any one member is liable to be employed at the behest of any other. A map of power that associated specific routines with specific power-holders could actually mislead in these circumstances, and a better reckoning of the powers of a given individual be obtained simply by identifying him as a member of an elite. In a political or professional elite access to powers will delocalize over all members, and being available to all members in this way such powers will become matters of interest and importance to all members. Elite members will have vested interests in all the powers available to the elite, and will have an incentive to preserve them and sustain them for general use. The existence of the elite will be a collective good for all its members, and there will be a general incentive for members to sustain its overall form as individual components thereof come and go.[37]

Wherever discretion in the use of power is concentrated, yet still widely distributed and complexly differentiated, elites will exist, exclusive interacting sets of agents engaged in the trade and exchange of powers. Modern societies are shot through with elites of this kind. Capacity for action is ordered, arranged, deployed and set in motion on the large scale precisely by such elites. We know no other way of doing things.[38] The systematic interlocking of vast blocks of capacity for action is accomplished by the systematic interlocking of specific sets of agents.[39]

Elites are usually strongly bounded groupings with devices routinely available for keeping their membership small. Small size is essential to the frequent interpersonal interaction that engenders trust and allows power to delocalize. It is nonetheless a mistake to imagine that the effectiveness and continued predominance of elites is the consequence of their small size and exclusivity. Small strongly bounded groups are found at all levels of society, not just at the top. It may be just as easy for a given number of peasants or workers to band together and trade powers as for the same number of landowners or employers to do so. Needless to say, the combination of elite members will be the more powerful, but this will be because of the overall pattern of routine practice in the society as a whole, the practice which maintains them as elite members and power-ful agents. Fundamentally, the dominance of elites, where they exist, is based on the power concentrated in their hands, and resides in the pattern of the distribution of knowledge throughout the entire elitist society. It is sometimes tempting, as for example when explaining the outcome of strikes, to note how the few may organize and co-operate more readily than the many, as if this size-effect serves as the crucial advantage for employers over labour. The true advantage that employers enjoy is that only a few of them have to organize. A few of them prepared to act in concert possess a capacity for action as great as that of many workers likewise prepared to act in concert. The reason for this is the existing overall pattern of routine action and interaction in the society, established in the course of a long historical development. This allows a trifling amount of new organization by an employer to counter-balance a much larger effort at organization and organizational inno-vation on the part of his work-force.[40]

Self-referring knowledge and the delocalization of power

I have now discussed the delocalization of access to powers through acts of delegation and through more or less deliberate practices of trade and exchange. But there remains a set of important and widespread processes whereby access to power becomes delocalized inadvertently, not so much by action as by inference, so that power-holders are unable to prevent some diffusion of their rights and powers to those in close proximity to them.

Any power-holder, however formidable, however exalted, will seek to live an everyday life with others based on something like respect and reciprocity: he will value family, friends and comrades or some thereof, and in his relations with family, friends and comrades, whether one describes those relations in the dry discourse of the economist or the richer language of everyday life, he will put his powers at their disposal or use them on their behalf.[41] In the course of interacting with the power-holder they will gain access to his powers, and to that extent come to count as powers themselves. Similarly, any power-holder will have advisers who, to the extent that they are able to generate confidence in what they say, may hope to influence how powers are deployed, and to that extent come to count as powers themselves.[42] Even the servants and menials of a power-holder may find that the power rubs off, as it were. They have the ear of the power-holder, and may be able to regulate access to him. And the very depth of their dependency upon him may induce him to place trust in them, to charge them with demanding tasks, to allow them to metamorphose into respected subordinates. These, at least, will be the typical conditions in the proximity of a major power-holder. Hence, even if they are not the actual conditions appertaining, they are likely to be presumed so to be. Friends, family, advisers, servants, will generally be presumed to have access to power, for all practical purposes to possess power, and to that extent they will possess power, since power is an aspect of the general distribution of knowledge.

A power-holder stands at the centre of a field of power, like a magnet at the centre of a magnetic field. Those who approach him are acted on by the field and become powers themselves, as pins around a magnet become magnets. Those whom he approaches feel the field strength increase with his onset: lesser powers take care to obey and defer, multiplying his power even as it acts upon them; comparable powers mobilize their strength just in case, opposing and repelling the approaching centre of force, just as one magnet repels another.

Having earlier discarded an emanationist account of power, I have now reintroduced it, although admittedly only for some figurative and metaphorical speech. But consider seriously the metaphor here. Someone adopting an emanationist view would not go seriously wrong when using it to predict the consequences of the actions of a major power-holder. Indeed, if he was not privy to the fine structure of the interactions of the power-holder it is not clear that he could understand him any better than in terms of an emanationist view. The emanationist view might perhaps provide as good a small-scale map of power as any possible small-scale map. No doubt large-scale maps are more accurate and informative than small-scale maps, on the whole, but if a small-scale map must be used perhaps we should not criticize one which represents power as an emanation.

An emanationist theory of power, used by a member, would be confirmed as readily as any small-scale map of power and would accumulate credibility once adopted. As it accumulated credibility, it would serve as a basis for action and would thus become recognized as a basis for action and institutionalized as a basis for action. Concurrently the reality being mapped would change: it would become a social reality wherein action based on the map figured more and more prominently. But action based on an emanationist theory of power is precisely the kind of action which confirms an emanationist theory of power. Action and knowledge of action, knowledge and action based on knowledge, would be moving towards a self-reconstituting equilibrated state. The power-holder himself could well recognize the move that was occurring: given that he was supposed to be radiating power from within, he could well decide to appear more radiant, to encourage the theory, as it were. Intimates of the power-holder, with their detailed large-scale maps of his power, could actually find the reliability of these maps being undermined as the power-holder came to command a generalized instead of a specific and delimited obedience. It would be time for them to set aside their large-scale maps and replace them with something more accurate, the simplified small-scale representations of the distant onlooker.

If an entire society ends up accepting an emanationist theory and the emanationist theory is confirmed in practice, what is the status of the theory? Presumably it is as plausible as any accepted natural-scientific theory involving invisible substances or invisible forces, and, being self-confirming, it must presumably be recognized to be as adequate an account of the distribution of power it describes as any alternative social-scientific account could be. Indeed a social-scientific theory would perhaps merely say that social life in that context proceeded *as if* power resided in and emanated from certain sources. Such an 'as if' theory would be largely indistinguishable in its predictions from the emanationist theory itself. What then makes the 'as if' theory superior? Fundamentally, nothing at all. It is merely that social scientists are likely to have the robust prejudices against invisible emanations typical of most professions in modern secular societies, so that *their* theory of power, whether it is power in their own society or another society, is unlikely to be an emanationist theory.[43]

A distribution of power exists as an aspect of a distribution of knowledge – knowledge that is confirmed or disconfirmed by actions calculated on the basis of it. Accordingly, change in a distribution of power will occur as a sequence of interrelated actions and inferences – actions following from knowledge, inferences following from actions feeding back to knowledge. It is important not to take an unduly behaviourist viewpoint in understanding such change. People may indeed act to change the distribution of power, as in a simple visible act of delegation. But they may also change the distribution of power by reflecting upon it, learning about it, seeking better to understand and represent it; for a distribution of power is an aspect of a distribution of knowledge and what it is known to be cannot be separated from what it is. This is particularly clear when agents adopt a simplifying metaphor or theory, such as the emanationist theory, because simplified cognition generates simplification at the level of action, and hence simplification of the phenomena described by the theory. Full institutionalization of such a theory produces the maximum simplification of what it describes, and hence coincides with the point of maximum validity for the theory.[44]

Power is a social phenomenon. There cannot be more to it than there is known to be. Thus the capacity of people to grasp and represent a distribution of power sets limits on the possible form that such a distribution can take; and how the capacity is actually used shapes the actual form that any such distribution does take. This is not an esoteric philosophical point; it has great empirical significance. In modern, highly differentiated societies particular powers may be elaborately specified and widely distributed at the formal level and intricately connected and delocalized at the informal level. Yet such a complex system is always complemented by something simpler, something based on generalized deference. The reason is that only a few 'local' members will be able to learn and thus constitute an elaborate 'local' system of powers and rights: most members will be obliged to develop and use a much simpler map and even local members will find a 'simplified' map invaluable, much of the time, as the basis for routine informal business. Such simplified maps of power may often provide little more than rough-and-ready indications of the 'overall' standing of specific agents, their possible value as allies or the extent of the danger they constitute as opponents, but such maps have to suffice, if for no other than logistic reasons. For the users of such maps the necessary concomitant is generalized deference and the undiscriminating grovel. For those marked as peaks on such maps the consequence is a useful generalization of capacity for action. For the system as a whole the result is a continuing affinity with baboon society.[45]

All political systems involving concentration of discretion in the use of power are shot through with relationships based upon generalized deference. In all such systems cognitive maps are in routine use which allow agents to be assigned, in seconds where necessary, a generalized standing, a rough position in some overall hierarchy.[46] In all such systems power-holders recognize the existence of such maps and take care to encourage and proliferate their use; for generalized deference is invaluable to power-holders. Indeed, even deep within the political and administrative hierarchies of modern societies where rights and powers are specified in great detail and generally known in like detail, most interaction is structured around generalized deference, and the larger-scale maps are kept in the drawer for occasional reference and use in emergencies. It is important that such maps are there, and are known to be there, but in most political and bureaucratic contexts, most of the time, such maps tend to become maps of reserve powers, rather than counting as the basis of routine interaction.

As a basis for the understanding of routine interaction in bureau-cracies and administrative hierarchies, an 'official' map of rights and powers never serves anywhere near so well as a rough-and-ready sketch of relative standings and the use of an emanation theory.[47] Innumerable incidents would serve to illustrate what is implied by this: consider the case of Leila Khaled. In 1973, Khaled, a Palestinian imprisoned in Britain for an aircraft hijacking, was released and flown abroad in a matter of hours, after British lives were threatened in yet another hijacking. The business was arranged by the British Prime Minister, who was able to order Khaled's release through the prison governor, supply an army escort to an airport and provide the necessary air transport, merely by use of the telephone. Yet as Mr Enoch Powell indicated to a completely uninterested House of Commons immediately afterwards, the Prime Minister had no standing whatsoever to entitle him to order the release; the action of the prison governor was a clear dereliction of duty; and a great chain of people at every level of the administrative and military hierarchy took as a matter of course actions which rode roughshod over the entire explicitly acknowledged system of law and order. No doubt powers and rights embedded in that system of law and order would have been invoked if any major body of opinion had wished to dispute or delay Khaled's release, but nobody did and the informal baboon-type system was allowed to operate; the system that every prime minister has conveniently to hand.

Prime-ministerial powers in Britain, like those of any great office in any political system, are highly generalized and the occupant of the office enjoys ready access to the powers nominally held by others. There is no need to allocate generalized powers to an office in order to secure them for that office: any recognition of extensive specific powers associated with an office guarantees that extensive general powers will come to be associated with it. Power will generalize by inference: effort is needed only to establish and maintain its boundaries.[48]

4

DIVIDE AND RULE

4.1 CONDITIONS FOR A RELIABLE HUMAN MACHINE

An individual possesses power by being a referent in a distribution of knowledge. Others know what is routinely done on his instructions, and what is routinely done in the way of sanctioning when his instructions are ignored – and others know what others know on these matters. Everyone is able to calculate accordingly how far to accede to his instructions. In many cases, the instructions have consequences which are in the interest of those who obey them, and sanctions have a secondary role. No doubt pilots obey air traffic controllers out of an interest in living longer and staying in one piece. But other instructions may call for the performance of repellent actions, or actions with adverse consequences for those performing them, when the problem of securing obedience is altogether more serious and resort to sanctions becomes essential. Sanctions add an extrinsic value to actions which can outweigh their intrinsic features or direct consequences and make non-performance more costly than performance. The more costly or distasteful the action, the more severe is the sanction needed to routinize it. The study of the extremes of domination is the study of what is possible on the basis of sanctions.

What is possible on the basis of sanctions? What is the most that can be achieved through their use? In opposition to the view currently accepted in the social sciences I shall argue that in principle there is practically no limit to what might be so achieved. In practice, compliant activity is never wholly intelligible in terms of extrinsic considerations but in theory it could be so. A vast range of actions may be invoked and directed through the threat of sanctions. A despot may enjoy recognized priority in the direction of all that vast range through the threat of sanctions. Almost any level of hostility may be neutralized through the threat of sanctions. No case of this kind is so extreme that it is impossible in principle.[1]

Enforcing compliance

Consider first of all a single power-holder and a single subordinate. The power-holder seeks unconditional compliance with all conceivable orders, whatever the plans or inclinations of the subordinate. He does not think of the subordinate as we customarily think of a fellow human being: he seeks instead to treat him as a human machine, a reliable instrument which will carry out any required task, however demanding and however repulsive. Clearly, weak sanctions will not reduce an individual to the status of a reliable instrument, nor will any limited set of positive rewards and incentives. The power-holder must be in a position to threaten violence and extremes of coercion if he is to enjoy priority, whenever he so desires, in the use of the capacity for action of his subordinate.

How though should the power-holder make good the threat of violence? Should he assail his underlings with the force of his own body? This is always insufficient. The natural inequalities between individuals simply do not permit it as a persisting strategy: even the most muscular thug has to sleep, and is then vulnerable to a rock in the head. Should then the power-holder call in coercion? If so, by what means does the power-holder exercise discretion over the routine activities of the coercers? Basically, we are trying to understand the basis of a power relation, and we must not presume what we are trying to understand. This seems to imply that if direct understanding of the relation cannot be produced then indirect understanding is not to be looked for either. If we do not know how A controls B, then we do not know how A controls C to control B, or how A controls D to control C to control B. Sociology texts often roll in a 'coercive apparatus' as a *deus ex machina* to explain how it is that someone has power, but it is more often than not a potentially endless regress that is thereby created.

Our power-holder seems something of a broken reed. He cannot himself enforce compliance, and he cannot enforce the coercive actions necessary to produce compliance. As an independent agent it would seem that he is nothing. Yet power-holders manifestly do enforce compliance upon unwilling, uncooperative underlings. How then is it done? One plausible conjecture here is that power-holders never act alone, but always as members of a co-operating community. If they are not at one with their subordinates, holding power with their acquiescence, exercising it with their collective support, then they must be at one with others; they must be members of a power-holding community. For such a community the coercion of underlings may produce a collective good, like for example bridge-building does, and hence may be morally approved and mutually sanctioned, with the fruits of coercion available to all, like a bridge is available.[2] Now any single power-holder can truly exercise power, enforce his discretion as he will, given only that he depends upon the power of a dominant community and holds his power as a part of the power held by that community.

An analysis of this kind makes coercion the child of co-operation, obedience of trust, repression of love. If the power-holder finds no co-operation, no trust, no love, amongst those below him, he must have it from those above or beside him. He must act in some kind of solidarity with others. If his solidarity is with other power-holders alone, and if he is typical of all power-holders, then indeed his human machine may figure in the awareness of the power-holding community like a physical machine in the awareness of a normal community. The community of the powerless may figure as a part of the technology of the community of the powerful. The needs of the powerless may be catered for merely as the servicing needs of artefacts and instruments are catered for.

This is a familiar kind of situation. In societies relying upon slavery one dominant co-operating community coerces others, thus allowing its individual members to enjoy discretion in the use of slave power. In caste systems, predatory military communities overcome others and instal themselves as rulers parasiting on the labour of the subjugated for generations after. In such conditions all kinds of symbols and cultural devices are employed to define the continuing separateness of the power-holding community and to reinforce its solidarity: separate language or separate dialect may be carefully preserved; separate classification as noble or of a special worth; separate uniform or adornment; where nature is helpful in the matter, separate physiognomy may be appropriately displayed and celebrated. Provided it maintains its separation and solidarity a dominant community may hope to hold down any other community or group of individuals with a markedly smaller general capacity for action than its own, and with but little effort to take a good deal of that general capacity onto itself as an enhancement of its own power. Just as a community may add to its power by making the effort to build a physical engine or machine, so it may by making the effort to subjugate others and build a human machine: in the one case it 'has' the extra resource represented by the machine it has made, and in the other the extra resource represented by the people it has subjugated. The only difference is that whereas there may be no clear limit upon the power of any physical machine that a community may build and exploit, there does appear to be such a limit upon the power of a human machine. It would seem that its power must remain very much less than that of the community exploiting it, if it is not to be beyond coercion and hence a threat rather than a resource for the exploiting community.

We ought to feel some unease at this point on empirical grounds. Power-holding communities do successfully hold down and exploit others, as described above. But they seem able to do so much more extensively than the above description allows, sustaining their dominance over vastly greater numbers of subordinates, imposing rule by a few upon legions of unwilling underlings. It is true that a few may have a greater general capacity for action than many, if they are superior overall in knowledge and technique. It must be borne in mind also that general capacity for *violent* action is of most relevance here: a few with arms may overawe many without. But the capacity for violence of a power-holding community can go a very long way, and it is hard to believe that it always exceeds that same capacity in those it subjugates and exploits.

Needless to say, it does not. A power-holding community may enjoy further advantages which allow it a greater scope for dominance than first appears. In particular, it may stand as a united community dominating subordinates who are several distinct communities, or fragments of many communities, or, in the extreme case, so many disorganized individuals. In these circumstances subordinates will be unable to make the most of their potential to act; they will be unable to sustain fully *concerted* action against power-holders.

The difficulty of concerted action on the part of subordinate individuals is a crucial element in understanding most highly developed forms of systematic exploitation and domination. It is a difficulty that may be experienced in many ways. The powerless will find that they do not know what others, similarly powerless, are about to do or likely to do: their actions will be plagued by ignorance. The powerful will encounter this ignorance as ineffective opposition. Their small but reliable capacity for violence will destroy resistance here, overawe it there, nip it in the bud somewhere else, thereby dealing with an overall potential many times its own, an overall potential which, if expressed in concerted action, would surely prevail. And as they triumph here and triumph there, so the powerful will appropriate the resources of the powerless to themselves piecemeal, and use them as part of the very apparatus which is their power: a captured gun here will blow up the enemy there; a captured regiment here will lead the charge there and so on. The powerless will become part of a differentiated system, a complex interlocking human machine, every part of which will serve to control every other part whilst the whole continues to yield up a surplus output to those in control of it. A simplest possible case of this is set out in figure 4.1. It is little more than a representation of the principle of divide and rule.

In a system where subordinates are divided, each group of subordinates will find its own local actions pressed upon by the rest of the overall system, and will find it difficult to do anything but comply so long as it calculates the consequences of its own actions in isolation. Even in the simplest possible case of figure 4.1, A may find itself outweighed by

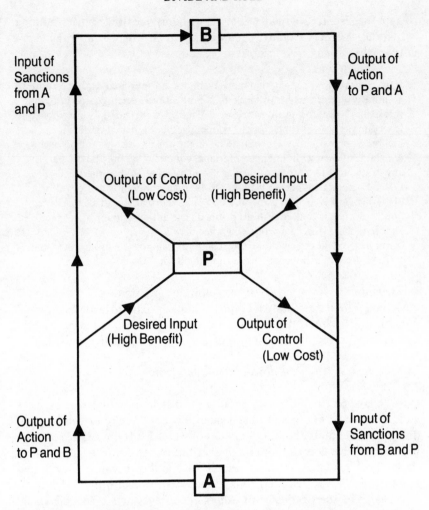

Figure 4.1 Cycles of control: relationship of power-holding community,
P, and two subordinate communities, A, B

power-holders plus *B*, and *B* may find itself outweighed by power-
holders plus *A*. The community of power-holders may be smaller than
either *A* or *B*, and with a lower inherent capacity for action, because they
are able to use *A* to control *B*, and *B* to control *A*. In the extreme case,
the community of power-holders may reduce to a single person. The
regress set up when one individual seeks to control another, the regress
noted at the start of this section, may be ended by tucking the tail into the
head. A cyclic system of control may be established in which agents are
both coerced and resources in the coercion of others. Such a system can

be kept in existence, in theory at least, with but one single power-holding individual. Michael Polanyi offers an example where something reminiscent of this may have occurred:

> It is commonly assumed that power cannot be exercised without some voluntary support, as for example by a faithful praetorian guard. I do not think this is true, for it seems that some dictators were feared by everybody; for example, towards the end of his rule, everybody feared Stalin. It is, in fact, easy to see that a single individual might well exercise command over a multitude of men without any appreciable voluntary support on the part of any of them. If in a group of men each believes that all the others will obey the commands of a person claiming to be their common superior, all will obey this person as their superior. For each will fear that if he disobeyed him, the others would punish his disobedience at the superior's command, and so all are forced to obey by the mere supposition of the others' continued obedience, without any voluntary support being given to the superior by any member of the group. (1958, pp. 224–5)

The empirical accuracy of this account does not matter: no doubt it is incorrect. What does matter is that Polanyi points to a real empirical possibility. He shows that all the power in a society may indeed be held over a long period at the disposal of a single unsupported individual.

Knowing and complying

Power may be held in this way because the distribution of power exists as a distribution of knowledge. The leader may continue to exercise a prior discretion over all the routine activities of which his followers are capable because of the overall patterned distribution of knowledge amongst them. That distribution has a degree of stability because when acted upon it generates self-confirming and self-reconstituting inferences. Knowledge of the obedience of others encourages acts of obedience by every knowledgeable individual. These acts confirm that particular individuals are indeed obedient. Others act accordingly, that is obediently, and so the cycle of inference and action continues, sustaining the power of the leader as an aspect of itself. The power continues to exist as an aspect of a stable overall distribution of knowledge, and it is not only that it continues to be exercisable over calculative, reflectively aware individuals; it continues to be exercisable *only because* those individuals are calculative and reflectively aware. Their reflective awareness, their basic nature as free human agents, is responsible for their desperate condition as an exploited human machine. The context of reflection and calculation is such that action, whilst remaining genuine human action, becomes effectively subject to another's discretion.

Polanyi shows how a cyclic system of control may thereby continue to operate with every individual being at once coerced and a resource in the coercion of others. It is indeed a *reductio* of divide and rule, but not unfortunately a *reductio ad absurdum*.

For effective domination of large numbers of subordinates in extreme conditions of divide and rule it is important that those subordinates should possess so much knowledge and no more. They should lack whatever knowledge might inspire profitable forms of individual deviant action, and they should lack whatever knowledge might help them to establish co-operative interactions with others, and hence create the possibility of concerted organized deviant action. Nor should it be easy for them to learn, to acquire the knowledge which initially they lack. This suggests that subordinates should be isolated from as much as possible of their social environment, and hence that the society in which they exist should be highly fragmented and compartmentalized. Individual subordinates should live as atoms, wholly in the public realm, under surveillance, but as far as possible without social relationships, so that opportunities for the planning and execution of concerted action are minimal. On the same grounds, subordinates should be well aware of the direct connection between their behaviour and possible sanctions, but unaware of the longer-range indirect connections by which their (compliant) behaviour feeds into the social order generally and actually helps to constitute and sustain the feedback of coercion and sanctioning that controls them (figure 4.2).[4]

Appropriate limitations upon the scope of subordinates' knowledge may be maintained in many ways. Time and space may be ordered and arranged to minimize the interaction and mutual awareness of subordinates, or even to render one group of subordinates invisible to another. Such an ordering becomes more effective the more extensive and all-embracing it is made, so that ideally it should extend through the whole of the life of the subordinate, who should not be allowed to possess a significant degree of privacy. Public activity should be created for its own sake: time should be filled with pointless routines, fatuous projects, bureaucratic impositions, all demanding and difficult, all to be performed under the gaze of others – unknown others, alien others, untrustworthy others.

On the same grounds, the flow of information to subordinates should be relentlessly interdicted, filtered and distorted. Every significant medium of communication should be monitored and controlled. Information should never pass directly from one subordinated sector to another. In particular, information about deviance and concerted animosity to the system should not pass. Lies and mythology should be substituted. Where some contact between groups or sectors is essential,

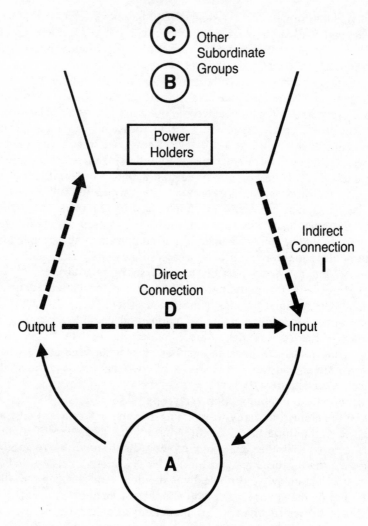

Figure 4.2   Consequences of compliance

the individuals involved should be cycled rapidly and kept under
specially close surveillance; in the ultimate human machine their lifetime
would be short.

Any means of setting limits upon the knowledge of subordinates and
restrictions upon their ability to learn is a valuable resource in the
continued enforcement of their subordination. But although ignorance
may help to sustain power based on the principle of divide and rule, it is
not *essential* for its continuation. Consider Polanyi's example once

more. Is the ruler's power based squarely upon the ignorance of his subordinates? It may seem to be so, but it is not. Any given subordinate in the example could well reason thus: the others are treated just as I am; they are human beings as I am; they will feel as I do; hence they will truly hate and oppose the leader. Suppose, then, that every individual were to reason in this way and gain the conviction that the leader was universally hated. Would this lead to the destruction of the system? Not necessarily. Who would strike the first blow? What consequences would that blow have? Might it not have better consequences if struck another day, or in another situation? And in the meantime might it not be necessary to maintain the mask of devoted obedience?

In principle the system could continue without being underpinned by ignorance. A hated ruler, and one known to be hated, may nonetheless continue to rule, just as a technically insolvent company, and one known to be insolvent, may nonetheless continue to trade. No doubt ignorance of the actual state of affairs would add to the stability of rule, just as ignorance adds to the stability of an insolvent company, but in neither case is ignorance essential to the continued existence of the state of affairs in question.

Restrictions upon what is known and what may be learned may greatly enhance the stability of a universally detested system of rule, but fundamentally such rule rests not upon ignorance but upon knowledge. Subordinates may with advantage be kept ignorant, but they absolutely must be knowledgeable. Their lack of awareness of the indirect connection in figure 4.2 is an advantage for the power-holder; their proper awareness of the direct connection is a necessity. Subordinates must recognize that the output of appropriate action which they produce is what minimizes the input of coercion and sanctioning which they receive. Invincible ignorance of this would actually save them from being controlled: knowledge of it is what allows their subordination. Wholly coercive systems, extermination camps, slave-labour camps, or whatever, have to rely upon the knowledge and reflective awareness of their inmates. Accordingly, power-holders will seek to inculcate and reinforce awareness of the direct connection, to educate people in regard to its existence, in order to sustain and guarantee that distribution of knowledge which makes them power-holders.

Hence the direct connection will be prominently displayed, dramatized, celebrated. Deviance, systematically concealed across groups, will be systematically displayed within groups, along with the condign punishment it calls forth. Vertical relationships of order and control will be given visible embodiments in uniforms, badges of rank, symbols and gestures of obedience and deference. The resources of coercion will be paraded up and down in processions and marches. Prisoners will be released to tell the tale. The rules of the game will be freely available and examples of the rules constantly to hand. Everyone will live in an environment where they come to know what they have to know, where they know it better than they would want to know it.

Rituals, ceremonials, symbols and symbolic displays are well recognized as means of supporting and reinforcing a system of routine practices, and they are also recognized in the role of mnemonic devices which facilitate cognition and the retention of culture. Even this, however, probably represents an understatement of the extent of their importance. Ritual and ceremonial action are information which people assimilate, appearances from which people infer, evidence on the basis of which they theorize. They are part of the raw material from which knowledge is made, even as they are also products designed and developed on the basis of existing knowledge. Thus they are part of the continuing process wherein knowledge is replicated and recreated. They are part of the tradition wherein past knowledge becomes present knowledge, wherein inherited knowledge is rediscovered and reaffirmed. But the distribution of knowledge is the social order, and a part of that distribution is the distribution of power. Rituals and ceremonial acts therefore do not merely reinforce an independently existing pattern of power. They are part of the process wherein power is constantly replicated and reconstituted.[5]

In summary, priority in the use of social power may be concentrated very heavily indeed by exploitation of the appropriate techniques of divide and rule. In principle, every first priority could fall into the hands of a single individual. One would never find such an extreme situation in practice, but there is no a priori reason why an appropriate distribution of knowledge should not come into existence and remain stable. It is perfectly possible for practically every individual in an entire society to conclude, on the basis of what he knows and what he is able to learn, that there is no realistic alternative to acquiescence in subordination – that there is no promising alternative individual action, no sensible possibility of alternative concerted action, even no plausible way of organizing for future concerted action.

Using the machine

A ruler in this situation enjoys the use of a maximally reliable human machine. So long as its human components remain reflectively aware and calculative, and do not lapse from that state, their compliance may be enforced over the greatest possible range of requirements, with the minimum of attention to the details of their individual ends and desires, simply by the threat of devastating sanctions. Acting on their own discretion they will choose to act at the discretion of another.

The detailed characteristics of the human machine cannot, of course, be ignored altogether. Just like a physical machine it will break down through over-use or lack of servicing. It needs the minimal attention due to any machine, unless the ruler is willing to treat it as an expendable resource to be used for present pleasures with no thought for the morrow. Most rulers are not so willing. The patience and concentration of a Stalin are more typical than the impetuosity of a Caligula. The human machine is normally preserved as the capital that yields a steady income of power, not exploited to destruction. But to operate the machine at a level consistent with its own continued existence may be to use it at very much less than its full capacity – its maximum instantaneous output. It may even be that when it is used in this way discretion over most of its operation may no longer actively be exercised; large numbers of routine actions become essential, or alternatively, unthinkable, so that there is no leeway in their use. The power-holder may only feel able to direct at whim the lesser routines of a great array under his formal control. This indeed is probably the normal state of a powerful agent: he may enjoy a vast income of power, but a much smaller disposable income. Much of the discretion formally and indeed actually, available to him he may never dare to use, since to exercise it actively would be to destroy the whole system. Nonetheless, this discretion, never exercised, still represents an asset to the power-holder. It may become usable at a later time without disaster; it may at some point be renounced for compensation; or indeed it may in the end be used disastrously after all, when disaster looms in any case: the defeated dictator may make his stand in the bunker; the declining aristocrat may make his last ruinously expensive act of conspicuous display.

In principle, the cost of machine maintenance may actually exceed output, and the power-holder may find his position a continuing burden. In Mervyn Peake's marvellous comic epic *Titus Groan* (1946), Lord Sepulchgrave, seventy-sixth Earl of Groan, trudges round the immense decrepit castle of Gormenghast for practically the whole of his waking life, grinding away at a long succession of wearisome ritual tasks. This is the only way in which the vast ramshackle system of the place can be maintained, and Sepulchgrave's discretion as its ruler kept in being. Sepulchgrave retains his discretion in the only possible way, and thus he finds himself living a life wherein he never actively exercises any discretion at all: he is more constrained than any of his subjects. It comes as no surprise to watch him pass through depression to madness, and eventually to the suicide which allows his dubious inheritance to pass on to another.[6]

Polanyi helped us to imagine a human machine with but a single controller, but Peake offers the imagination still more. Consider that the controller himself may be constrained in what he freely does, that he may often find all actions but one intolerably costly. Now we may have a machine without external control, an entire society calculatively imitating an automaton.[7]

4.2 SUCCESSION

The relative merits of individualistic and structural explanations are much debated and will continue to be debated in the social sciences. Some readers may be tempted to dismiss what has been said in the preceding section as unduly individualistic. It has made scarcely any reference at all to social formations or social structure as commonly understood; it has avoided discussion of the complexities of social organization; it has been more concerned to show how far powers may concentrate in a single individual than with asking how they distribute themselves across many individuals or an entire society. Yet despite all this the approach being taken here is not at all an individualistic one. Indeed, fundamentally, it is structural. That it is structural will only be overlooked if limited and inadequate notions of structural analysis are entertained – if, for example, structures are regarded as wholly independent of individuals, as separate entities that condition or determine what individuals do, from the outside as it were. When the question of where social structure is located is pressed as hard as possible, it transpires that structure is best thought of as residing, at a given time, in specific people and as constituted, at that time, by those people.[8]

I have made the suggestion that a society may be regarded as a distribution of knowledge. A given individual will relate to such a distribution in two ways. First, he will be a carrier of knowledge, one of the individuals who in knowing what he knows, carries a part of the overall distribution of knowledge and to that extent, along with any number of other individuals, helps to constitute it. Secondly, he will exist as a *referent* in the system that he, along with all the others, carries, and he will help to constitute it in that different sense. As a referent in the distribution of knowledge he is known about, and his powers are known about. Everything of social significance which he as an individual is able to do is a consequence of his being known about. How his directives fare depends on what others read off from their knowledge of him, or infer from their knowledge of him. To refer to the powers of an individual simply is to refer to the features of a distribution of knowledge, and hence to an aspect of the structure of a society. To describe an individual action is to describe something intelligible only by reference to a distribution of knowledge, and hence intelligible only as social action.

There are social scientists who consider individual actions to be the concern solely of the psychologist, and who will speak only of social formations (usually treated as surrogate individuals), or of the tendencies of heaps of individuals (usually treated as crude aggregations of independent, unconnected individuals). Both these attempts at structural analysis are unduly individualistic, and merely hide individualistic modes of thought by confining themselves to large numbers. Any properly structural or holistic account of society should be indifferent to the level of detail at which it is obliged to proceed, equally applicable to large-scale changes in routine practice and specific individual judgements and actions. Among the accounts that meet this requirement is that which treats a society as a distribution of knowledge.

Any individual has a role in constituting a distribution of knowledge as a carrier, and a role in constituting it as a referent. The demise of any individual is on both grounds a disruption of the distribution of knowledge. In this sense we may say that it is a cause of damage to the social structure, which structure is constituted at any time by the knowledgeable agents of the society. As a carrier of knowledge an individual will usually be little missed; the damage and disruption caused by death will usually be small and easy to repair. But as a referent in the distribution of knowledge an individual may be crucially important, and his death a major trauma. Major power-holders are important components, even as unique individuals, of the overall network of knowledge, and their death may leave a tear in the net, a tear that may be extensive, difficult to mend and detrimental to the strength and integrity of the whole. Thus, the death of even a single power-holder in a society of calculative agents may greatly diminish the strength of the power structure, increase its vulnerability, render it liable to further damage, even prove to be the crucial lesion that leads to its collapse and dissolution.

Effects of this kind are likely to be most clearly and dramatically evident at the very pinnacle of a power structure, particularly where the structure is that of a despotism involving something close to absolute personal rule. Here a death, the demise of but a single individual, may inflict considerable damage on the overall structure, radical change on the generally diffused distribution of knowledge. This is what makes the phenomenon of *despotic succession* so intriguing. At the point of succession the power structure is massively disrupted by an exiguous event; the context of calculative action is radically redefined. Whereas calculative action may have reconstituted the power structure before, confirmed the existing distribution of knowledge, now it may do so no longer. Whereas calculation may have been largely routine and largely invisible before, now it may be so no longer. For a time there will be an opportunity to study the calculative basis of power structures in peculiarly favourable circumstances.

The despot's dilemma

When the occupant of a position of supreme power dies, whether or not his system was loved or hated in his lifetime, there will usually be widespread incentives to take it over, to capture and to fill the vacated position.[9] Control of the existing system will be the key to continuity or to change, to its own continued existence or its abolition. There will be no lack of aspirants to the succession. But in a society of calculative agents succession cannot be determined by rule or norm. In the anomalous situation created by the death of the ruler, a successor must be capable of enforcing his claim and resisting the competing claims of others. This means that the problem of succession is plagued by a fundamental dilemma, a dilemma beautifully set out and illustrated in an extended study by Burling (1974).

The conditions for a smooth transition from one ruler to another largely concern the powers of the new ruler at the point of succession, and hence his career previous to the succession. If he is not actually to be opposed, if there is not to be strife and civil war, then he should have powers sufficient to overwhelm any coalition which rises against him. To have such powers he must be known to have them and be known to be competent in their exercise. Thus, he should already have possessed and exercised discretion over a great amount of capacity for action. He should have had the opportunity to learn how to use and exercise power effectively, to build up a working map of the society wherein it is to be used, and to establish securely his relationship to his subordinates or followers. But such a successor, ideal though he may be as a successor, is likely to be an impossible subordinate. He has, after all, no reason to await the decease of his predecessor. If his capacity for action is sufficient to succeed, then it is likely to be sufficient to take over the polity at once. Thus, there is no easy way of ensuring the continuity and stability of the system in the future without destabilizing it in the present.

Burling illustrates the dilemma with a range of anthropological materials. He shows how chiefs and despots have been vulnerable to rebellion from any subordinate who accumulates sufficient power. He shows too how the clear designation of a successor provides a focus toward which opposition to existing rule moves, and around which power consequently accumulates, so that warfare between father and son, or father and nephew, or ruler and brother or half-brother, becomes a commonplace. Conversely, he shows how rulers seek to pre-empt such threats to their position. No rules for succession may be formulated, or they may be formulated so vaguely and ambiguously as to indicate no clear successor, or they may be procedural rules and relate to procedures that can be carried out only after the death of the ruler, and which have no outcome predictable in advance. Where there are widely known and widely recognised rules of succession already in existence, anyone unfortunate enough to be marked out by them is liable to be eliminated. Indeed, a whole sequence of indicated successors may be purged, with considerable numbers of people suffering death, imprisonment or exile, until at last the perceived implications of the rules themselves become sufficiently vague and contestable, and it is no longer possible clearly to state who in the society is the next in line to rule.[10] Nor are informally recognized successors or promising candidates for succession likely to be tolerated by such careful rulers. Immediate subordinates will be balanced against each other. Anyone who becomes too visible, too successful, too prominent, will be cut down. Where there is a loosely hereditary system sons may be excluded from powerful positions, administrative experience, even normal social intercourse of any kind, through exile or imprisonment. Or their 'education' may be carefully designed to exclude all worldly knowledge and training in the skills of rule, and to offer instead homiletics of obedience, desiccated religion, incentives to passivity and other-worldliness.

These are the techniques of the successful despot, but they are a recipe for strife upon his death. The decapitated power structure is then headed by a small number of equally powerful figures, probably representing opposed interests, familiar with each other as rivals and opponents in the earlier system of divide and rule, knowing nothing of each other to encourage trust and co-operation. If there is a nominal heir or inheritor, he will lack established powers, knowledge and experience, and will be liable to become a pawn in the games of others, a figure-head. Thus, despotisms are likely to be punctuated by violent and destructive succession struggles, which either bring about the demise of the incumbent ruler or are brought about by it. The ideal of the 'smooth transition' is rarely realized.

One of the merits of Burling's presentation is that, unlike many anthropologists, he is willing to take a historical perspective, even to discuss political change over several centuries. Thus he is able to show not only how despotism created problems of succession, but how *learning from experience* fed back into the practice of statecraft and conditioned the nature of successive succession disputes. A despot coming to power at the end of strife with rivals would typically be harsher than his predecessor, and more ruthless in the use of prophylactic executions. His own successor, if similarly troubled, would be more ruthless still, remembering the inadequacy of earlier practice. The extent of slaughter might increase in this way from generation to generation, as it did, notably, amongst the Baganda of Uganda, where the accession of the Kabaka came to be marked by a comprehensive elimination of kinsmen including even his own grown sons (Burling, 1974 pp. 39–45). No doubt learning from hard experience explains why similar practices have been so widespread, as for example in Moghul India, the Ottoman Empire and in that spectacular and comprehensive reordering which established the Japanese Shogunate as such a marvellously durable and thus enduring political system. Equally, one could look earlier, to the despots of Imperial Rome, whose families served as crude stone blocks, to be carved into imposing pyramids of power. Such sculptures, cut deep into the texture of individual lives, could last but a generation before their points were lost through death, and the hammer and chisel were required once more.

Despots, by definition, possess immense personal power. Whatever seems conducive to the stability of their rule they are likely to be able to provide. Ritual, ceremonial, symbolism and display all lie easily to their hand, and indeed are invariably provided in liberal measure. Legitimations and justifications of their rule lie even easier, and are invariably poured forth freely by innumerable sycophants. Religious, educational and legal practices are generally open to manipulation. An entire normative order may be created at the ideal level, to sustain rule. Yet it is never enough. Laughter stays in everyone. Despots have to deal skilfully in the deployment of violence. They have to learn the techniques of repression and control. Many despots have learned so well, and used their knowledge so well, that their last unconscious breaths have been taken in complete security, even where violence and upheaval have been but minutes away.

But where the despot is concerned with the present, others may have an interest in the future, in a smooth transition to whoever follows, with a minimum of debilitating violence. Thus, procedures for settling the succession are likely to evolve in despotic systems, procedures that can be brought into play once the present incumbent has indeed breathed his last. Learning from experience may be expected to refine and develop such procedures over time. In all despotic systems there appear to be some rules and practices related to succession, which serve to make it less problematic and more a matter of routine. Needless to say, such rules are neither designed to serve the 'social function' of accomplishing succession, nor do they determine how succession actually is accomplished. It is not possible to construct good succession rules, insert them into so many individual heads, and sit back to watch those individuals act out the implications of the rules. Such rules must be sustained calculatively. They must exist as exemplified guides to action which a sufficient number of calculative agents find it expedient and profitable to support.

It is indeed just this kind of rule that is in practice encountered in actual situations.

Burling documents the existence of prohibition rules in many despotic systems, which explicitly exclude from succession some proportion of those who find themselves possessing power at the crucial time.[11] Such rules may range from the very general to the highly particular. The generation of the deceased despot may be excluded from the succession; all of a certain race or caste may be, or all the members of a given class or family; or specific individuals may be specifically debarred, the first-born son of the previous ruler, for example, or the occupant of some senior office or position. Provided that the proportion of the powerful thereby excluded is not too large, the acceptance of such a rule need not be problematic: all those not excluded by it may be expected to support it once it exists. The use of this kind of prohibition rule does not merely reduce the number of contenders for the succession, it creates an interested and powerful set of outsiders, and often these outsiders are explicitly allocated the task of selecting the new ruler. Amongst the Manchu, the generation of the old ruler was expected to choose a successor from amongst the younger men. Amongst the Baganda, the most powerful office-holder amongst commoners played a major role in selecting a royal successor to the Kabaka. Such a figure might be expected to see more clearly, from the outside, where the most promising choice for future peace and stability lay, whilst having himself an interest in such peace and stability. Even where no clear and obvious choice existed, his actual choice might serve as a 'prominent solution': where having *an* agreed solution was more important and beneficial than having any *particular* agreed solution, support might be expected to move to his choice simply because it stood out in the general distribution of knowledge as a choice that had been made, a choice which could be supported.[12]

Prohibition rules have been used in the achievement of succession. They have existed and hence have been known to exist. They have been cited, invoked, appealed to, articulated and applied. Sometimes their perceived implications have been observed and enforced. But, needless to say, their existence has by no means always served to ease the succession process, and indeed they have frequently been ignored or set on one side. Where the death of a ruler has left some individual with a great preponderance of power, the mere fact that the individual has fallen under some prohibition has not prevented his use of that power to take overall control. Interestingly though, figures of this kind have varied in their attitude to the prohibitions that have disadvantaged them. Some have been content to rule as advisors, or ministers, or regents, behind a puppet of appropriate status, even to establish a dynasty ruling behind the facade of another. Others have simply swept the old prohibitions away. It would be interesting to learn what considerations of policy favour the one solution over the other. It would be interesting, too, to consider whether the widespread practice of ruling in the name of another, as in Tokugawa Japan, or Maratha India, should be seen as evidence of the insignificance of explicit rules of succession or of their importance.[13]

Prohibition rules are just a minor class of all the many and various kinds of rules and conventions associated with succession. I have referred to them simply to illustrate the part played by rules: rules do not determine agents' strategies, but are aspects of agents' strategies and the interaction of those strategies. They are not programmes that determine action, but conventions sustained by action. When an individual recognizes a succession rule as compelling and unalterable, he does so because he perceives not a fixed characteristic of his own mind but a fixed characteristic of his context, sustained by powers against which his own capacity for action would avail nothing.[14] Needless to say, this does not make the study of rules of succession and their use in selecting successors any the less interesting. On the contrary, Burling's survey of such rules and their use serves as a study of calculative collective action of great sociological interest and importance.

Where despotic systems persist over long periods the rules and procedures surrounding succession change. Many strategies may be tried out in what possibly is an unending search for 'the smooth transition': the lack of persisting, settled patterns leads Burling to the speculation that 'Perhaps every rule of succession is so imperfect that it leads to the establishment of a revised rule.'[15] Given the extent of this experimentation with succession practices it is intriguing to note how rarely collective actors have featured at the head of despotic systems. A collective actor has the immense advantage of immortality: its individual components can be changed slowly like the cells of a human body, whilst it nonetheless remains recognizable as 'the same' entity. But collective actors have not in general lived long under the stresses of absolute rule, and in most cases though not all seem to have metamorphosed, by one route or another, back into individual mortal actors once more.

Retirement is another strategy employed rarely in despotic systems, although Burling mentions one or two examples. One might think that retirement with sufficient pension and a modicum of honour would attract many an aged tyrant, and cause no significant problems for his successor. But in practice it has been unusual for one absolute ruler to use his power and position to clear the way for another, to establish a smooth transition to a new regime in which he might live out his life in obscure contentment. Perhaps we should take this as testimony to the social character of power, its nature as an aspect of a distribution of knowledge. Since this is how power exists, the power-holder alone is in no position to destroy it, or even permanently and decisively to alienate it from himself. Such a divestment of power must be a long and difficult social process. But to the extent that it is accomplished less than completely the power-holder remains a threat to his successor, and hence the power-holder will be unwilling to initiate it, since to pose a threat to his successor, however weak and however inadvertent, will be to pose a threat to himself. It is often said that despots become psychologically addicted to power, but before this is accepted we need to appreciate the problems they may have in getting rid of it.

Death need not be fatal

The problem of succession becomes less acute as rule becomes less absolute. The fewer the powers that lie at the disposal of the ruler, the less the disruption caused by his demise and the lower the vulnerability of the polity to external threat. The fewer those powers, the more remain undisturbed to be used in repairing the power structure and the less the cost of the repair itself. The fewer those powers, the smaller the prize they make and the smaller the risk or sacrifice worthwhile in the attempt to secure them.

It would seem that a spreading of powers makes a social order much less vulnerable to the disruptions associated with matters of life and death. So too, no doubt, does a differentiation and specialization of powers, which makes for trading and the interdependence of power-holders. Just a modest spread and a modest differentiation may well produce a power structure with considerable self-healing and self-reconstituting properties, a structure wherein succession may be achieved co-operatively, with little trauma. For power-holders in such a structure it may matter less how well anyone in particular stands than how well the power structure itself stands. Thus they may seek to repair the structure with persons, like a bridge is repaired with stone, taking more heed of the general character of the human material than of the individual characteristics of any given unit thereof. This may be true even when the keystone of the power structure is being replaced, the head of state, the chief executive, the Bishop of Rome. The imperative need to have a keystone may be overwhelmingly more important than the matter of who in particular constitutes it. On this Hobbesian basis, we are told, the Tsarist bureaucracies accepted Lenin and his Bolsheviks.

It would seem that in most modern industrial societies there is a sufficient spread of power to allow for bland and non-traumatic processes of succession. Such processes may even be routinized without danger,

and successors marked out in advance with no more inconvenience than
that regularly tolerated in the United States when the President becomes,
for a time, a lame duck. Indeed, it is tempting to suggest that many
modern societies have solved the problems of succession altogether
through the use of regular electoral processes and the custom of pressing
leaders into retirement after a period of service. But this is perhaps to be
unduly incautious and complacent. Stalin and Hitler both ruled in
industrialized societies, and in their deaths both revealed how extensively
they had accumulated personal power, and thereby transformed themselves into prodigious social institutions. Even today in the most
sophisticated societies matters of individual life and death may have a
profound and far-reaching social and political significance, reflecting the
ability of individual leaders to accumulate an inordinate amount of
personal power.[16]

In some respects, indeed, the death of a leader may take on an enhanced
significance in the context of a modern developed society. One of the
interesting features of death is that it occurs, or is made out to occur, in
an instant of time. In some societies the effect of this may be weakened
by poor communications: a death may occur in an instant, yet not
instantly be known to have occurred. In a modern society, on the other
hand, that which becomes generally known somewhere tends very quickly
indeed to become known everywhere. Everyone immediately knows that
the death has occurred, and that everyone else knows that the death has
occurred. The tear in the institutional structure is thus itself an
institution, made in an instant, without teaching, without negotiation,
without legitimation. With respect to the tear everyone will think alike,
and such uniformity at the level of knowledge and cognition may often
carry over into uniformity at the level of action. Now may be the time for
coup, or revolution, or secession, when the centre is weak and its
opponents are all aware of that weakness, and aware that all are so
aware. Death may be the signal that initiates action as well as that which
affords hope of success. Indeed there may be no need to let nature do the
signalling: assassination may be a potent weapon in political conflict,
where in eliminating an individual it is a significant part of the social
order that is removed.

At this point we have moved away from the problem of succession as
such to consideration of death as a solution to a co-ordination problem,
an event that aligns cognition and generates shared dispositions to the
same forms of action. Events of this kind may be immensely important
to uncompromising opponents of the existing power structure. For them
every death may mark a recurrent time of opportunity, every grave and
monument a place. Deaths, funerals, anniversaries, commemorations,
acts of worship and remembrance may all become direct actions against

the existing order or contexts for organization against the existing order. Those walking together for one purpose may find, being together, that they have the capacity to act for another purpose. Or they may merely discover their overall strength and take confidence in their planning of future concerted action, knowing that so many others share their objectives. For the business of organization is very much a matter of people getting to know about each other, and becoming able to act with knowledge of how others are likely simultaneously to be acting. An event that draws large numbers together, for whatever purpose, facilitates their organization, for whatever purpose.[17] As the radio station is to the attempted coup, so such events may be to more broadly based movements of social unrest.

4.3 ACQUIESCENCE AND LEGITIMACY

Where there is a society, the calculative, reflectively aware activity of its members must be activity that largely reconstitutes it. A possible society is one which may be constituted and reconstituted in this way. I have argued that a society wherein power is maximally concentrated, and wherein the powerful are able to make practically unlimited demands upon the powerless, is in this sense a possible society, and by making reference to succession in societies where power is highly concentrated I have tried to provide some justification for the view that calculative action is indeed the basis of their persistence, and hence of their existence. Having considered these extreme cases, it would seem reasonable to suggest that societies of calculative agents wherein power is concentrated less strongly, and wherein the position of the powerless is less disagreeable, may likewise be possible societies. If sanctions are unrestricted in magnitude; if there is efficient and thorough surveillance so that the threat of sanctions is ubiquitous; if subordinates are insulated from each other and suffer restrictions upon knowledge and cognition, so that concerted deviance cannot be planned and organized; then powers can hope to exert reliable control whatever actual set of demands, few or many, moderate or severe, they are accustomed to make.

Severe sanctions, extensive surveillance, impediments to interaction and controls upon knowledge and cognition are, of course, all difficult things to create and sustain. But the burden does not have to rest upon power-holders themselves. Subordinates may be at once controlled by others and agents in the control of others. The principle of divide and rule may be followed, and the fragments of a society used to control each other in cyclic patterns. In principle such a strategy may allow priority in the use of most of the capacity for action in a society to concentrate even into the hands of one single individual, feared by everybody yet obeyed by everybody, because of what everybody knows about everybody else. Accordingly, the general logistical problems involved in the domination of many by a few may be presumed always to be soluble without *fundamental* difficulties.

Needless to say, no actual society has ever developed a fully effective system of sanctions, surveillance and social isolation. Nor should it be thought that there is any 'natural' tendency for societies to develop in this direction, or for individuals to seek controls of this kind as part of their 'natural' inclination to increase the extent of their powers. A human machine of the kind just described may be reliable, but it is not particularly efficient. Much of its output must be expended in overcoming its own internal friction. Other forms of organized interaction may be comparably reliable and more productive. As for individuals, there is nothing to suggest that they have a 'natural' tendency to maximize their social powers. A power-holder may exercise discretion as a pleasure or an obligation: he may use it much or little, with relish or reluctance, to further private ends or the ends of others. Powers are avoided as well as sought after. There is nothing inherently desirable about their possession.

Nonetheless, the study of the extreme case may help in an understanding of what is actual. We may compare existing societies with the hypothetical human machine. To the extent that they resemble it, we come to appreciate the practical importance of sanctions, surveillance and social isolation. To the extent that they differ from it, we come to appreciate the role of additional factors sustaining the distribution of power, and to gain some indication of where to look for them.

Many organized activities in modern societies are profoundly reliant upon sanctions, surveillance and social isolation, and embody in subtle ways much of the social technology of divide and rule. Bureaucratic and administrative hierarchies are obvious examples. Let it be accepted that such hierarchies are often in practice monumentally inefficient, that their 'official' representation is usually very far from their actual manifestation, that they are shot through with, and sometimes undermined by, countervailing patterns of informal organization. It remains the case that there are many points of analogy between a bureaucracy and a reliable human machine. Indeed, the human machine is the fall-back operating mode of practically all bureaucracies, and the implied ideal whenever the system is reflected upon by those high within it. Max Weber's characterization of a bureaucracy as directed to the imposition from above of a systematic discipline and control may be called into question, but it does tend to capture the perceptions of those at the top of the bureaucratic structure. Such power-holders look to the system below them to work come what may. No more than extermination-camp guards do they wish to be *forced* to rely on active support. They take comfort in the availability of sanctions and the possibility of surveillance. They keep the iron hand beneath the velvet glove. Using bureaucracies as instruments, they have come to conceive of them as instruments, receiving the conception of bureaucracy as available instrument as a part of their inherited knowledge.

Rich resources for sanctioning, surveillance and social isolation lie embedded in every modern bureaucratic hierarchy. An elaborate and refined system of sanctioning is potentially available as a consequence of the existence of the career structure, and the fine gradations of opportunity and reward that may be associated with the career structure. An elaborate system of surveillance is potentially available as a consequence of the existence of extensive written records of all decisions and exchanges – or, more precisely, as a consequence of the existence of visible, long-lasting records of these things. An elaborate system of social isolation is constituted by the bureaucratic hierarchy itself. The basic tiering of a bureaucratic hierarchy is an embodiment of one of the basic principles of divide and rule. Typical of practically any organization chart is the 'tree' form, whereby every official directs two, three or more immediate subordinates. In military hierarchies three immediate subordinates is commonly the minimum. In such a hierarchy, every individual subordinate deploys only a minor proportion of the power nominally possessed by his immediate superior, and knows that the major proportion remains at the call of the superior even if he (the subordinate), with his delegated powers, opposes him. Individual deviance is hence everywhere discouraged: the system is nominally stable at all points under reflective awareness. Presumably this is one reason why the 'tree' pattern of bureaucratic organization is now everywhere found. Hierarchies should flare out very rapidly indeed towards the base if they are to be everywhere stable. (Indeed, the pyramid, that ubiquitous symbol of hierarchical ordering, grossly understates the rate of this flare and to that extent systematically misrepresents the nature of hierarchical organization. The layers of a pyramid define an arithmetical progression of magnitudes, but those of a bureaucratic hierarchy should define a geometrical progression.)

In a bureaucratic hierarchy every individual interacts predominantly with immediate superiors and immediate subordinates. In every such interaction the superior has access to a greater capacity for action than the subordinate, and in that sense is more powerful. This truth is emphasized ritually and symbolically, so that it continues to be believed and hence continues to be true: symbols of relative standing and prestige make statements carefully arranged to correspond with the overall distribution of access to capacity for action. Every individual is brought to know that his immediate superior outguns him and outshines him, so that deference to his requests is expedient. And that superior is likely also to discourage concerted deviance, typically by deterring his subordinate from unstructured 'horizontal' communication, and often by similarly restricting interactions between non-adjacent vertical layers; the official can expect trouble if he speaks too freely in the adjacent office, or if he gives the impression of going over his superior's head.

When a modern bureaucratic hierarchy is compared with the kind of maximally reliable, maximally oppressive power structure considered earlier, it is not immediately obvious where the *fundamental* difference lies. In both contexts it is sanctions and surveillance which ensure that subordinates perform tasks as required, whatever they think of their intrinsic value or desirability. Both the income tax office and the extermination camp have the character of economies wherein the performance of routine actions is guaranteed by the extrinsic values that attach to them. The basis of control is the same in both contexts, and indeed in all contexts wherein sanctions guarantee conformity. Whether sanctions are mild or extreme, positive or negative, used or merely threatened, they allow people to be manipulated in just the same way. They decouple agents' calculations from the intrinsic significance of their actions, and fasten them upon an extrinsic significance. Evaluation of the intrinsic significance of what they might do, and hence an effective discretion over whether or not it is done, accrues to the power-holder.[18]

The limited role of sanctions

There is nonetheless, one important respect in which all the hierarchies and power structures extant in modern societies fall short of being complete and comprehensive systems of control: the intuition that there is a fundamental difference between the tax office and the human machine is sound. Almost without exception, every organized distribution of power in a modern society sustains itself on the basis of a *limited range* of sanctions. The extremes of physical violence, physical intimidation, physical cruelty, are no longer institutionalized, and the continuing tendency is for the range of routinely applicable sanctions to become ever narrower and their maximum impact less and less.[19] As sanctions weaken, so the range of actions which can be reliably controlled narrows, and hence the range of actions where surveillance is profitable and a serious attempt at control worthwhile. Thus, in modern societies it is invariably the case that people act at the discretion of others only in so far as a narrow range of alternative actions are concerned, and a limited set of times and contexts.

This was a point fully appreciated by Max Weber in his seminal remarks on bureaucracies and officials (1968). Weber emphasized the personal freedom of the official and the way that his duties were limited and bounded, in extent by the recognition of working hours and a specific place of work, in nature by rules and regulations. As Weber rightly points out, what any official may require of others is restricted to what he is readily able to present as consistent with the specifications of his legitimate authority, and hence, conversely, what he may be required to do by others is similarly restricted. The general recognition of the existence of rules specifying correct official activity and the legitimate authority (in Weber's sense) of particular offices allows officials to resist tendencies toward arbitrary and unduly demanding control.[20]

In Weber too we find the clue to how weak sanctions may suffice as a basis for immense power. Weber's bureaucrat is scarcely affected by the intrinsic consequences of the actions he takes or the decisions he makes: his private world is dissociated from them; his public world is kept beyond his control and maintained stable in the face of them. The intrinsic costs and benefits of what he does are negligible as far as he himself is concerned. Accordingly he will be highly sensitive to extrinsic costs and benefits, and hence tolerably well manipulated by weak sanctions.

Within a bureaucratic system routines may be directed on the basis of weak sanctions with very little loss of efficiency. Weak sanctions may imply extensive limitations on what a given subordinate may be induced to do, but not on what a set of subordinates may be induced to do. The need is merely for ingenuity in the allocation of tasks: the income tax officer will still reliably ruin strangers, and should deal with strangers; the professional bomber pilot should operate from 40,000 feet and not over his home town. An enormous amount may easily be obtained from people provided one only expects a very little from them. This is the principle that lies at the very heart of our modern institutional arrangements, the secret of our current success.

In the absence of the relevant structure of sanctions and rewards neither the tax officer nor the bomber pilot would act as they do; in this respect their actions are like those of the camp inmate. Nonetheless, the role of sanctions in the latter case is more profound than in the former. The extermination camp inmate may be presumed to be opposed to the camp, lock, stock and barrel, and to refrain from acting against it only because of constant surveillance and the threat of sanctions. But for the tax official and the bomber pilot there is a private realm: surveillance is incomplete; restrictions on interaction are incomplete; constraints upon knowledge and cognition are incomplete. Accordingly, whilst the tax official and the bomber pilot may still find it expedient to conform and comply with the direct instructions of superiors, they actually have ample opportunity to oppose or criticize the context of their subordination, or to plan and pre-organize concerted action against it, on a recreational basis, as it were.

More generally, since sanctions are weak and surveillance limited in modern societies, since there is a private realm, all hierarchies and bureaucratic systems are vulnerable to pressure both from their own members within, and from those same members and complete outsiders without. Yet in most modern societies pressure of this kind is usually weak, whether from subordinates within the hierarchies or from others. Even unionized subordinates, adept at extracting considerable extrinsic rewards for the activities they perform, refrain from using their organization to attack hierarchies themselves, or to modify or redirect their activities – the intrinsically significant activities which they themselves perform to gain their extrinsic rewards. In practically all modern developed societies a highly skewed distribution of discretion in the use of power is sustained in a way that cannot be sufficiently accounted for by sanctioning and the rest of the social technology of divide and rule. How then is it to be accounted for? What else is implicated in its stability?

It would be a mistake to imagine that there is insufficient capacity for action available, beyond the reach of the pinnacles of power as it were, for any effective opposition to our existing order. Although modern societies are efficient, comparatively speaking, in their mobilization and use of capacity for action, they remain vastly inefficient in absolute terms. There is, always and everywhere, a vast spare capacity, and there is always capacity which could be created but is not, latent power as opposed to immediate power.[21] Far from effectively maximizing general capacity for action, power-holders in modern societies often encourage its under-utilization, or alternatively seek to divert it to the fulfilment of grandiose but trivial projects. Above all, they like to ensure that spare capacity for action which they themselves do not control is not set to the manufacture of yet more capacity which they do not control. In thereby acknowledging the virtues of high levels of 'depoliticization', power-holders also implicitly recognize what a wealth of resources might be brought against them if 'politicization' were to occur.[22]

It would also be mistaken to attribute the stability of the distribution of powers to any systematic manipulation of the knowledge and information that passes into the private realm. It it true that in all societies without exception efforts are made actively to shape and order knowledge in attempts at social control, and that the flow of information is everywhere censored, restricted and distorted for the same end. Nowhere is the nature of society as a distribution of knowledge more clearly evident than in the efforts people make to adapt and modify that very distribution, in efforts to manipulate the actions of others. But this is a ubiquitous exercise in modern societies, not one directed from the pinnacles of power.[23] Nor could systematic attempts at such direction take on a fundamental significance in the absence of strong sanctions and extensive surveillance.

In the last analysis, we refrain from acting to change the skewed distribution of power neither out of ignorance nor disinformation. We continue to reconstitute that distribution through the totality of our knowledgeable calculative actions, many of which stand unaffected by external coercion or association with sanctions.

Legitimacy

Considerations of this 'kind have led sociologists, philosophers and political theorists to claim that the distribution of power in modern societies has a general, extended legitimacy,[24] and is based in the last analysis upon widespread active approval and support. Whether it is based on rational understanding, or on shared values and norms, or on delusion and the power of ideology, approval and support of some kind must be postulated to account for the uncoerced component in the acceptance of the status quo. This is a difficult kind of argument to deal with systematically and it is one that is put forward in many different ways. Nonetheless, I want not only to demonstrate weaknesses in specific examples of this kind of argument, but also to cast doubt upon it in its most general form and to suggest that it needs, to say the least, some radical revision.

Let me begin with a specific case of the argument. It is widely held in the social sciences that although states may be conquered by force and initially held down by coercion, the continued predominance of conquerors involves their establishing their legitimacy as rulers and transforming rule based on might into rule based on right. 'Naked power', which is difficult to sustain, is transformed into 'legitimate authority', which may be maintained on the basis of less extensive and less expensive sanctions. I have already, in my earlier discussion of authority, rejected this mode of thought implicitly, and refused to define authority in terms of the evaluations of those over whom it is exercised, but I shall now attack it directly and attempt to clarify its weaknesses.

Lenski (1966) describes the transition from might to right in a typical, but particularly straightforward and readily intelligible manner. Force, he says, may indeed conquer. But a nation continually held down by force must be subdued over and over, at great cost to its conquerors. In the words of Edmund Burke, 'A nation is not governed, which is perpetually to be conquered.' The continued reliance on force may be possible in theory, but its possessors will nonetheless find it to their own advantage to switch the basis of their rule, to gain, as far as is possible, acceptance and support from the ruled. Thus, says Lenski, *'those who seize power by force find it advantageous to legitimise their rule once effective organized opposition is eliminated'* (1966, p. 52, Lenski's italics). Legitimacy will be achieved by encoding the privileges of the rulers in law, wherein they may be clothed in universalistic language and made to appear just and natural, and by supporting them with propaganda readily generated through control of educational and religious institutions and the media of communication. Using these resources, Lenski believes, a new ruling elite 'can usually surround itself with an aura of legitimacy within a few months or years' (ibid., p. 53).

Note how Lenski's account requires the existence of two distinct kinds of human agents. Elite members are stereotypically active, reflective and manipulative in their use of knowledge, ideas and information; the ruled are passive, credulous, manipulated. Yet no account is offered of the provenance of the basic distinction, nor is any clear and obvious explanation of it available. Why should there be this systematic variability in the relationship between human beings and their knowledge? The lack of any answer to this question constitutes, in my view, a fatal weakness in Lenski's account, and indeed in all the innumerable accounts of the role of knowledge in society that rely on a basic distinction between those who are the manipulators of ideas and those who are the dupes of ideas.

It remains the case that conquerors are able to rule, in many cases, with less and less reliance on force as time passes. Why is this? What is it that actually makes rule more and more secure in such cases? If we think of societies as constituted of knowledgeable, reflectively aware agents, the answer to this question is not difficult to provide. We may then think of the stabilization of a new regime as a typical example of the validation of a new distribution of knowledge, which process of validation is at the same time one wherein the distribution is constituted and established.

Note first of all that Edmund Burke was wrong to think that a society secured by force must 'perpetually be conquered'; and Lenski was wrong to think that changes in the basis of rule only begin 'once effective organised opposition is eliminated'. Conquest precisely involves the destruction of the organization of the opposition, and in so far as this is done, the same society does *not* remain to 'perpetually be conquered'.[25] Analogously, as a pattern of organization is destroyed, so the orientation of knowledgeable agents to other patterns of organization will change: 'the transition from might to right' is crucially facilitated and in many cases mainly accomplished in the process of conquest itself.

Whatever act of violence is counted as initiating a new regime, whatever battle is won or city captured or surrender received, it will not be instantly known everywhere. Unquelled opposition will continue to exist in ignorance of the act, and may count its chances of resistance the higher out of ignorance. It will only move to a more realistic assessment of its chances as knowledge diffuses through to it. Similarly, the more the new regime suppresses some outstanding opposition the more likely is remaining opposition to forego further violence and make its peace. Success will breed success, so that remaining threats to the regime become smaller and smaller, and need matching with fewer and fewer countervailing coercive resources. Success will breed success as opponents lose their allies and turn out of necessity into supporters, depriving yet other opponents of allies. Eventually calculation will indicate to everyone that concerted opposition is not feasible and isolated opposition is pointless. There will be a general move toward making the best of what exists. Erstwhile opponents will calculate on the basis of the regime's continuing and come to develop vested interests in it. Shortly they may be its defenders. Finally a stable distribution of knowledge may emerge, wherein everyone knows that everyone else acquiesces in the regime, wherein this is known to everyone, and wherein the general knowledge of the general level of acquiescence is what sustains the acquiescence of which there is general knowledge. This is the point at which the power of the regime achieves both its greatest stability and its greatest extension, and the minimum in the need for coercive resources that appertains at this point is a simple correlate of this. It is not that power changes into something else – authority – at this point, but that power achieves its greatest magnitude as a resonance in a distribution of knowledge extending across both rulers and ruled. Knowledge of might may thus diffuse and transform itself into knowledge of right.

Needless to say, a new regime is likely still to take an interest in whatever legal system it inherits and to adjust it to its purposes: it may well establish legal bounds to its privileges and legal protection for those it rules, in order further to encourage acquiescence by giving the ruled a stake in the system and hence something positive to lose by opposition. Similarly, a new regime will probably concern itself with propaganda and the media of communication, in order to facilitate the required shifts in the distribution of knowledge and to prevent the re-emergence of the old distribution. It will be important to the new regime that people know what they have to know. But, for better or worse, this process of assisting the diffusion of knowledge does not need a passive and credulous audience: although the learning of the new official version of society may possibly be not to the collective good of the ruled, it will generally be useful and beneficial at the individual level, so that there is no fundamental difficulty in understanding why it should occur. Just as people find it all too easy to over-graze the common land or to have too many children for the collective good, so they may find it all too easy to assimilate the emerging system of self-referring knowledge. The very fact that this knowledge, far from being incorrect or inadequate, will, even as it is being diffused, have strong tendencies to be confirmed will make its assimilation all the easier.

As rule is established, so the amount of force at the disposal of rulers may itself be reduced, and the amount of sanctioning and surveillance in the society. This is because the immediate capacity for action of the ruled is itself progressively reduced and hence their disposition to active opposition. In these changed conditions the availability of force continues to underpin rule, but force, through sanctions and surveillance, does not provide anything remotely like a sufficient explanation of conformity. On the other hand, legitimacy and active support may throw little light on the basis of conformity either. People may simply be adjusting to contingencies they find themselves unable to change. Consider actual situations where the underpinning role of force is important and clearly evident. No doubt prisons could not continue on any other basis. Yet prison activity is far from explicable as activity determined wholly by the threat of coercion. One that might even say that prisons are co-operative enterprises, kept going by the efforts of all their inmates. Sadly, one might rightly say this even of those prisons that were extermination camps. The availability of coercion, the threat of sanctions and the use of surveillance, is massively insufficient as an explanation of actual conforming activity, even in the context of a prison. Yet we surely would not wish to say of a prison that it is a general acceptance of the legitimacy of rule that allows that rule to continue on the basis of less coercion than might otherwise be required. Rather, we would be tempted to think of interaction winding itself around those features of prison life that were directly sustained by the threat of force, and for all practical purposes beyond alteration. It would be a matter of interacting individuals making the best of things as they saw it.

Having considered one particularly relevant and interesting example of the argument, it should now be easier to see what is dubious about appeals to legitimacy and approval in general. What such appeals basically involve is an inference to *specific* attitudes and evaluations, from actions of a kind which are actually consistent with a *vast range* of such evaluations, and may be indicated by innumerable different kinds of considerations, given agents' knowledge and its distribution.[26] It is a straightforward fallacy to claim that because some of the actions that contribute to the continuation and reconstitution of a distribution of powers are performed freely, some level of approval of the distribution, or some recognition of its legitimacy, must be postulated in order to explain them. It is difficult enough to find evidence of the existence of approval and legitimacy in some specific situations, some of the time, and to establish that such problematic entities may be given an explanatory role as causes of specific actions. It is next to impossible to demonstrate their essential and ubiquitous importance. In practice, in almost every case, references to legitimacy and approval serve more to mislead than to enlighten. In societies like our own, the only clear indication of a generalized support or approval for the existing distribution of powers would seem to be the lack of any systematic movement for change in that distribution – the very thing that references to approval are most commonly invoked to explain.

Because it's there

Approval is altogether the wrong kind of notion to invoke in the explanation of the persistence of large-scale distributions of power. If our failure to assail and demolish the existing power structure indicates a general approval for its existence, then presumably we also approve of the Bass Rock, or Ben Nevis, which likewise we have failed to assail and demolish. And indeed there is a useful analogy lying latent here. If we could understand the sense in which we tolerate the mountain, acquiesce in its existence, drive round it instead of hacking through it, we might have a template for understanding something of our toleration of a distribution of power. For clearly there is a sense in which we acquiesce in the existence of the mountain without actually, or even metaphorically, approving of it.

A distribution of power is an aspect of the overall distribution of knowledge, and since the knowledge in question is self-referring knowledge, the distribution is something well known to agents themselves. Its major features have scale and prominence in agents' cognitive maps of social order, just as mountains have in their maps of the physical environment, and scale and prominence in both cases is an indication of something difficult to shift. Such prominences are liable to be taken account of and planned around more then they are appraised and evaluated. Their very existence is a key factor which, being taken account of in calculative action, may help to explain their continued existence. [27]

The prominent features of any routinized social order always have some stability deriving from the costs and uncertainties involved in destroying them, changing them or replacing them. A given distribution of powers may be perceived merely as one of many possible locations in a vast landscape of social possibilities. But that one location is invariably a valley surrounded by vast mountain ranges of conversion costs, and although there may be other valleys not too far away, deeper cut, richer, more alluring, the route across the passes may be closed to a small number of individuals and difficult and unpredictable even to large numbers moving in echelon. And even this is to assume that there is a map of the route and a clear vision of the valleys not too far away, not merely a hazy awareness of towering windswept summits to inspire the thought: better the devil you know.

Modern societies are not total institutions or even near approximations thereto. We are not divided into power-holders and their instruments, with the former acting at discretion with a mind to the intrinsic significance of what is done, and the latter acting, calculatively true, but only in relation to sanctions and rewards, and hence the extrinsic significance of what is done. Discretion is indeed concentrated in modern societies, its distribution markedly skewed, but discretion remains nonetheless distributed over the whole. That discretion may often be freely used: everybody is in a position to act some of the time without regard for sanctions and with regard for the intrinsic value of what they do, and everybody does so act to some extent. The skewed distribution of powers, which is as a matter of fact in existence amongst us, is to that extent the product of the unconstrained action of all of us.

Power-holders 'highly placed' in modern societies are in no position to enforce compliance through a ubiquitous direct control. They have to rely upon the outcome of calculations carried out beyond the reach of their systems of sanctions. But the systems of activities wherein they enjoy discretion have low running-costs, high output and large conversion-costs and power-holders have become adept at directing them with an eye on the longer term. Hence calculative actions largely sustain the status quo, and even long-term imaginative projections are hard-pressed to produce credible blueprints of an alternative order of things and how to get there – blueprints such as are the essential cognitive institutions of major movements of concerted deviance. Thus, much of our present social order with its skewed distribution of powers is reconstituted by calculative action, even though it is neither secured from 'above' through coercion and pervasive sanctioning, nor sustained from 'below' by approval and active support.

That said, it must be acknowledged that a specific skewed distribution of powers will be more likely to persist in the long term, on the basis of weak sanctions and weak controls, the more it is operated with regard for the interests of those who act to reconstitute it. Power-holders can reasonably expect increased toleration if they make few demands, sustain the supply of goods, respond to changing pressures, incorporate significant opposition, create vested interests in their own predominance and generally maximize the range of attitudes and evaluations that are consistent with acquiescence in what they do. This, of course, is very much how powers are exercised in societies like our own.[28]

5

UNITY IS STRENGTH

5.1 ACTING FOR THE COLLECTIVE GOOD

The effect of sanctions in a repressive society is intelligible without the use of any elaborate theory of individual human behaviour. People may reasonably be expected to avoid death or imprisonment out of self-interest, or out of concern for the fate of their loved ones, or simply to keep open the chance of future action to further whatever ends are meaningful and important to them. Similarly, in modern societies, sanctions and rewards serve as incentives to action for individuals with a vast range of diverse personal concerns and objectives. Indeed, one of the marvels of a monetary economy is the way that innumerable individual objectives can all alike be turned into motivations for routine, conforming behaviour. So long as a person has a fancy for something that money can buy, whether for himself or others, he has an incentive to conformity. The efficacy of monetary reward is compatible with a vast range of conjectures about the nature of individual human ends, about what individuals find intrinsically desirable and what unpleasant, and being compatible with so many psychological conjectures it is, in itself, evidence for none.

Thus, it was possible to discuss sanctioned actions in the preceding chapter without an assumption of self-interest, although the discussion was for the most part compatible with such an assumption, and no doubt would have lost credibility if it had not been so compatible. It seems to be widely accepted that calculative action will predominantly be self-interested action, that where an individual evaluates actions in terms of ends or interests it is his own which will have priority. This is taken for granted in many areas of economics, just as it is, much of the time, in everyday life. Even sociologists tend to divide action into the 'calculative' and 'self-interested' on the one hand, and the 'moral' and 'principled' on the other: where they see self-interest being set aside or systematically overridden they are often reluctant to speak of calculative agents. Economists frequently define 'rational' action as that which is both calculated and self-interested: sociologists often implicitly agree.

It is nonetheless a mistake so to link these things together. How far actions are calculated to be consistent with ends, and how far these ends are the immediate ends of the calculating individual should be kept as separate questions. How far actions are themselves ends, intrinsic goods in themselves, and how far they are ends solely of the individual performing them, should likewise be considered separately. The need to do this becomes clear when we seek to understand how individuals act together in the absence of external coercion or external incentive, to further ends and interests in co-operation with each other. It is especially important when we consider, not actions which benefit individuals separately and which may clearly be inspired by particular individual wants or interests, but actions which generate *collective goods*, and which are not clearly and directly inspired by any particular individual want or interest at all. The explanation of collective action of this kind, action which furthers the collective but not the individual good, is widely recognized as a major problem for any social theory that bases itself upon references to calculation and intentionality.

The free-rider problem

Nobody can be excluded from a collective good: the benefits it brings are indivisible. By definition, it may be enjoyed not just by its producers but by everyone in their vicinity. When a bridge is built, all may cross it. When clean air is produced, all may breathe it. When a high wage is negotiated, all may earn it. When a revolution succeeds, all may be relieved of oppression. Needless to say, in modern societies self-interest can be coupled to the production of collective goods: builders may be paid to construct the bridge, or mercenaries to make the revolution; laws may be passed against pollution and paid officials set to enforce them. But imagine a tribal society getting together to build the bridge by direct action, or a sect of activists furthering the revolution, with the individuals involved looking simply to their own future individual benefit. How far would self-interested individuals participate in such activities?[1]

It may seem that all those individuals who gain from the provision of a collective good have a direct personal interest in providing it, and that when the overall benefit exceeds the overall cost of production the good will be produced. But as Moncur Olson pointed out in his *Logic of Collective Action* (1965), this is bad economics. A calculative agent would note that he could not be excluded from the enjoyment of the good, once provided, whether he had borne a part of its cost or not. Often, therefore, he would see no point in contributing to the cost, and would leave it for everyone else to provide. In a society of self-interested calculative agents everyone would act in this way, and the good would therefore not be provided at all, despite its being a benefit for everyone. Olson thus highlighted the rationality of the blackleg, and raised the question of why there should ever be a strike. Why not let the others do it? Why not free-ride?[2]

The nub of the free-rider problem is the clash between calculations of the overall benefit of collective action and individual calculations of cost and benefit on the margin. Concerted action for the collective good may offer immense benefits to the collectivity, and every single individual member thereof considered separately may profit from it, and yet it may still involve every individual in far more effort than can be balanced by his own individual returns on that effort. Consider a project to build a bridge. Participating individuals may each have to carry out several days of labour, accepting arduous physical demands and some danger. In a community of any size a given individual will note that his own private loss in refusing to participate is negligibly small. It may be but a few hours delay in his having use of the bridge, whilst everybody else makes up for the loss of his labour. Hence every individual will see his marginal contribution to bridge-building as not worth making, and will refuse to participate. They will all seek a free-ride on the efforts of others. The bridge will not be built. And yet every individual might separately consider a few days even of arduous and risky labour a small price for the subsequent continuing use of a bridge. The opportunity for every individual to make a profitable investment of effort is destroyed by the operation of individual rational self-interested calculation (Olson, 1965; Hardin, 1982).[3]

More generally, suppose that the overall cost of the provision of a collective good is C, and its overall benefit is B, and that both are to be spread evenly over a society of n agents, if each voluntarily participates. Suppose also that each increment of cost generates the same increment of overall benefit. Then for his individual contribution to costs of C/n a given agent may expect an additional benefit of B/n^2 – the overall benefit generated by his own personal contribution, B/n, divided by the number of individuals over whom it is spread, n. It is to the individual's advantage to pay the cost only if $B/n^2 > C/n$, i.e., if $B > nC$. All projects which fail to yield a benefit n times larger than cost are discouraged.

Note how in these circumstances the size of the collectivity which benefits from the good is crucial. A very small group will be able to develop the capacity for action needed to generate many of its collective goods: its small size will actually be a factor that contributes to its power.

A larger group of self-interested individuals will find it more difficult to develop an analogous collectively sustained power: individual contributions will matter less in larger groups, and there will be incentives to make them much less often. In very large groups it is difficult to think of collective goods to which members would find it profitable to contribute: very large groups will be prone not to produce such goods at all, but to remain, in Olson's terminology, 'latent groups'.[4]

On the face of it, if individuals are calculative and self-interested then they will make no significant level of direct voluntary contributions to the provision of collective goods for large groups: they will leave them to others to provide. Conversely, if collective goods of this kind are in fact provided voluntarily, then individuals cannot be wholly calculative and self-interested. What then does the empirical evidence suggest? Olson inclined to the view that collective goods are not provided voluntarily for large groups, and sought to show that cases where they were apparently so provided usually involved actions orientated to self-interest. The joining of trades' unions, for example, was in his view largely to be explained by the coercion of closed-shop arrangements, or by the *private* benefits of membership, such as reduced insurance and the discounts on goods and services negotiated for individual members by union officials. Generalized concern to advance the cause of an occupation or a social class did not suffice to generate union members. More recently, Hardin (1982) has offered extensive evidence to support much the same conclusions. If he is right then people do not significantly inconvenience themselves or their pockets to provide collective goods. Thus, Hardin notes that although concern for environmental conservation and for racial equality have been intense and pervasive in the United States for many years, the sums contributed by individuals directly to the general furtherance of these causes have been derisory. Hardin is prepared to admit the existence of a small amount of universalistic and altruistic activity in society but, as he sees it, self-interested calculation predominates.

For all that Hardin's conclusions are based upon extended empirical study and are argued with immense skill and care, I think that they nonetheless deserve criticism. Nor is this simply because they are general assertions about human behaviour made on the basis of evidence drawn overwhelmingly from one specific society, the United States.[5] More important is the treatment of the evidence itself. It is a tribute to the quality of Hardin's work that his own data may be used to call into question his own favoured line of interpretation, and to support alternative forms of conjecture. Consider some of the 'exceptional' cases to which he draws attention. Hardin admits that he is unable to account for the British practice of blood-doning on the basis of rational self-interest, and has to propose that it is sustained by a tiny amount of atypical altruism, which suffices to supply the good in sufficient quantity. He is without recourse in the face of the vast queues of volunteers who typically besiege army recruiting offices at time of war: would it not be far and away more 'rational' for such individuals to free-ride, and let others do the dying? Finally, Hardin can offer no satisfactory resolution of the standard problem of voting. Voting seems to be unintelligible by reference to self-interest: no individual vote ever makes a difference at election time, so why should a self-interested calculative agent ever take the trouble to cast one? Voting, of course, is a crucial case since, indirectly, it is through voting and representation that so many collective goods are provided in modern societies: the 'irrational' practice of voting is what makes it 'rational' for representatives to take decisions furthering the collective good, and so to modify the distribution of individual rewards that the capacity for action of the community is directed to their provision.

A great deal of human activity can be reconciled with the conjecture that individuals operate on the basis of calculation and self-interest. Hardin shows us how much might be accounted for on that basis. At the same time, he provides convincing evidence of the existence of activities which are difficult indeed to reconcile with the conjecture. First of all, his materials remind us of how effective communities and societies of all kinds actually are in providing collective goods: goods of this kind are provided in all social contexts and any general account of the basis of social order should be able to explain their provision. Secondly, he establishes that collective goods may in some cases be provided directly, by individuals who could readily free-ride yet do not: the free-rider problem is in this sense, in many particular cases, a soluble problem. Collective goods *are* provided; the free-rider problem *is* frequently solved.[6] Whatever else, it seems to me, these two points should be clung to as trustworthy matters of fact, and preserved in the course of any discussion of collective action. For the moment, theories and speculations should be wound around these points, and not allowed to conflict with them.[7]

How people solve the problem – a conjecture

One way of accounting for the provision of collective goods is, of course, to postulate the existence of internalized moral rules which function precisely to provide such goods. That collective goods are actually provided may be used as an argument for the existence of firm individual commitments to rules or principles. The difficulty here is that collective goods are not always provided, and the free-rider problem is not always solved – even in cases where it would appear highly 'functional' for it to be solved: bridges often remain unbuilt; pollution often continues needlessly to kill and erode; attacked workers often fail to organize strikes. Much here depends on the view one takes of a great range of empirical materials, but in my judgement there is far too much free-riding to vindicate a view of society as being based upon commitments to internalized norms, yet far too little to allow its reduction to the actions of so many independent, self-interested agents.

Are there any interesting differences between situations wherein the free-rider problem is solved and those wherein it is not? I think there very well may be. Hardin's empirical materials suggest an important contrast between the two kinds of cases. When he focuses upon privately executed individual actions – the signing of cheques and the posting of letters – Hardin documents a very low level of provision of collective goods. But when he considers things that people do together – publicly visible actions – his 'exceptional' cases arise: communities vote on the same day, and as communities rather than as isolated individuals, even though the vote is secret; members of communities go to war together; in Britain, a great deal of blood-doning is communally ordered and communally encouraged. This suggests that interactions between people, and the effects that people have on each other in the course of such interactions, may be what largely account for the provision of collective goods – where they are indeed provided.

Hardin's general picture gives insufficient emphasis to the effects of interaction. It is not that his picture is unduly individualistic: this common criticism of 'economic' approaches is misplaced; there is everything to be gained from the study of society at the highest level of detail possible, which is the individual level. What is wrong is the tendency to atomize the individuals of which society is composed, and to decouple them from each other into independently operating units. Marx put his finger on this right at the beginning of his work:

> The members of the civil society are not *atoms*. The *specific* property of the atom is that it has *no* properties and is therefore not connected with beings outside it by any relations determined by its own *natural necessity*. The atom *has no needs*, it is *self-sufficient*. . . . It is . . . not the *State* that holds the *atoms* of civil society together, but the fact that they are atoms only in *imagination*, in the *heaven* of their fancy, but in *reality* beings tremendously different from atoms, in other words, not *divine egoists*, but *egotistic human beings*. (1845, pp. 162–3)

'Egotistic human beings' in interaction are capable of constituting a moral community in which collective goods may be provided directly, even for large numbers. Let us take this as our hypothesis. Let us postulate that norms for collective action must be sustained in the public life of an interacting community, and collectively sustained and enforced. Where the provision of a collective good may be established as or through such a public norm, which people press upon each other as they interact, then the good may be provided and free-riding kept at bay. Where this is not possible the good is much less likely to be provided, and large-scale free-riding may well persist.

If an hypothesis of this kind is to be made plausible three basic points must be established. It must be shown, first that people are profoundly affected by each other as they interact, secondly that they are prepared to affect each other for the collective good, and finally that they are capable of developing shared conceptions of what the collective good is.

The first point raises few problems. For all the diversity of view and extensive disagreement about the nature of interpersonal interaction, all who study it agree upon the far-reaching consequences it may have. People need interaction with others as a matter of 'natural necessity'. Its effects, whatever they may be, are such that 'egotistic human beings' become vastly different from 'divine egoists'. In the literature of the social sciences this vastness is well documented: the arguments tend to be at the level of whether human beings are merely deeply *affected* by interaction, or whether they should be said to be *constituted* by it. Certainly, such interactions are not mere means of exchange, routes to extrinsic benefits; they have an inherent value. They do not simply convey information via the symbols which constitute them; they have a larger significance related to the evaluations they also convey. A continuing feedback of signs of acceptance and recognition of competence seems essential to the continued possession of individual competence. Continued approval and respect seem essential for an individual's sense of self-esteem, and perhaps even for his maintenance of personal identity and sense of self. Whatever else, a constant flow of acceptance, recognition and approval is of sufficient importance to make participation in some form of ongoing collective life intrinsically valuable for practically all individuals. Conversely, a sustained flow of rejection, disapproval, even mere indifference, is intrinsically unpleasant, not to say traumatic or in some cases life-threatening. There is surely enough here to reinforce universalism, and to discourage or realign self-interest, so that the provision of the collective good is massively increased. Setting aside the details, there is every reason to accept that there exists, in the public domain, in the texture of interaction itself, sufficient resources to override or transform inexpedient individual ends, and to sustain collectively advantageous action.

The next, much more difficult question, is whether and how far these resources will be put to the appropriate use. Let me make a massive and grotesque simplification at this point and simply speak of people informally *sanctioning* each other in the course of interaction. Some actions will attract approval and honour. These may be thought of as intrinsically desirable things which, when attached to actions, give those actions an additional extrinsic significance: approval and honour serve as positive sanctions. Some actions will attract disapproval and contempt. These will serve analogously as negative sanctions. Might collective goods be generated using these resources? Might powers be ordered and aligned appropriately? Might people build a bridge as a mutually approved project, gaining the respect of their fellows by their participation and avoiding the disapprobation directed at free-riders?

I believe a bridge might indeed be built in this way, its building standing as a public norm enforced in the course of ongoing interaction. But some difficult and intricate problems are involved in understanding how it is possible to build bridges in this way. If a collective good is generated, in the last analysis, by mutual sanctioning, then it is necessary to understand the basis of the sanctioning itself. On the face of it this raises once more the very problem we have been trying to overcome, the free-rider problem. Is not sanctioning for the collective good a privately costly but publicly beneficial activity, just like bridge-building itself? Does not this mean that any move from bridge-building to sanctioning will preserve all the problems of the original situation? Why not let other people sanction the norm of bridge-building? If 'rational' individuals are moved by expediency to free-ride on the building activity of others, why should they not be similarly moved to free-ride on the sanctioning activity of others? Is it not utterly futile to account for the performance of publicly valuable but privately profitless action by appeal to sanctioning, when sanctioning is precisely that kind of action?

The answer must be that the sanctioning involved in symbolic interaction is quite different from bridge-building or any other form of purely instrumental activity. Sanctions involving physical coercion or violence may indeed be costly collective goods like bridges. But symbolically transmitted sanctions embedded in informal interaction may explain the provision of such goods, bridges, coercion, violence, or whatever else, because sanctions of this kind are not costly in any clear sense. It is at this level of human behaviour that the cost/benefit frame of reference starts to disintegrate, that actions have to be considered as ends as well as means. It may be plausible to treat the loss of a right purely as a cost, as when a cheque is signed or property is made over to another: Hardin documents the reluctance of people to incur such losses for the public good. It may even be acceptable (although far from unproblematic) to extend the concept and speak of unpleasant and dangerous tasks like bridge-building merely as costs. But where is the cost of praise or blame, of approval or disapproval? What is the cost of a specific facial expression, given that some such expression must be worn? What is the cost of a specific sequence of noises, given that the larynx is constantly emitting noises of some kind?[8] How much of a sacrifice is it to stand with one's peers on a picket line, urging and approving courses of action, when one would otherwise be standing with one's peers on the football terraces, urging and approving courses of action?

Needless to say, one cannot legislate against cost/benefit analysis. It may be taken up and applied to acts of informal sanctioning by anyone of a mind to do so. Presumably, the cost of generating a sanction, a gesture or symbolic expression of approval or disapproval, is more or less zero. The benefit of the sanction will derive from its effect upon its target, and its effects within the context of the sanctioning group, presuming that people are acting together to sanction a collective good. The target may be profoundly affected, so that a massive benefit results, albeit an indivisible benefit, a collective good. The sanctioning group may approve the action of the sanctioner and all the approval may count as his individual benefit. Looked at in this way, sanctioning for the collective good may be cost-effective for the individual after all.[9] Perhaps rational, self-interested agents might build a bridge on that basis. Be that as it may, what should in any case be evident is that there is no clear-cut, demonstrable inconsistency between sanctioning for the collective good and acting calculatively, even in the extreme case where calculation proceeds wholly on the basis of self-interest. Sanctioning for the collective good is like cheering on one's team at a football game. No doubt the cheer is lost in the noise of the crowd generally. No doubt its role in raising the spirits of one's team is very small. Considered as an instrumental action, the individual cheer is a waste of time, and one could as well leave everyone else to urge on the team. Is the action then irrational, or contrary to any sense of individual self-interest? Not at all. Is the action inconsistent with reflective awareness and the full use of calculative capabilities? In no way. Even if we forget that the cheer may have an intrinsic value as an end, and even if we forget that the cheer is an approved action, a recognized action, we are still left with the fact that no loss is involved in its production. The worst-case ratio of benefits to costs in this case is found by dividing zero by zero.

It may be that a cost/benefit mode of analysis could be extended by a determined advocate right into the fine structure of interaction and discourse. But the attempt would be forced and artificial. There are more appropriate modes of thought available. In an interesting attempt by an anthropologist to deal with the free-rider problem we find a useful pointer in a more promising direction: 'How a system of knowledge gets off the ground,' Mary Douglas suggests, 'is the same as the problem of how any collective good is created' (1986, p. 45). This is not exactly right, since without helping to constitute and sustain the shared knowledge of one's community one does not benefit from its existence either. But the profound analogy between sustaining collective action and sustaining shared knowledge is invaluable.[10] Both require that people affect each other in the course of interaction so that a degree of standardization of action or of cognition ensues. Both entail a kind of ongoing mutual sanctioning. But the mutual sanctioning which allows agents to carry along a shared body of knowledge simply cannot be considered as expedient activity taken on the basis of calculations of profit and loss, cost and benefit. To make such calculations it is necessary to think, and to refer to what is known. One cannot cost one's thought before one thinks or the knowledge one needs as the basis for thought before one acquires it. The development of thought and the acquisition of knowledge are just going to go ahead whatever, as a continuing fundamental social process. 'Our colonisation of each others' minds is the price we pay for thought' (Douglas, 1975, p. xx). And nobody is ever allowed credit on this kind of transaction.

That which is necessary for the continuation of calculative action does not lend itself to treatment as a free variable within calculation, a good the supply of which may be switched on or off according to circumstance.[11] Whatever is so necessary is simply going to continue. Ongoing interaction and the mutual sanctioning involved therein are so necessary, and are going to continue. These things are prior to individuation and self-awareness, and cannot be treated as mere instrumentalities: we will not decide whether or not to continue with them any more than we will decide whether to continue to think or to take decisions. Their existence, in some sense or other, has a natural necessity. Mutual sanctioning continues all the time, as breathing continues all the time, and like breathing it may be adjusted to specific requirements on the basis of conscious calculation, even though much of what it does never becomes the subject of conscious calculation.

The matter of the sanctioning of actions conducive to the collective good must accordingly be considered in a larger framework than that of purely instrumental calculation. Life continues. Life is ongoing interaction and mutual sanctioning. It is a process that generates and sustains agreement in cognition through our intense susceptibility to each other in ongoing interaction. It is a process that moves us in the direction of a shared conception of what there is and what there ought to be (with the 'is' and the 'ought' not necessarily set apart or differentiated in that conception). It is vanity to imagine that we can sit above the process itself as a whole and pretend to appraise it as a whole. But the *specific* shared conceptions of 'is' and 'ought' that it sustains *can* be reflected upon and no doubt are. What shared conceptions are best sustained? What standard understandings may be supported with a generalized approval? When the question is put in this way then the answer must often be: those that further the collective good. If there are going to be public norms, and the question has to be 'which norms', then the clear answer, even for single individuals giving priority to their own concerns, will often be 'those that further the collective good'.[12] Alternative public norms will either be impossible to sustain and standardize, or less valuable in the life of the individual himself, given that the individual as a member of the collective benefits considerably when the collective good is provided. Hence, in many circumstances people will indeed sustain norms that further the collective good. Whether the collective good is always furthered as a consequence is, of course, another matter.

What kind of action is sanctioning for the collective good? For present purposes it scarcely matters how it is labelled. Those with a taste for taxonomy might wish to describe it as moral action. But if it is moral action it is moral action which emerges from our orientation to other people, and not from our orientation to rules or norms or principles or values.[13] It is a reflection of our nature as social beings with a deep susceptibility to each other. It is, moreover, a form of action which does not have to run counter to self-interest, and which is perfectly compatible with a calculative, reflectively-aware attitude. It seems plausible to suggest that this is why collective sanctioning is in practice the most important factor making for the actual production of collective goods even if it is not the only factor. Needless to say, in so far as people are prepared to calculate in ways which take direct account of the good of others, in so far as they calculate universalistically or altruistically, there is a further impetus to their provision. Nor is there any reason to doubt the importance and significance of these modes of calculative action, even if Hardin is right to imply that a direct sympathetic orientation to the ends of others is generally neither strong nor widely extended.[14]

If mutual sanctioning is capable of generating collective goods in the way that I have suggested, then there seems no reason why the size of the group enjoying the good should be of crucial importance. It should not be assumed that because people sanction each other in the course of local interactions the overall consequences of mutual sanctioning must be restricted and local. A public norm, I have suggested, may most readily be sustained and mutually sanctioned where its existence as a norm benefits all the members of the interacting, mutually sanctioning group. But this does not preclude the maintenance of the norm from being a benefit for others beyond such a group. The extra spreading of the collective good is irrelevant. The argument has *already* treated the direct marginal gains to the individual that arise from his contributing to, or sanctioning of, the good as negligible. Thus, given only that the basic argument is correct, there is no reason why, say, a strike of some hundreds of thousands should not be sustained by mutual sanctioning in many local contexts. There is absolutely no reason to imagine that the larger the football crowd the less people will cheer.

Consider, too, that individual people move between contexts, and often need to make their actions conform at once to the public norms of many contexts. Mobile agents tie contexts together: the fact that they are sanctioned by two groupings serves as an incentive for them to fuse the good of both together as one good. In particular, *representatives*, who are both members of local communities and members of a community of representatives, have for that very reason strong incentives to define and provide highly generalized, widely enjoyed collective goods. If a small community can produce a bridge through mutual sanctioning of its members, then the representatives of many such communities can produce a bridge-building programme. As a small community comes to know that its representative and his fellow representatives are capable of initiating such a programme, its demands for a bridge may be transformed into local pressure for the programme; local concerns may generate local pressure for very general collective goods.

Collective goods and the co-ordination of cognition

One final general issue remains. People are profoundly susceptible to each other as they interact: the resources for effective mutual sanctioning are indeed to hand. The actual use of such resources in a society of calculative agents is intelligible: they may indeed be deployed to further the collective good. But for this to occur it is necessary that the collective good itself is generally recognized and agreed upon.[15] This may be a much more serious problem than first appears, and indeed in some circumstances an insoluble one. But it is not insoluble in all circumstances. Acceptable solutions may be expected to emerge in many conditions so that collective goods are provided after all.

Consider the bridge once more. Its building may be made into a mutually sanctioned public norm or set of norms. But for this to occur it is necessary for those involved to know which bridge they are building. There must be an accepted plan for the bridge, an accepted location, an accepted procedure of construction. The bridge must exist as a *cognitive institution* if collective action is to proceed. The main problem in establishing such a cognitive institution is that different versions of the bridge will suit different people to different degrees. One person may want the bridge here, another there; one may want it wide, another narrow; one may propose stone, another wood.[16] The resulting conflicts might indeed be sufficiently severe to prevent the emergence of agreement in some circumstances. But in other circumstances one might reasonably expect that such problems would be overcome. Nature may be helpful and mark out one version: there may be just one narrow point on the river, or just one suitably placed island. Even where nature offers no help, agreement should eventually emerge from ongoing social interaction, given only that the costs and benefits of different feasible versions of the bridge are not too different for different individuals. In these cases agreement itself will be recognized as being more important than what precisely is agreed upon (Schelling, 1960). Individuals will support alternatives which already have support, precisely because these are the ones with the greatest chance of eventual general acceptance: a little support will attract more support, and hence more again and so on. Thus, initial random fluctuations of support for different alternatives may eventually metamorphose into a coherent movement to the acceptance of just one of them, whereupon mutual interaction will serve to transform agreement in cognition into agreement in action.[17]

At last, then, we have arrived at a plausible account of the provision of collective goods in a society of calculative agents. Such a society may hope to sustain privately unprofitable but collectively valuable activities after all – in some circumstances. The actions that most individuals would wish everyone else to perform may be transformed into the actions that most individuals actually do perform – sometimes. Public norms for the public good may be sanctioned, and possibly enforced, in a society of calculative agents. And since they are sanctioned by calculative, reflectivity aware individuals, they may be set aside immediately the public good is no longer served. In such a society consciences will not become cluttered with norms, nor will rivers become cluttered with bridges.

5.2 THE INCIDENCE OF COLLECTIVE ACTION

Collective action may be implicated in the persistence of the status quo or in its transformation: it may hinder or bring about social change. There is no fundamental difference between the two kinds of collective actions. A society is calculative activity based on a distribution of knowledge. People know what is implied by the various alternative courses of action available to them. They act on the basis of what they know. Their actions, being perceived, recognized, learned-about, thereby feed back and affect the distribution of knowledge itself. In such a society there is no special problem of social change, no difference in kind between actions that reconstitute a stable state and actions that transform it. A stable state is merely a state which ongoing calculative activity happens fully to reconstitute.

A changing society may accordingly be studied in just the same way as a stable society, as calculative activity, and analogously a changing distribution of powers may be studied in the same way as a stable distribution. Thus, if we are able to specify the conditions in which people will act for a collective good, we may hope to explain both the routine activity that supplies existing collective goods and innovative activity wherein people organize themselves in order to supply new ones. We may hope to account for existing powers within a society and the emergence of new powers, the processes which sustain existing organized capacity for action and those which transform latent into actual capacity for action through organization.

Nonetheless, in modern societies readiness to act directly for the collective good has a particular importance in relation to efforts to bring about social change. Within the existing order collective goods tend more and more to be provided by hierarchies, which, once established, minimize the need for widespread direct collective action. Once there is a hierarchy the many separate decisions of interested individuals are replaced by a single decision of one agent, so that the problems created by one decision being dependent on another, and notably the free-rider problem, are eliminated. Moreover, the structure of decision-taking at the head of the hierarchy may be such that all individuals are affected equally by its outcome. There may be power to print the money to buy the nuclear submarine, but no power to make some individuals pay and not others. Individual or factional interests may be incapable of affecting decisions, because decision-takers are unable to act in relevantly discriminating ways. Decisions may involve affecting everyone alike one way, or everyone alike another way, without the possibility of further alternatives. They may involve the choice of the collective good or the collective harm, which gives the collective good some chance.

Here is an effective solution to the problem of producing collective goods. The head of the hierarchy acts somewhat as a Hobbesian sovereign enforcing the individual costs of production. Note, however, that the powers of such a figure cannot be freely delegated to him from below, so that he represents nothing more than the collective will of those he rules; for a power of this kind would itself be a collective good, and individuals would leave everyone else to constitute it and support it and decline to do either themselves. If hierarchy is to ease the provision of collective goods it must have powers over and against the individuals it rules. The head of the hierarchy must be obeyed to some extent out of fear. In this case as much as any other, 'Covenants, without the sword, are but words, and of no strength to secure a man at all' (Hobbes, 1651, p. 173). This means that the hierarchy and its powers must be constituted as a distribution of knowledge which self-validates inductively, so that people know by experience that others routinely conform and that failure to conform brings loss or retribution.

Hierarchies may save people from the disasters which would otherwise arise from unduly self-interested calculations. Such hierarchies cannot, however, themselves emerge as the products of those calculations. Nor, once they have emerged, are there clear grounds for any individual to treat their persistence as itself a good. But once, by some accident, they have emerged, and persisted for a time, the inductively-based conviction that they will persist further will generate the actions which ensure that they do persist further, binding even self-interested individuals to the enacting of the collective good, and hence of their own individual good.

But if the agent at the head of a hierarchy thereby acquires powers which cannot be withdrawn at whim, which are more than what those 'below' allow him, 'by consent', to exercise, why should he be bound solely to the collective good in the use of those powers? The answer is, of course, that he is not so bound. As providers of collective goods, hierarchies may solve problems of free-riding and individual co-ordination, but at the same time they create problems of exploitation. The sovereign individual is a guarantee of collective goods only in so far as their provision coincides with his individual good. There is, however, always some degree of coincidence here. Even the director of a fully reliable human machine will take care to provide the collective goods required for it to persist and continue: individuals may often lavish greater consideration upon possessed objects than upon free and equal fellow human beings. Less secure power-holders will have regard to the collective good as a way of making opposition less attractive: it will be in their individual interest to further general interests. It may also be that power-holders take pleasure in living in a well-provisioned and harmonious society. On the whole, what we should expect here is what in fact we find: those in modern societies at the head of hierarchies, with powers conducive to the production of collective goods, will indeed involve themselves in generating such goods, whilst at the same time diverting a proportion of their available capacity for action to the production of a private rake-off; where hierarchies are effective in solving co-ordination problems and their conversion costs are high, that private rake-off can be very large.[18]

Hierarchy may breed hierarchy. Once specific collective goods are provided through hierarchical arrangements other collective goods may be provided by adjusting and extending those arrangements, as part of the business of rule. More problematic are attempts to work against 'the system', to redirect its existing output to new beneficiaries, to eliminate its existing powers, to dismantle it and replace it with something else. Such attempts involve getting organized, sometimes *ab initio*, and this almost always must be a matter of direct collective action.

Organizing for collective action

Suppose there is a collective good potentially available to some subset of individuals in an existing society. What are the conditions which permit them to organize in order to further that good? It is sometimes assumed that the emergence of such organization is merely a matter of time. Conversely, the argument from economic 'rationality' has been taken to suggest that only very small groups are able to organize themselves directly and that larger groups will never organize in however long a time. But if the argument of the preceding section is correct, then the ability of people to affect each other in the course of interaction must have an overriding importance. Organization may be generated, and free-riding in relation to it minimized, if appropriate public norms can be established, and enforced by what for the sake of simplicity I have described as mutual sanctioning.

What then are the conditions for successful mutual sanctioning? Basically they are very simple. The relevant set of people must be able to engage in frequent interaction, and be obliged to do so whether because of mutual interdependence or because of the overall organization of the context of life. In a nutshell, what is required is shared culture, separate culture, strongly-bounded culture, and frequent interaction within the culture. Shared culture is the condition for communication and interaction. Separate culture is required to confine interaction to those who define the collective good. Strong boundaries prevent escape from mutual sanctioning.[19] Frequent interaction provides the occasion for such sanctioning.

Needless to say, such a simple recipe must fall far short of being a satisfactory account of the conditions for successful collective action, but it does, in a rough-and-ready way, help to make some sense of where such action arises and where not. Immigrants have to suffer discrimination as immigrants, but countervailing collective action on their part is discouraged by their cultural diversity and the weakness of cross-cultural interaction. Women would benefit from changes in routine discriminatory practices, but even within a single form of culture they find it hard to act together to further such changes. Although changes in their routine activity are encouraging them to get organized for their collective good, that activity still isolates them from each other and generates too little interdependence between them; they may readily withdraw from each other and avoid mutual sanctioning whenever they so wish; they are obliged to interact strongly with the opposite sex upon which they remain heavily dependent. In contrast, military officers in many societies are bound into interaction with each other in situations which are difficult to leave, and which isolate them from outsiders. Notoriously, they find it easy to organize and act for their collective good, using their available military capacity for action for their own ends. Whenever it is not heavily dependent on external supply and external expertise, military organization is liable to become political organization. Similarly, industrial workers must often interact with each other in circumstances that require relations of mutual dependence and cut participants off from outsiders. Mutual sanctioning may be highly potent in these conditions and escape from it difficult, especially when the social context beyond work is largely an extension of the social context within work. Industrial workers are correspondingly successful in organizing for their collective good.

There is nothing at all original in this account of the basis of successful collective action. It appears in many guises in the sociological literature. As one might expect from someone who treats social relations as constitutive of human nature, Karl Marx offers an account that comes very close to it. Although he makes no explicit mention of the problem of free-riding he emphasizes the role of interaction in overcoming the disunity engendered by opposed individual ends. Thus, struck by the rapidity with which the new industrial working class was organizing itself to resist exploitation, particularly in comparison with the longer-established and equally exploited independent peasantry, he attributed the difference predominantly to the form and intensity of the interactions that economic circumstances obliged these classes to engage in. Industrial workers were brought together in one place by capital and forced to interact. This allowed them to overcome the individual competition for work which naturally divided them, to organize and to act in concert. 'The advance of industry . . . replaces the isolation of the labourers, due to competition, by their revolutionary combination, due to association' (Marx, 1848, p. 58). In contrast we have the smallholding peasants described in *The Eighteenth Brumaire*, living alongside each other but not entering into 'manifold relations' with each other:

> Their mode of production isolates them from one another instead of bringing them into mutual intercourse. . . . Their field of production, the smallholding, admits of no division of labour in its cultivation . . . and, therefore . . . no wealth of social relationships. Each individual peasant family . . . acquires its means of life more through exchange with nature than in intercourse with society . . . the great mass of the French nation is formed by simple addition of homologous magnitudes, much as potatoes in a sack form a sack of potatoes. (Marx, 1852, p. 332)

Although the peasantry was, according to Marx, a class with a separate mode of life, a separate culture and separate and distinct interests, it was able to beget 'no community, no national bond, and no political organisation' (ibid., p. 332): peasants interacted insufficiently to further their collective good by organization of their own, and had to further it instead by support of powers originating outside themselves. Needless to say, Marx was quite wrong about the peasants: they did have manifold relations with each other, and they could organize and act for their own collective good.[20] But because he was doubly wrong here about the empirical realities, his basic claim is not vitiated. It remains plausible to hold that interaction and mutual sanctioning during interaction is what allows the collective good to be furthered.

Interests and opportunities

Marx does not refer directly to collective goods; he speaks of peasants having shared interests and failing to organize to further them. He speaks similarly of the shared interests of workers, and of the bourgeoisie, and such speech is not peculiar to Marx or Marxists, being widely used and widely found intelligible. But what are the interests spoken of here, and how do we ascertain who share them and who do not? Interests are sometimes defined entirely in individualistic terms without reference to the social circumstances in which they are furthered: they may be equated with the wants of individuals or their desires or their needs. This serves only to confuse and mislead. Individuals are neither united nor divided by their wants and desires as such, and no clue to the likely social actions of individuals will be obtained by taking them one by one and ascertaining the constellation of their wants and desires.

If co-operative action is to be viewed as in some sense the consequence of shared interests, then interests cannot be the characteristics of independent individuals; they cannot be 'psychological' properties, definable independently of social circumstances. Imagine a set of individuals, all of whom do have the same wants or desires, conceived of as 'psychological' characteristics consistent with their own individual human nature. Needless to say, such shared wants could be expected to generate conflict as much as co-operation, just as diverse and opposed wants could encourage co-operation as much as conflict: desiring the same things is, to say the least, no more conducive to peaceful coexistence than desiring different things. Fundamental difficulties remain even if we assume that co-operative activity will in fact emerge as a way of satisfying shared wants. What patterns of co-operation should be expected? The answer must be no particular patterns at all. Consider that amongst n individuals any subgroup might profitably organize to expropriate or enslave everybody else and share the gains: something of the order of 2^{n-1} patterns of organization might thus prove profitable in fulfilling shared wants and desires; even from thirty or forty individuals millions of alternative patterns of profitable alliances might be generated. If we insist upon thinking of isolated individuals without reference to existing society and social organization, then we are led to conclude that individual wants and desires may inspire innumerable alternative patterns of organization equally. If 'shared interests' are simply shared wants, then they can tell us little or nothing about collective action.

References to 'shared interests' in sociological theory are useful because they do not emerge from this individualistic approach but from a structural, contextual approach to human activity. If we are to understand these references and evaluate them fairly, what we must start with is individuals as they actually exist, already engaged in action and interaction, in an already ordered and organized set of social contexts. We must start, that is, with individuals in historically given circumstances, constituted by their knowledgeable activities and understood in terms of their inherited distribution of knowledge. No such individual will perceive 2^{n-1} alternative possible groupings for concerted action. What then will be perceived? First, there will be a number of possible strategies or projects which represent possible adjustments or transformations of existing states of affairs: we may think of these projects as defined by the existing order, rather as the natural planes of cleavage of a crystal are defined by the crystal structure. Secondly, a number of possible ways of affiliating or further affiliating and organizing with others will be perceived. It is out of the totality of these two kinds of perceptions, which are both perceptions of the existing order and perceptions constitutive of the existing order, that successful collective action must emerge.

In a given social context, any particular project requiring collective action will benefit a specific set of individuals: for every such individual it will offer the prospect of fulfilling some of his individual wants or desires, whatever they may be. Every such individual may be said to have an *interest* in the project. All the individuals in the set may likewise be said to *share an interest* in it. This is to define interests as implying 'potential courses of action, in contingent social and material circumstances' (Giddens, 1979, p. 189), and hence to treat them as more than the products of individual psychology. It is only when considered in this way that interests may be said to inspire attempts at further co-operation and organization. It is not a matter of people being alike at the level of wants or desires, but of their benefiting alike from some available innovation or project. Thus, it may very well be plausible to say that a work-force shares an interest in higher wages: this may serve as a partial explanation of some of the activities of the work-force. But little is thereby implied about the specific wants or desires of any member of the work-force, or about the extent to which such wants and desires coincide. A cursory reference to wants and desires is necessary. This, presumably, is how one recognizes that concerted action for higher wages furthers interests, whereas concerted action for lower wages does not. But once the check is made, the explanation of action will largely refer to a shared interest rather than to the wants of diverse individuals, and the specific shared interest referred to will be defined by 'social and material circumstances'.[21]

Every routinized order defines certain lines of change or transformation as the most readily available lines: it defines a number of available projects. Every such project defines a set of agents who stand to benefit by it and thereby share an interest in it. All the available projects taken together, therefore, define a number of interest-sharing sets of individuals. Similarly, every routinized order makes some developments of organization more readily attainable than others. Some specific sets of individuals will find it easiest to get organized. To identify the strongest possibilities of collective action in a given order is a matter of ascertaining which sets are identified by *both* methods. Where available interest-furthering projects coincide with realistic prospects for organization, collective action is most likely to occur.[22]

I have specified the location of likely collective action in what might seem an unduly individualistic way, but once the specification is used in any particular case it immediately leads back into structural description. Available interest-furthering projects will generally involve a change to an existing routine or set of routines, and those with a shared interest in the change will be those affected alike by the routine or routines. Almost invariably such individuals will be known as specific kinds of individuals or as occupants of specific kinds of social positions: as a set they will define a class or kind in the existing distribution of knowledge. Similarly, prospects for organization will almost invariably be most promising for sets of individuals already possessed of a special taxonomic status in the existing order of things. Indeed, the categories and classifications of the existing distribution of knowledge will themselves facilitate organization: they will offer prominent solutions to the problem of how profitably to employ spare capacity for action in co-ordination with others (Schelling, 1960). Hence, in seeking to identify likely bases of collective action investigation will almost invariably, if not quite necessarily, come to focus upon some already known and categorized set of agents or interactions. The existing concepts and classifications will nearly always specify the directions of maximum cohesion and the planes of easy cleavage in the crystal of society.

I have suggested how we might identify the most favourable locations for innovative collective action in a given society at a given time. But if we turn to the actual historical development of societies over a long period it is necessary to think in a slightly different way. At any given point in such a development people are already organized to some extent, and already generating collective goods to some extent. It is now a matter of what *changes* will encourage *further* collective action. And since there are already some organization and some set of available projects, changes to either factor separately may suffice in this respect: increased interaction *or* increased opportunities to further interests may suffice separately to get collective action under way.

It is interesting to note that the historical changes in nineteenth-century England which directly inspired the work of Karl Marx and Friedrich Engels included vast alterations in the conditions of social interaction. New urban populations were indeed thrown together and obliged to live in close proximity, as Marx described. Organizational innovation was more or less inevitable: there was little need to consider what projects might be furthered thereby, since they were legion. Collective action duly got under way.[23]

When people are first thrown together into interaction in relatively unstructured conditions, that interaction will become co-ordinated and routinized to further whatever specific concerns and objectives people may have. Informally co-ordinated interaction will be found preferable to chaotic interaction on practically every ground, in relation to practically all conceivable goals and objectives, whether of individuals or collectivities. Such informally co-ordinated interaction is itself a simple form of social organization, on the basis of which more elaborate and explicitly conceived forms of organization may be built, directed to the achievement of more narrowly defined goals, including the provision of specific collective goods. Initially, in a still half-formed community, the provision of such goods will be inadequate, and organization for their provision will proceed apace. Such organization will increase both specific collective capacity for action and general capacity for action. However it organizes at such a stage, and whatever for, a community will increase its overall power. Industrial workers in the nineteenth century increased their power not only by organizing specifically against their employers, but also by organizing for mutual assistance, co-operative trading, insurance, even on occasion religious worship. Indeed, perhaps religious organization should be treated as paradigmatic here, given that it emerges out of the activity of a solidifying community and is not imposed upon it.[24] Religious organization is organization for no worldly end in particular and hence for every worldly end in general: its ubiquity serves as testimony that proximately located persons will organize themselves come what may, that in the early stages of organizational evolution there is no need to seek out precisely identifiable projects and specific shared interests. The key to collective action is the ability to organize: once organized there will be projects enough.

Status groups and their collective good

Whereas Marx was vividly aware of new communities in the early stages of organization, the experience of Max Weber encompassed long-established communities extensively and elaborately organized. Hence, Weber's work throws an altogether different light on the problem of collective action. When communities have attained a high level of organization and are not in a position markedly to increase their overall production of collective goods, it may be that those remaining projects still attractive to individuals involve a narrowing of the collectivity itself. Gains may be made by exclusion of current or potential members. Boundaries may be narrowed or new boundaries defined, with the maintenance of such boundaries becoming itself a collective good, mutually sanctioned by those standing within them. Thus emerge status groups, with members maintaining exclusivity on the basis of their alleged right to a special esteem or honour. This may happen even if members are competitors in a market situation:

> Usually one group of competitors takes some externally identifiable characteristic of another group of (actual or potential) competitors – race, language, religion, local or social origin, descent, residence, etc. – as a pretext for attempting their exclusion. It does not matter which characteristic is chosen in the individual case: whatever suggests itself most easily is seized upon. Such group action may provoke a corresponding reaction on the part of those against whom it is directed.
>
> In spite of their continued competition against one another, the jointly acting competitors now form an 'interest group' toward outsiders; there is a growing tendency to set up some kind of association with rational regulations; if the monopolistic interests persist, the time comes when the competitors, or another group whom they can influence (for example, a political community), establish a legal order that limits competition through formal monopolies. (Weber, 1968, pp. 341–2)

Status groups will tend to emerge at sites where there is a realistic opportunity for dominating or monopolizing the supply of some essential resource or skill, or where access to rights, privileges and opportunities may be controlled effectively. Members of such status groups gain in absolute terms from the monopoly profit they are able to share amongst themselves, and they gain also in relative terms: their resources are enhanced in relation to others, which may count as a good in itself as well as facilitating the domination of others, and hence the prospect of still further gains from control and exploitation.

Clearly, the maintenance of the group boundary brings substantial benefits, but in the first instance these are collective benefits accruing to members as a whole as the outcome of many costly individual acts of boundary maintenance. Boundary maintenance is a collective good with costs borne separately by every individual member: members must not trade with outsiders, or supply them, or train them in requisite skills, or give them employment, or whatever else involves a breakdown of insider privilege, even though such actions may be highly profitable at the individual level. The free-rider problem arises here. Within a status group the conditions for successful collective action must appertain. The status group must sustain itself as a distinct pattern of interaction wherein mutual sanctioning can operate. This, no doubt, is why in practically every case he considers, Weber finds the status group established as a distinctive style of life, replete with symbols of its own separateness. And this, just possibly, is also why Weber so stressed the pre-eminent role of honour in the maintenance of such groups: honour is the individual benefit won by acting for the collective good.

There is, in the work of Max Weber, a monumental survey of all the many and various kinds of status groups and of their bases and significance: every kind of demarcation is considered, from the traditional discriminations by ancestry, sex, religion or language to modern variants such as nationality, occupation or educational credentials; all kinds of monopolies are involved, from the crucial case of property ownership *per se* to narrowly defined occupational niches and professional skills and techniques. This survey offers innumerable insights into the emergence and dissolution of status-group boundaries, the dynamics of the processes through which groups appear and disappear. Indeed, it almost amounts to a general theory of the incidence of collective action. Almost, but not quite. Weber would occasionally generalize about what favoured the emergence of status groups and what discouraged it, but he was not prepared to be systematic here. He preferred to remain at the level of taxonomy and to eschew formal theoretical assertions.

It is easy to sympathize with this restraint. Not only is it extraordinarily difficult to sort out the essential from the accidental in all the complex processes internal to nascent groups, but there is also the fact that their external environment will be far from indifferent to their nativity. In the first instance, claims to a special honour are likely to be based upon invidious distinctions, and monopolistic strategies are likely to be resisted. The nature and the basis of such 'external' resistance may be just as difficult to understand in general terms as the 'inner dynamics' of group formation itself, particularly when it is recognized that many different status-groups may be in the process of formation in the same context at the same time, possibly competing for members, possibly dividing the forces of opposition. How are we to calculate the interaction between diverse forms of collective action, emerging at different sites with different objectives?[25] How are we to calculate the response of existing power-holders threatened by collective action, when power-holders themselves may be unclear as to their best response, or torn between conflicting strategies? Consider that the two fundamental objectives of communities of existing power-holders responding to threat require strategies which are incompatible with each other. A threatened community will seek to strengthen itself and realize its own latent power to the maximum, which involves increased exclusiveness and intensified internal interaction. It will also seek to weaken and divide the opposition, but this involves incorporation, compromise, exchange, weakening of cultural boundaries.[26] It may plausibly be suggested that the first strategy will be favoured where the powerful have confidence in their strength and independence, and the second, a strategy of caution, will be favoured when there is interdependence, or when the opposition is truly to be feared. But between the one state of affairs and the other there is an infinite number of intermediate states: at some point the expedient strategy must be less than clear, and where this is so that very lack of clarity may be a factor with a less than clear relevance to the calculation of strategy itself.[27]

Weber's restraint, however, understandable as it is, must still evoke pangs of regret. From the point of view of sociological theory the boundary around the group is the most interesting and important of all collective goods, and the fact that such boundaries are known everywhere and enforced everywhere speaks volumes for the ease with which human beings in the right conditions may solve the free-rider problem. Max Weber's insight into boundary maintenance in status groups still counts as one of our most valuable resources as we seek to understand the incidence of collective action.

5.3 UNIVERSALITY

Membership of society is often thought of by analogy with membership of a small group. This may be a useful and sensible way of thinking. Indeed, a society may simply be such a group, wherein everyone knows everyone else individually and all outsiders are avoided, ignored, or even in some cases immediately eliminated. Alternatively, however, many millions of individuals, most of whom will forever remain strangers to each other, may all acknowledge their common membership of a single society, and act in ways that recognize their membership and the membership of all the others. Similarly, at the level of cosmology and ideology, the immediate environment may be held to contain the whole of existing humanity: it may be that the world is thought to end just over the horizon, or that the inhabitants of distant realms are, by definition as it were, something less than human. But there are also those who extend conceptions of fellowship and obligation so that they encompass not just every conceivable variation of human kind, but plants and animals and even the whole of inanimate nature.

Variations in the size of 'society' and in the range or scope of recognized social obligations have not usually been found problematic in the functionalist tradition of sociological theory, since norms once internalized may bind indifferently any number of persons and specify obligations of any extent. But if it is not possible to make free with norms for explanatory purposes, and interpersonal interaction is regarded as crucial to the sustenance of order and routine, then important questions remain. Order in face-to-face situations, or in groups of people known to each other and in continuing interaction with each other, is not enough to account for order across situations and between groups.

Like many other ways of thinking about social activity, that adopted in this book makes the orderliness of specific contexts and situations more readily intelligible than that of extended 'societies' or 'social systems'. Individuals living in proximity in some specific environment exchange information, explicitly and implicitly, through speech and through action. They exchange sanctions, as they evaluate each other, each others' information, each others' evaluations of information, each others' informed actions. They learn from the information and suffer from the sanctions. From these processes, running together, order emerges and persists as a distribution of knowledge; from them powers develop, and discretion in their use is established as an aspect of the distribution of knowledge; because of them, people are able to pool their powers and act in concert for the collective good. Two dimensions of interpersonal interaction – informing and sanctioning, learning and suffering – allow the emergence of order and serve as the ultimate basis of social power and of its distribution at any given time. But they allow the emergence of order only in specific social situations. In so far as there is a 'social order', which transcends specific situations and extends across many such, some additional explanation is required.

The key here, needless to say, is the fact that individuals may move from situation to situation, with given individuals having standing as members in many situations, and relating to different kinds of others in different situations. Because individual lives transcend specific situations individuals bind these situations together. The question is how they do so. The answer favoured here is that they do so fundamentally as learners. As they move between situations they develop beliefs about situations, about persons and offices and relations in different situations, about the properties of situations, which apparently persist independently of any particular situation. Such beliefs crystallize into knowledge, of all kinds of entity or process, at all levels of generality. Such knowledge includes situation-transcendent knowledge, which, in so far as it is generally acted upon, generates an order that also is situation-transcendent, and serves to validate the situation-transcendent knowledge.

This is to treat the problem of how a conception of 'society' may emerge from a series of situated interactions as analogous to that of how a conception of 'nature' may emerge from a series of situated observations. In both cases, people make analogies from one situation to another, abstract common features from different situations, project from existing present situations to anticipated future situations, forget the 'situated' basis of knowledge altogether, in developing formulations to apply to any and all conceivable future situations. In both cases, persons exchange information about specific situations at specific times in the course of negotiating agreed understandings of many or all situations at future times. As knowledge is generalized and standardized, conceptions of 'nature' and of 'society' are defined and established. Just as interaction across contexts may allow the emergence of a generally accepted 'context-independent' representation of natural order, so similarly may it allow the emergence of a generally accepted 'context-independent' representation of social order.[28] It is immaterial here that knowledge of social order emerges as people learn about each other, that the business of learning changes people and hence changes that of which they learn, and that the knowledge of social order which emerges is knowledge of something which can only exist as an order in what people know. Society has already been identified as a distribution of self-referring knowledge, and it is a property of such an entity that it is constituted and reconstituted as it is learned of.

It may be objected that the precise identification of a society could prove impossible if it is conceived of in this way. Agents with standing in several contexts may perceive no primary or overriding category of membership amongst those that apply to them; where they do recognize their membership of an overriding 'society' they may disagree with others about who properly constitutes it and who lies beyond it; if they agree who constitutes it they may nonetheless differ as to how. These are indeed legitimate points, but they should not count as criticisms. We do not know what precisely societies are, because precision is not of their nature. There is no method of drawing their boundaries in a precise yet unproblematic way: any particular way of achieving a precise delineation will have pragmatic value at best, and no standing as a 'real' or 'true' boundary. Not even the most advanced and sophisticated theorists of 'society' or 'social systems' can hope to be clear as to what these entities 'really' are, and indeed they are not at all clear. When they study social life they tend to solve their problems of definition arbitrarily: generally they equate 'society' with whatever order exists amongst the heap of individuals who inhabit the territory of a nation-state. This is acknowledged as mere expediency, but it is worth emphasizing that what is involved is not an expedient approximation, as though there is some better definition which would come closer to the true state of affairs: the expediency lies in the initial recourse to definition.

To resume, in so far as people develop context-transcending or context-independent knowledge, their activities will manifest a pattern and order extending beyond specific contexts. Often it will make sense for theorists to speak of 'society' as a way of referring to this extended order and/or the knowledge that is associated with it. Often members themselves will refer to 'their' society in the course of reflecting upon and acting in relation to such an extended order. Society is thus something which comes into existence as it comes to be known, and the fundamental relationship between members and their society is that, in more than one sense, members know their society.

Needless to say, this is merely a minimal account, which attempts to state the conditions in which it is meaningful to speak of whole societies, rather than simply of groups and situated interactions. The basic condition for the existence of a society is that its existence is known and taken account of by members. But this is not to say that the only relationship between the individual and society is necessarily at the level of knowledge and cognition. Whatever comes to be known becomes a possible focus for attitudes and evaluations, passions and emotions. The precise nature of such attitudes and emotions, which can only be ascertained in any given case by empirical investigation, may have important implications for the extent of the power attributable to a given society and for the manner of its distribution over that society.

Sociological theorists often identify a direct emotional bond between the individual and his society, and account for aspects of social solidarity by making reference to it. Durkheim offers the most extreme position of this kind: at least in his early work, he regards the sentiments which bind the individual to the social whole as essential to the very existence of society itself. Weber is more cautious, but nonetheless he attributes an important role to such sentiments in his account of the nature of the modern nation-state. Yet Durkheim and Weber are in profound disagreement on the nature of these sentiments, and on what their effects actually are. The disagreement probably stems from their divergent understandings of the nature of human groups and the basis of group cohesion and solidarity. Both reason by analogy from 'group' to 'society', so that opposed understandings of social life on the small scale generate divergent accounts of the nature of large-scale social formations and the basis of their persistence.

Group and society in Durkheim

In *The Division of Labour in Society* (1933, first published 1893), Durkheim asserts the altruism of the individual with regard to his group. It is an altruism deriving first from his love of interaction with similar individuals within the group, their company, their confirmation of his sentiments, their own selves; and secondly from his awareness of the extent of his dependence on the group, which engenders sentiments making for sacrifices in its favour. Altruism generated in these ways is readily extended to 'society' as a whole; at least, this seems to be Durkheim's conviction, since he makes the necessary moves smoothly and unselfconsciously: in conditions of low division of labour, 'Not only are all the members of the group individually attracted to one another because they resemble one another, but also because they are joined to . . .'. the society they form by their union. Not only do citizens love each other . . . they love their country' (p. 105). As division of labour intensifies, altruism continues to be the fundamental basis of social life, increasingly sustained by the sentiment of a 'state of dependence' on society (p. 228). In addition, the individual is thrown into increasing contact with 'the State', which 'is entrusted with the duty of reminding us of the sentiment of common solidarity' (p. 227).

Many years later, in *The Elementary Forms of the Religious Life* (1915, first published 1913), Durkheim produced some marvellous pioneering insights into the cognitive basis of social life. His study of aboriginal religion represented totemic ritual primarily as an intellectual activity in which participants developed an understanding of themselves and the social relations in which they were involved.[29] Yet there remains, in this work, the same persistent conviction that sentiment is essential as a basis for solidarity, and the same easy movement from group to society, society to group. The members of the aboriginal clan spread wide and thinly, as they hunt and gather food. Their continuing awareness of who they are and how they relate to each other is heightened and reinforced by the ceremonies of their totemic religion. In coming together for the totemic ritual, the clan simply becomes a group, and the 'effervescence' its members experience is simply group experience of the most intense kind. Clan solidarity is, in effect, a variation upon group solidarity. It is the solidarity based upon resemblance identified previously in *The Division of Labour*. But beyond the aboriginal clan is the aboriginal tribe, and beyond the tribe are other tribes and beyond those tribes are other peoples altogether. As social interaction extends, sentiments of resemblance or of dependence may likewise extend, and the question of who one is and how one is related to others may become more complex and multifaceted. Thus will emerge ritual orientated to the god of the tribe, or the gods of many tribes and thus eventually the 'great, international gods' (1915, p. 415). These 'advances' in religion will all correspond to parallel 'advances' in the extent of society and the scope of social obligation; the bonds initially established within the group will generalize more and more, toward limits coextensive with humanity itself. Durkheim's sociology points toward Kant's morality.

Durkheim's imagination is dominated by the image of a small group held together from within by positive forces of attraction: the social bond, as it exists within the group, is sustained by positive emotions, love, fellowship, loyalty, deriving from sentiments of affinity and similarity, indebtedness and continuing dependence. Durkheim simply takes this image, which makes solidarity within the group unproblematic (and incidentally solves the problem of collective action by the assumption of generalized altruism) and projects it onto 'society'. So long as similarity and/or dependence are recognized affective links may extend and proliferate, an emotionally underpinned altruism may sustain a social organism of any size (1933, p. 228).

Such a projection invites two forms of criticism. First there is the question of how 'society' is known and how its structure is perceived and recognized. Durkheim takes the existence and visibility of the social organism for granted; he even assumes that the existence and role of distinct 'organs' like the state, within the social whole, can be perceived unproblematically, and a uniform affective orientation to them adopted. He does not allow for different perceptions of 'society', or even of the proper role of its various 'organs'. It is possible to argue that, as a matter of history, those who 'love their country' have been moved to more and greater treasons in consequence than those who are indifferent to it, but a Durkheimian perspective makes this hard to conceive. For Durkheim, people not only have a love of their country, they all know alike what that means and agree on what may be demanded in the name of it.

Secondly, there is the question of the role of emotional and affective orientations. Durkheim regards these as the essential basis of altruism, and hence of society itself, which cannot endure other than upon the moral, altruistic action of its members. But there are many modern anthropological studies which cast doubt on this conception of what is fundamental to social life. Nor, indeed, is there need to refer to modern studies. There is the evidence of Durkheim himself to bring to bear, who drew attention to social forms sustained by coercion and force, and others characterized by avarice, before, notoriously, casting his examples aside as 'pathological' (1933, Book 3). It is tempting to conclude that the affective link of individual and society is crucial in Durkheim not because it is *necessary to* society, but because it is *desirable in* society.[30]

Group and society in Weber

The wish is never father to the thought in this way in the austere sociology of Max Weber: quite the contrary. Like Durkheim, Weber builds an image of society from an image of a group, and again we find the assumption of strong direct connections between the individual and the group. But here the group in question is the status-group, a group held together against the outside as much as for the inside, a group sustained by members not out of love so much as its obverse. Here society is not an expanded version of life within a group but the totality of relations between groups, so that the direct emotional relationship between the individual and society is a possibility not so much because it is always clear what and where society is as because it is sometimes clear what and where it is not.[31]

Like Durkheim, Weber is interested in the large-scale organization of the many millions of persons living within the territory of a modern nation-state, but unlike Durkheim he does not proceed on the assumption that they are unproblematically all members of a given 'society', and that they all somehow constitute an organic whole. Instead, Weber begins by identifying specific smaller communities, crucial amongst which is the 'political community'. 'A political community is a community which subordinates a territory and the conduct of the persons therein to orderly domination by its readiness to resort to force' (Weber, 1968, p. 901). What the political community subordinates will count as a collective good for its interacting members, so there need be no difficulty in understanding why those members should act, not merely to serve the state, but to generate the self-confirming convictions that establish the very social reality of the state and its standing as an entity to be feared and respected.

Alongside the political community Weber identifies additional groups and communities for whom the existence of the state will also count as a collective good: for obvious reasons senior bureaucrats and military officers will constitute such communities; so also, in some circumstances although not others, will capitalists and financiers;[32] so will intellectuals, who are likely to find it advantageous to involve themselves in the construction and development of appropriately related nationalist ideologies: 'It goes without saying that, just as those who wield power in the polity invoke the idea of the *state*, the intellectuals, as we shall tentatively call those who usurp leadership in a *kulturgemeinschaft*, are specifically predestined to propagate the "national" idea' (ibid., p. 925).

Following Weber, it is possible to analyse the nation-state as an entity sustained by an alliance of factions within it, all of which stand to benefit from its continued existence and act co-operatively to ensure its continued existence. But Weber regards such an account as insufficient. The dominant political community within the state must, he believes, possess legitimacy, and the source of its legitimacy lies in its prestige and the prestige it brings to the state it dominates; such prestige is 'the prestige of power', which 'means in practice the glory of power over other communities' (ibid., p. 911). To generate and sustain its legitimacy, the dominant political community of a nation-state must secure the prestige of that state in relation to other states, controlling or influencing those states by use of the capacity for violence routinely available to it. With the emergence of modern nation-states, 'Great power structures *per se* are then held to have a responsibility of their own for the way in which power and prestige are distributed between their own and foreign polities' (ibid., pp. 921–2).

The prestige of power intensifies allegiances and generates convictions of legitimacy, according to Weber, through the emotions. People come to regard themselves as fellow members of a nation or nation-state through facing violence together, using violence together, tasting the fruits of military action, particularly military victory, and hence developing emotionally charged 'memories of a common political destiny'. Such memories create a strong affective bond between the individual and 'his' nation-state, and make the international power-prestige of that state a matter of personal emotional significance. Such an individual will readily mobilize the war.[33]

Characteristically, the way in which Weber describes the acquisition of this emotional orientation to the nation-state distinguishes between the higher and lower reaches of society. In the former the emotions would seem to be very much under the control of will and reason: 'It goes without saying that all those groups who hold the power to steer common conduct within a polity will most strongly instil themselves with this idealist fervour of power prestige' (ibid., p. 921). In contrast, the emotions of the lower orders are described in terms of an external determination. Their willingness to take risks on behalf of the state, unlike that of their betters, is imputed not to do-it-yourself but to suggestibility: 'The masses as such . . . have nothing concrete to lose but their lives. The valuation and effect of this danger strongly fluctuates in their own minds. On the whole it can be easily reduced to zero through emotional influence' (ibid., p. 921). Nonetheless, one way or the other, all groups and communities within the nation-state come to develop a direct emotional investment in its international power-prestige, and hence a personal readiness to assist in increasing it, whether through direct violent action or otherwise.

Thus Weber identifies the basis of a specific form of power, that generated from individual orientations to the nation-state and accruing in consequence to its dominant political community. Because individuals find the increased prestige of their nation-state emotionally satisfying, and hence an end in itself, they are willing to act to secure such increased prestige with less extrinsic incentive than would otherwise be necessary, or even without extrinsic incentive. State powers may thereby be increased and the dominance of the state within the nation rendered more secure.

Notice that the direct connection being asserted here between the individual and his nation-state is altogether less problematic than that which Durkheim asserts between the individual and 'society'. The individual does not need to know what precisely comprises 'his nation-state', or how precisely it is ordered. So long as there is awareness of membership on the one hand, and awareness of non-members and outsiders on the other, he can reap the emotional benefits of 'state success':[34] others will then make the prestige of his state, which is his vicarious pleasure, clear and visible to him; he will then be in a position clearly to perceive, not the state itself, or the nation, but their external success and their external reputation. Moreover, it is not a matter of this success binding the individual to 'society' or even to nation-state; it is a matter of success making it sensible to give support to the political community which has produced the success. National prestige, desired by individuals and secured through and/or by the political community, justifies further support for the political community on grounds of expediency, and thus affords it a continuing if still temporary legitimacy. If the political community delivers the goods, it will continue to have active support; if it fails, active support will lapse or decline. Those in control of the state have no automatic standing: the state is not an 'organ' of the social whole, partaking directly of the emotional loyalties directed to the whole. Rather, those in control of the 'state apparatus' justify themselves by satisfying the demands that arise from the emotional relationship between the individual and the nation.[35]

Weber's view of the precise emotions which link the individual to his nation also has a certain plausibility. The prestige of national power generates a welcome awareness of distinction and especial worth, a sense of superiority associated with such negative feelings as disdain, contempt, pity, for outsiders who necessarily must be diminished to some extent in standing and dignity. The prestige of national power is merely an extension of the prestige, the special honour, associated with membership of the status-group, consciousness of which honour is again, necessarily, consciousness of the diminished honour of outsiders. Everybody enjoys membership of some status-group or other, some group with a perceptible boundary and distinctive orientations to insiders and outsiders, and everybody is aware of the increased sense of worth and standing which correlates with acceptance into membership, and the diminishment associated with expulsion or persistent exclusion. The complex of emotions and sentiments Weber gives weight to here have a claim to consideration as cultural universals.

If a sense of especial honour or prestige, of exclusivity, distinction and superiority to the outsider, is intrinsically satisfying and sustains emotions which are found inherently desirable as ends, then the ubiquity and persistent stability of status-groups becomes easier to account for. Weber notes how status-groups lay claim to particular economic privileges and seek to monopolize access to scarce goods or positions. But to sustain these collective economic benefits group members have to accept costs that fall upon them as individuals, the costs of restricted trade and exchange with outsiders. I have already indicated that mutual sanctioning for the collective good may suffice to explain why individuals accept such losses, but this does not preclude alternative or supplementary explanations that make reference to emotional orientations. If outsiders are felt to be inferior, it may be argued, contact with them may be experienced as intrinsically unpleasant, even as degrading and polluting, so that exchanges with outsiders will be discouraged. Similarly, if life outside the world of the status-group is perceived as degraded and diminished then the perceived costs of leaving the group increase, and the ability of group members to sanction for the collective good increases correspondingly. In stressing the intrinsic honorific rewards of exclusivity, rather than the economic rewards that he also recognized, Weber identifies that aspect of status-group advantage which most readily accounts for independent individual commitments to such groups: at the same time, he inadvertently offers a solution to the problem of collective action, a solution that invokes emotional and affective linkages but linkages quite the opposite in character to those invoked, for much the same purpose, by Durkheim.

As a final argument on behalf of Weber's analysis it is interesting to note that the emotions linked with the honour and prestige of membership are likely to be especially intense and uncompromised when state membership or nationality is involved. Within the boundaries of nation-states there is a greater level of perceived interdependence than there is across those boundaries. Status-groups within a nation-state will usually, if far from invariably, find that relationships involving exchange and reciprocity set limits on the extent to which they can emphasize their own peculiar merits and openly indulge in the celebration of invidious distinctions. Similarly, the hierarchical arrangements of the nation will set limits on the extent that any group, save perhaps that at the very pinnacle of power, can convincingly assert its own clear superiority: pity or contempt for those one obeys, by whom one is controlled, is hard to sustain without implying an even greater pity or contempt for oneself. In so far as people at the bottom of hierarchies have a taste for uncompromising assertions of their own superiority, a comparison with outsiders promises better than one with those above. Perhaps considerations of this kind were what prompted Weber to the comment that 'Ethnic honour is a specific honour of the masses' (1968, p. 391), although it must be emphasized that Weber did not equate ethnicity and nationality.[36] In any event, it is notoriously the case, so far as modern history is concerned, that where individuals have orientated their actions with regard to the fate of large-scale social entities, nations and nation-states have figured more prominently than entities extending across their boundaries.

No doubt Weber's discussion of the nation-state was the product of its time. It remains, nonetheless, impressive in its coherence and in its consistent application of the basic themes and assumptions running through the whole of his sociology. This coherence and consistency give it a continuing relevance. It is hard to understand the lack of attention it currently receives.[37] Equally, it is hard to understand why it is sometimes considered relevant to politics but not to sociology: what can be relevant to politics yet not to sociology? Perhaps it is actually that modern European sociology is a product of its time, and is inclined to squeamishness with regard to nationalism. On the other hand, Weber's account of the nation-state is not a theory of the nation-state, as Weber himself clearly recognizes, just as his discussion of status-groups is not a theory of group formation.

Suppose that the account is treated as a systematic theory, which indeed actually occurs in Randall Collins's exposition and development of *Weberian Sociological Theory* (1986). Such a 'theory' does indeed make sense of many aspects of the relations between states, and usefully highlights the connection between the external success of a political community and its level of active internal support. International prestige is sought after for internal consumption (Lynn and Jay, 1986, pp. 59ff). Economic resources are invested heavily into generating the prestige of power. The internal political value of overt violence is well recognized: politicians appreciate the convenience of having weak nation-states available to overawe or brutalize. But here, of course, is the problem. For there to be domination there must be subordination. For every political community that legitimates itself through successful use of violence or successful pressure against an enemy, there is another political community that loses out. For every nation whose members can realistically hope for high international prestige and a corresponding 'special honour' there must be others where there is no such hope. Yet such nations exist, and their political communities often retain their position without difficulty, even in adverse conditions, even when the nation lacks a territory.[38]

It is possible to seek out ways around this problem. Lacking a suitably weak enemy beyond its borders, a political community may perhaps stir up support by violence against an enemy within (Collins, 1986, p. 160), or it may simply make out its actions on the international stage as successful and prestige-enhancing. The extensive secrecy surrounding foreign affairs in most modern societies, a secrecy primarily directed toward keeping citizens rather than aliens in a suitable state of ignorance, allows many clashes between states to be claimed as prestige-enhancing victories by both: on this basis political communities may come to love their enemies. In the last analysis, however, these are feeble arguments. It has to be acknowledged that the nation-state does not have to be nourished by an emotional fervour of nationalism; the political community within the nation-state does not have to look to the prestige of power as the sole basis for its active support. Collins himself comes close to conceding the point: 'Much of the time the state can survive by routine, or by a relatively low degree of "legitimacy arousal"'; 'The cognitive complexities of changing the physical organisation of things tends (sic) to require more energy and more coordinative activities than simply leaving things as they are' (ibid., p. 160).[39]

The emotions associated with the prestige of power, that is, with domination, glory, the diminishing of other people, may or may not be cultural universals: it is conceivable that people everywhere could readily experience them and find pleasure in the experience. But the conditions of that experience are not found everywhere, nor even everywhere where people know themselves to be ordered in nations or similarly vast entities. It is tempting to conclude accordingly that affective links are not of the essence of 'society': neither the positive emotions cited by Durkheim nor the negative emotions pointed to by Weber are constitutive of extended social orders or even an essential underpinning for such orders.

This is not to deny the importance of the passions in social life, or that objects like 'society' or the 'nation-state' can be foci of individual passions and emotions. On the contrary, the intensity of such passions may be all too evident when the symbols of the nation-state are insulted, or (what is perhaps the same thing) when its recognized territory is occupied or its individual citizens seized or mistreated. The general distribution of such passions may be important in understanding movements to secession or union within and between states, just as they are in understanding the formation and dissolution of specific groups, or their fusion and differentiation. Tendencies to universalism, generalized reciprocity and incorporation on the one hand, or to exclusivity and particularism on the other, may plausibly be related to distributions of positive and negative emotional dispositions. Whatever favours the development of the one or other kind of disposition must feature in any general account of the conditions of these contrasting kinds of social changes. All that is argued here is that the social objects that change, the extended orders recognized as 'societies', 'nation-states' and so forth, are primarily constituted and sustained by cognitive processes involving learning and calculation. No particular dose or flavour of emotion is essential to the continuing existence of a nation-state, although Weber was of course correct to emphasize that the greater the intensity of the emotions associated with the nation the greater the capacity for action of those who control the state. If the ability systematically to manipulate the emotions does actually exist as a skill then to possess that skill is indeed to possess power.

6

FINAL THOUGHTS

All the sciences deal in generalities, and in every realm of experience there is some level of detail at which those generalities fail to enlighten. The theories of the social sciences can no more hope fully to account for actual sequences of events in a society than those of the natural sciences can hope fully to account for the actual molecular motions in a roomful of air. The complex tangle of phenomena that make up our social life will always be incompletely understood, not, as is sometimes said, because it is especially complex, but simply because it is phenomenal. It remains worthwhile, nonetheless, to deal in generalities: there is, we may say, always and invariably a degree of orderliness in social life, and capacities and potentialities associated with that orderliness, just as there is always pressure in the air of a room and capacities and potentialities associated with that pressure.

Wherever human beings are found, whatever the situations in which they are found, social order and social power are also found. It follows that the particular features of a situation are insufficient as a basis for understanding the power available in that situation. Our understanding of power must involve a situation-transcending component: it must include a general conception of human behaviour and of how human beings interact with each other. Two general conceptions of this kind are currently available within the social sciences. One is sociological functionalism, which presumes that human beings are somehow predisposed to serve as the cells of an integrated social organism, constrained in what they do by the requirements of the organism as a whole. The other denies the existence of this kind of constraint and views human beings as active agents linked together through shared knowledge and mutual susceptibility.

Needless to say, the position taken in this book is of the second, anti-functionalist kind. As such it is in line with many other recent contributions to social theory, which for all their clear affinities reveal a striking diversity in their sources of inspiration. My own way of thinking derives from work in the sociology of knowledge and in particular from problems of the reference and self-reference of knowledge as they arise in that context. Others have developed closely related perspectives using the work of Alfred Schutz (Schutz, 1964; Berger and Luckmann, 1966; Thomason, 1982). Anthony Giddens has used the seminal sociological theorists to move in much the same direction (Giddens, 1979, 1984). Roy Bhaskar paints a similar picture of society in the course of constructing a realist philosophy of the social sciences (Bhaskar, 1979; Manicas, 1987). Many other approaches are equally deserving of citation. I would not wish to deny the substantial differences of view that exist in this body of writings. Every author has his own characteristic style, his own favoured images and metaphors. What does seem possible, however, is that as all these various strands of thought are further explored, extended and allowed to combine, a reasonably integrated vision of social life may well emerge. We can look forward to a systematic, general, yet non-teleological account of social order, and of the power it makes available, to stand as a viable alternative to the functionalism which has for so long dominated the social sciences.

My own favoured images and metaphors should now be all too familiar. I have conceived of a society as a distribution of self-referring knowledge substantially confirmed by the practice it sustains, and I have treated power and its possession as aspects of this distribution. Some readers may feel that I have made insufficient practical use of these metaphors and images. The overriding concern of my book has been to set out a theory and then to see whether its constituents remain robust and satisfactorily applicable even in the most unfavourable of conceivable circumstances. Unlike many contributions to social and political theory, it has made no serious attempt to make sense of the particular circumstances that appertain in actual societies. But this should not count as a criticism. To have offered commentary upon social and political states of affairs would have required compression of the basic exposition, and I am only too well aware that even my extended presentation fails to achieve a fully satisfactory level of clarity and consistency, and that the justifications for my claims all too often remain patchy and incomplete. The first priority, in attempting to move beyond what is attempted in this book, must be to give yet more attention to its basic themes, to concentrate upon difficulties and obscurities, to test and check and question its key claims, to modify, elaborate and develop them as necessary.

Modification and development are sure to prove necessary. Throughout I have followed a principle of maximum economy, and striven to rely upon as few general postulates as possible about the characteristics of human beings and their behaviour. I have made some simple assumptions

FINAL THOUGHTS   167

about human learning, cognition and inference, assumptions that are in any case necessary to account for the way in which we adjust to our physical environment and come to some extent to be able to manipulate and control it. And I have used the simplest possible assumptions that allow for our sociability and interdependence. I have tried to show that even on the basis of these rudimentary assumptions it is possible to understand how distributions of power can be constituted and sustained as continuing features of collective life. But economy is not an end in itself; to be economical is not necessarily to be correct, and indeed I have no doubt that the account of power offered here says far too little about the general characteristics of human beings as we know them and is diminished in consequence. The difficulty, of course, lies in deciding what more might be said, what further general postulates should be adopted and relied upon.

Take, for example, the matter of the routinization of social activity. In this book the distinction between routine action and calculative action is eroded, to the extent that it ceases to be of any fundamental importance at the collective level. Routinization is essential for calculation and systems of routine activity may at the same time be systems of calculated activity: routines may be thought of as co-ordination equilibria in societies of calculative agents, patterns of activity from which no significant number of individuals would wish to deviate so long as most individuals continue to conform. Thus, systems of routine activity may continue to be constituted and reconstituted even as the sets of involved individuals vary between being largely calculative and reflectively aware and largely creatures of habit: all roads lead to routine. This, I think, throws light on the ubiquity of routine, and calls into question the widely accepted view that routine activity needs a different kind of sociological explanation from non-routine activity. Economy in understanding is achieved. Nonetheless, it may yet be the case as a matter of fact that all human beings give a special significance to that which they recognize as routine and matter-of-course. It may be, for example, that routine is everywhere found familiar, safe, reassuring and hence desirable in its own right and intrinsically pleasing to follow and execute. This is an additional empirical hypothesis about the general characteristics of human beings, and if it is correct it has important consequences for our understanding of social life: it would imply that routinized systems of activity have still stronger tendencies to persist and reconstitute themselves than I have acknowledged in the main body of this text, that there is an additional inertia, as it were, in routinized systems, over and above that which I have already identified. The problem is to ascertain whether or not this particular hypothesis is correct. The same problem arises with any number of analogous general empirical hypotheses. If routines are everywhere found intrinsically desirable and their performance a pleasure in itself, might the same not be the case with hierarchies and orders of precedence, with the exercise of rank and the display of standing? For that matter, might the same not be the càse with deference and the manifestation of submission and subordination? Hypotheses of this kind cannot simply be dismissed; the fact that they are occasionally accepted crassly and employed polemically and disreputably does not make them false. On the other hand, caution and an inclination to frugality in the use of such hypotheses scarcely needs to be justified.

Suppose that the kind of position advocated in this book is satisfactorily developed and comes to deserve some kind of provisional acceptance. It will then be interesting to see how far it is compatible with those more specific social theories currently used as taken-for-granted resources in making sense of societies and social institutions. If social order is indeed co-ordinated calculative activity, if power is the capacity for action made available by such co-ordination, if co-ordination itself is based on what people know of each other and not upon functional imperatives, then only theories consistent with these assertions should continue in use. This is not to suggest that most existing social theories should be consigned to the scrap-heap. In most cases, where such theories are found wanting, it will be adjustment and adaptation that are required, in some cases merely a rereading. Most sociological theories have grown and developed in a context suffused with functionalist modes of thought, even if they did not always originate in such a context: what is required is that they be dug out of the functionalist context and transplanted to another, whereupon, in many cases, they are likely to continue to grow.

I have already hinted at both the opportunities and the difficulties arising here through my brief references to the work of the three seminal writers in the sociological tradition. Much of Max Weber's work is readily reconciled with the present standpoint, and actually suggests ways of solving some of the fundamental problems that arise when that standpoint is taken. Anyone who seeks to account for the provision of collective goods and who finds it insufficient merely to remark that they are 'functional' must be attracted to Weber's analysis of status-groups: the 'special honour' associated with status and its particular importance in the key activity of boundary maintenance continue to be promising subjects for further research. The theories of Durkheim and Marx are less easy to assimilate, even though functionalist modes of argument are very much less pervasive and significant therein than is generally thought. But although Durkheim on ritual and religion, and Marx on class and ideology, cannot simply and straightforwardly be made consistent with the point of view taken here, the intrinsic interest of the task and the potential rewards of success make it clear that the attempt is worth making whatever the difficulties (Douglas, 1986; Elster, 1985).

Finally, let me turn to the relationship between power and knowledge. First the general form of the relationship must be recalled. Imagine the individuals of a society in a given setting at a given time. If I am right then the distribution of knowledge over these individuals is what constitutes them as a society. But that distribution of knowledge specifies the capacity for action available in the society, its competences and capabilities. To specify what members know is to specify what powers their society embodies, and who among them has discretion in their use. For given human beings in a given environment any change in the distribution of knowledge entails a changed distribution of powers. It is not a matter of the one thing precipitating the other, or causing the other, or making the other inevitable: the one thing amounts to the other. In speaking of knowledge and of power we are referring to one and the same thing. A society, by virtue of being a distribution of knowledge, is an ordered array of powers.

If this is so, why is it not generally recognized to be so? Why is it not intuitively evident everywhere? The answer must be that, although the cognitive order and the power structure are indeed one and the same, the components of the cognitive order, conventionally analysed, are not the same as the components of the power structure, conventionally analysed: to put it crudely, we mostly concern ourselves with bits of power and bits of knowledge, and there is no simple correspondence between these bits. An architect, who thinks of rooms and corridors, may happily converse with a builder, who thinks of bricks and mortar, about a house or dwelling, since the two ways of breaking the house into components are easily related for most practical purposes: this is not the case with powers and items of knowledge. The existence of a specific power, available at a specific point in the social order, may be a matter of the existence of innumerable items of knowledge, spread over every part of the social order. The existence of a specific item of knowledge, at a specific point in the social order, may be implicated in the constitution of numerous powers available at many points. Immense powers may readily be wielded by a dolt and ignoramus, even by an entire caste or stratum of such. And the crucial tasks of preserving and transmitting knowledge may make occupations fit only for slaves.

Our awareness of knowledge is not in itself an awareness of power. We have, almost invariably, to move from the one to the other. Hence we are tempted to think of separate entities, and then of changes in the one causing or inciting changes in the other. What we have to remind ourselves of, if we are to curb this tendency, is that the movement that we recognize is simply a reorganization of awareness. Knowledge and power are the same things under different forms of awareness, and a change in the one does not cause a change in the other but rather entails it. Similarly, changing knowledge and changing powers do not stand in an external relation to social and institutional change: they are such change. The mainstream of social theory, inspired by the writings of Foucault, Habermas and others, is turning increasingly to the study of knowledge, culture and cognition: it should indeed continue to focus its attention on these things, not because they are relevant to understanding its subject-matter but because they are its subject-matter.

The fact that knowledge and society are inseparable, that cognitive order is social order, is equally relevant in the context of the sociology of knowledge. One of the long-established projects in the sociology of knowledge is to account for changes in myth, ideology or cosmology as the effects of changes in economic activities or in the routines of everyday practical living. Now there need be no fundamental objection in a sufficiently differentiated society to citing changes in one context as causes of changes in another. It is perfectly plausible to propose an economic change as the cause of, say, changing religious belief. It may even prove plausible to suggest that the sphere of religion is always secondary and that of the economy primary, in the sense that changes in the latter may routinely induce changes in the former but not vice versa. What is wrong is the implication that in the primary sphere there is activity without belief, as it were, and in the secondary belief without activity. If it is indeed the case that the religious realm is derivative of the economic it must be in the sense that changes in one realm of knowledge-able activity may derive from but not inspire changes in another. To account for change in a myth or in a 'religious cosmology' must be also to account for some change at the level of activity however apparently small or trivial. Successful explanation of this kind, if it exists, is explanation of social change, and any theory that allows such explanation must be a theory of social change in a general sense.

Consider too the more recent concern of sociologists of knowledge with the intellectual division of labour. The way that knowledge and competence is increasingly fragmented into bundles carried by bounded subcultures of scientists, experts and professionals has raised a host of important questions. How is knowledge evaluated in the esoteric sub-culture? How is it kept pure and separate, yet developed and adapted with a mind to its general utility? How is the general credibility of the knowledge sustained, and the standing of its expert carriers? Can credibility be built upon trust deriving from favourable experience, or must it be reinforced by monopoly-sustaining legislation and the powers of administrative bureaucracies? How far does differential access to expert knowledge constitute a differential distribution of powers? These are indeed appropriate questions for sociologists of knowledge to ask, but addressing as they do problems of social order, social organization, the maintenance and distribution of powers, they are the very questions a social theorist should ask. Once again we are brought back to the point that knowledge and society are inseparable, that social life is knowledgeable activity, that as Alfred Schutz recognized long ago the core of the sociological discipline is the study of the distribution of knowledge.

NOTES

Chapter 1 The Concept of Power

1 Throughout the book, 'he', 'his', etc. are used in a generic sense.

2 In such a sense-making system the standard insights of ethnomethodology may be brought into play. Power may be treated as the underlying pattern 'documented' by its effects. See Garfinkel (1967, ch. 3).

3 Thus, in one variant of the experiment 14 subjects regarded Y's behaviour as 'helpful' and 7 as 'forced' when Y was seen as 'high power', but only 6 plumped for 'helpful' as against 15 for 'forced' when Y was seen as 'low power'.

4 Given my concerns in this book it has only been necessary to offer an extremely brief and selective account of the problems involved in defining and measuring power. There is however an extensive literature which expounds and analyses these problems in depth. Amongst standard works which I have found useful in this regard are Lukes (1974, 1986), Martin (1977) and Wrong (1979). No less valuable have been Clegg (1975, 1979) and Ng (1980), wherein impressive literature surveys coexist with fascinating and original individual points of view.

5 What follows is not intended as criticism of the definitions of Weber, Dahl and Wrong. Because they do little to advance my objectives it does not necessarily follow that they failed to advance those of their authors. Nor is there any other way of assessing the merits of definitions, save in terms of their pragmatic value: definitions cannot be false, only more or less useful.

6 The reputational approach to measurement can be developed and elaborated endlessly. I merely present the crude basic form of it here. A fine example of the approach put into practice is Hunter (1953).

7 Just as Hunter (1953) provided a paradigm for the reputational approach so Dahl (1961) provided one for the event approach. An extended controversy between proponents of the two approaches resulted in the development of a vast literature in which the methodological problems of measuring power through its effects were debated with formidable thoroughness. For ways into this literature see Aitken and Mott (1970), and Bonjean, Clark and Lineberry (1971).

8   The event approach, just like the reputational approach, can be refined and elaborated endlessly; and indeed most of the important criticisms of Dahl are not rejections of his call for direct observation of the effects of power but attempts to make his basic approach more sophisticated and observationally adequate. Thus, Bachrach and Baratz (1962, 1963) lament Dahl's exclusive concentration upon formal decision-making processes. Before such processes get under way, agendas for them are decided and the range of alternatives to be considered are determined: power may be exercised and prove crucially important in these earlier stages; for example, it may be used to keep some alternatives off the agenda, and to ensure that some possibilities are never considered and fought over. By focusing solely upon the decisions actually taken and ignoring the issues that never even came up for decision, Dahl might perhaps have produced a systematically biased description of the distribution of power.

9   Clegg (1975, ch. 2) characterizes the community power debate in just this way. It is not a dispute to be settled by reference to the facts of the matter, he suggests, but a dispute about which methods should be licensed for the creation of what we shall call 'the facts'. Although his terminology is different from mine I would not disagree with Clegg's account.

10 Recently, Luhmann (1979) has built upon Parsons's work in an important essay which bodes well for further developments.

11 I have never been an enthusiast for the work of Parsons, and have a particularly negative view of his later work, from the mid 1950s on. The criticisms of Black (1961) seem to me still to be justified. However, I am only too happy to make an exception of Parsons's papers on power, and recognize their interest and importance.

12 Parsons's work does not *proceed from* this definition. It proceeds from the analogy with money, and the definition is a *product* of the use of the analogy.

13 What follows here does not follow Parsons precisely. Indeed I could not follow him precisely. Whether the fault is his or mine I do not know, but I am unable satisfactorily to understand Parsons's text at the level of fine detail.

14 Needless to say, runs become even rarer when there exists that remarkable institution a 'lender of last resort'. There should be a book on the lender of last resort: perhaps there is.

15 It is not only Parsons's theory which is arguably the product of a conservative bias; the particular way in which he applies it and illustrates it merits criticism on these grounds, as for example in Giddens (1968).

16 Admittedly it is necessary to refer to these phenomena using terms other than 'power' if one is willing to accept Parsons's theory. But what is the loss of a mere word?

17 Parsons develops the analogy between property and authority at considerable length, although not without effort and the accumulation of a number of problems and difficulties. I have not gone into this aspect of Parsons's account in detail, since I shall eventually offer an entirely different conception of authority.

Chapter 2   Social Order

1   Parsons's words echo those of Durkheim: 'There is nothing less constant than interest. Today, it unites me to you; tomorrow, it will make me your enemy. Such a cause can only give rise to transient relations' (Durkheim, 1933, p. 204).

2   It is interesting how, in the nineteenth century, great economic theorists and social philosophers, well able to see the skull beneath the skin in most contexts, seem to have had difficulty in treating ownership and property as anything other than God-given. Even as individualistic thinking became less predominant later in the century, and some of the seminal works of sociological theory came to be written, this particular institutional form tended to remain opaque and its study neglected.

3   Some accounts of exchange recognize their own limitations, their essential incompleteness as theories of social interaction and social order: others do not.

4   Not even Karl Marx provides what is needed here. Needless to say, there is no question of his treating property and ownership as God-given. He is perfectly clear that these things are social relations, and is not in the least reluctant to advertise the fact and its significance. But even Marx may to some extent have been mesmerized by this particular institutional form. Ownership of the means of production is the pivot in his account of social structure and social change. The basic Marxist terminology of societies is based upon ownership: ownership of land is definitive of feudal society, ownership of capital definitive of capitalist society. The dominant classes in these societies are likewise defined objectively in terms of that which they own. But although Marx's thought flows out from institutions of ownership with tremendous strength and penetration, it does not flow inward to anything like the same extent. Marx is surprisingly uninformative concerning the basis of the stability and persistence of such institutions, and indeed of institutions generally, and he does not explain systematically why his theory of society and social change has to pivot about this particular institution. Just like the utilitarians, Marx is insufficiently curious about ownership and property, and although, needless to say, his sin is an order of magnitude less than theirs, and perhaps simply reflects the meagre intellectual resources he inherited at the end of a long line of bourgeois economists, it still means that there is no developed solution to Hobbes's problem available in his work. Nor is this a weakness which has been cured or eliminated by later writers in the Marxist tradition.

5   Much of Parsons's work from *The Social System* (1951) onwards is concerned with elaborating the requirements that must be met by 'functioning social systems'.

6   The application of sanctions is considered to be secondary to the internalization of norms: it is precisely internalization, and the consequent conviction of the intrinsic rightness of the norms, which produces the systematic inclination to sanction.

7   Alfred Schutz's essay on 'Making Music Together' is the inspiration behind this example (see *Studies in Social Theory, Collected Papers*, vol. 2, 1964).

8 I consider first the case of a norm or a value separated from action because this tends to be how norms and values are thought of by Parsons. He constructs a hierarchy with very general fundamental values at the top and more specific and narrowly applicable norms at the bottom. Shared commitment to fundamental values is considered to be essential to the large-scale 'integration' of society, and these values are assumed to be very strongly internalized. Specific norms, on the other hand, may be less strongly internalized, and indeed much of the sense of their rightness may derive from their being seen as special cases of fundamental values, or as necessary for the sustenance of fundamental values. Accordingly, changes in a norm low in the hierarchy may always be made intelligible as an attempt to follow a norm more highly placed, or to further a value more highly placed, and social change may thereby be explained, as well as social stability.

Parsons assumes here that inference flows down from values to norms and thence to actions, so that norms and actions may be 'derived' from fundamental values. But in truth it is the significance of values which is derived by inference from the particular actions that people set under them. There is no other source that can imbue values with concrete significance. If values are separated off from what they are said to determine, from what allegedly may be 'derived' from them, the values themselves become meaningless, their symbolic expressions mere jumbles of empty signs. This means that it must be false to describe normative orders as hierarchies with values at the top, with more specific norms and rules at the bottom, and a flow of implication and determination downwards. Accordingly, Parsons's hierarchical conception of normative order, and his conception of fundamental values as the linchpins of such order, simply will not do and must be set aside. It is not the sharing of fundamental values that integrates us as a society; it is our togetherness, to the extent that it exists at the level of concrete practice, which allows us to subscribe in common to shared formulations of fundamental values and to agree on what they 'imply'.

9 One might ask why, if a value formulated abstractly and not exemplified in any way is devoid of significance, it is so common to find values being formulated in the abstract and used without exemplification. Part of the answer, perhaps, is that it is often convenient to employ formulations which commit one to nothing in particular. Certainly, this seems to be one reason why abstractly formulated values and principles are so popular with professional politicians, and often feature in the entertainment they provide on the mass media.

When in 1984 the British Home Secretary called for and obtained the suppression of a television programme, and then insisted that the informal pressure he had put upon the gutless wonders of the British Broadcasting Corporation was 'not really censorship', which indeed he passionately opposed as a believer in 'free speech', the minister was on safe ground in offering this legitimation of his deplorable act. There was no essence of 'free speech' or of 'censorship' at which to point to call him to account, nor was the significance of these terms illuminated by routine cases of usage in connection with particular instances and examples.

It tends to be the most general or 'fundamental' values in a society that are most commonly encapsulated in abstract verbal formulations and transmitted thus, in isolation from particular instances of action. This is why it is the most general and fundamental values which are usually the most empty and fatuous, and most appropriate for use in political rhetoric. Indeed these 'fundamental' values may be systematically ordered into pairs appropriate for *ex post facto* justification, and in this pattern become built into the reflexes of political speakers. Defenders of 'freedom' may then automatically make reference to 'licence' whenever they have a fancy for repression or censorship. Unrelenting, principled opponents of 'terrorism' and 'politically motivated violence' may happily support 'freedom fighters' and 'covert intelligence operations'.

10 This should be an immediately obvious point. That it is not always so is the consequence of a tendency to think of action only in regard to already socialized agents. This is to ignore the problem of how agents come to recognize the significance of symbols and hence how they come to be able to interpret instructions or formulated rules and norms in the first place. As a result of this, references to 'the norms' which treat them as a kind of rulebook set up above action do indeed occur again and again in sociological texts, and even, still, in the research literature.

11 Wittgenstein is seminal here. He recognized that the best way to establish the point securely and with maximum generality was to attack the hardest possible case. Hence we have his *Remarks on the Foundations of Mathematics* (1964), as well as his celebrated analysis of what it is to follow a rule or norm in the *Philosophical Investigations* (1968). See also Bloor (1983) and Kripke (1982).

The argument has been developed in the context of sociology by ethnomethodologists and sociologists of knowledge. For the former, see Garfinkel (1967) or the immensely clear and insightful exposition of his work in Heritage (1984); for the latter, see Barnes (1982).

12 This is not to say that problems cannot arise with sex; they can but they need not. Problems may arise with addition too.

13 Hart (1961) is excellent on the interpretation of legal rules.

14 This is the culmination of Wittgenstein's (1968) analysis of following a rule. See also Kripke (1982).

15 That individuals do, on some occasions, lose discretion to what they think of as the implications of norms is an empirical possibility which cannot be dismissed out of hand. It may well be that fixations of this kind, losses of autonomy in the face of inner promptings and inner fears, are widespread in some social contexts as the result of some forms of training, and influence the alignment of moral responses. All that is argued here is that such states of affairs cannot be the fundamental basis of social order; whether or not they are very commonly a nuisance as far as orderly interaction is concerned is a question which can be left aside. I do not wish to follow those social scientists who argue against the very existence of inner states or internal causation and deny the very possibility of internal constraint upon human action.

16 On the basis of some agreement people may move into closer agreement but some degree of uniformity in initial response is always necessary.

17 The basis of this shared tendency remains obscure. Perhaps we should accept
    some theoretical speculation which understands it in terms of a uniformity in
    human nature. Perhaps we should say that congenital proclivities account
    for the fact that, when exposed to the same social background and
    experience, we develop examples, by analogy, in the same way. Perhaps we
    should look to physiology and psychology as the routes to a final solution.
    Or again, perhaps we should not expect any such solution and resist the
    temptation to illegitimate speculation. For the two opposed arguments see
    Bloor (1983) and H. M. Collins (1985).
18 The problem of strife between individuals, the problem of egoism, is indeed
    Parsons's problem. In a sense it was Hobbes's problem too, but in another
    sense it was not. Hobbes did indeed refer to the 'war of everybody against
    everybody', but his observed problem during the English Civil War was the
    problem of *faction* not egoism.
19 It is not just semantics and syntax that become matters of habit and routine.
    Think of the refinements involved in inflexion, the learning of an accent and
    a style of delivery, and think how these things count as badges of
    membership of a culture or subculture.
20 Indeed, we should recognize that the very perception of disorder as a
    phenomenon is only possible against the backdrop of routinized activity: our
    existing common-sense understanding of disorder in activity is already
    parasitic upon our conception of order in that activity.
21 Satisfactory conceptions of the nature of knowledge are not of long standing
    in the social sciences, and the lack of such a conception may well have
    handicapped Parsons and other social theorists. If, for example, one believes
    that knowledge emerges directly from the interaction of reason and
    experience and is not embodied in the tradition of the culture, then one is
    liable to overlook important aspects of learning as a social process and to
    miss important features of the sociability of the learner.
22 These general themes concerning the nature of knowledge have been exten-
    sively illustrated and vindicated with reference to scientific knowledge, which
    stands as a hard case in relation to them. For relevant work in the sociology
    of science see Barnes (1982), Law and Lodge (1984), H. M. Collins (1985).
    The classic studies of Fleck (1935), Polanyi (1958) and Kuhn (1970) also
    bring out the relevant points admirably: knowledge is sustained and defined
    socially, so that if there is a problem of social order it is a problem of
    cognitive order as well as a problem of orderly action.
23 Ironically, Durkheim himself is the fount and origin of these ideas. *The
    Elementary Forms of the Religious Life* (1915) offers marvellous insight into
    the social character of knowledge and into the relations between cognitive
    and social order.
24 At the same time, calculations may lead to some departure from routine and
    hence eventually to change in routine, experienced as social change A
    changing environment, or a developing knowledge of a constant environment,
    may lead to changed calculations of expedient action as members reflect
    upon what it is possible for them to do, and which of the possibilities best
    advance their objectives or further their interests. In these circumstances

objectives and interests act as causes of change to the routinized system, although because of the persisting general tendency to routinization such change will typically not be in the direction of chaos but toward a new pattern of habituated routinized action.

It is to be expected also, if one views social order in this way, that against the general backdrop of persisting routine, members will continually be engaged in constructing and then setting aside any number of temporary systems of routine directed to the fulfilment of ephemeral ends and objectives. No fundamental problems need arise, from this perspective, in understanding how people make music together, or dance together, or climb cliffs together.

25 There can be no complete or fully satisfactory account of what a society is; different accounts have different pragmatic advantages. See chapter 5C.

26 If this move is accepted, then it becomes important to work with a naturalistic conception of knowledge, and to avoid thinking of ideal entities like 'statements' or 'theories', floating free in some separate immaterial realm. Talk about knowledge (as opposed to the referents of knowledge) is talk about people.

27 This mistake is made whenever we speak of 'the social effects of science and technology'.

28 Some sociologists of knowledge will be inclined to say the same of physical objects of all kinds, to say, for example, that what makes an object a sphere is simply general agreement that it is a sphere. An important source of confusion needs to be eliminated here. Knowledge is indeed a matter of agreement in belief. Nonetheless, we cannot know that a ball is a sphere simply by looking to other people, who will be looking to yet other people, and so on endlessly. We must all first look to the ball and decide for ourselves as to its shape – and only then look to others to discern the agreed verdict, if there is one. We have practices for determining the shapes of things which we apply to the things themselves and which tell us (collectively) what shapes the things are. In contrast, our practices for determining the leadership statuses of persons we apply to the contexts around those persons, in fact to other persons applying similar practices. There is a difference between material objects classified by intrinsic or internal properties and social objects classified by reference to contexts, and persons in the contexts.

29 Our usual conception has natural knowledge referring clearly and directly to the external world without any element of self-reference. It will be evident already that natural knowledge cannot be represented adequately in this way, but the usual conception remains useful for purposes of contrast. Indeed, although systems of natural knowledge are not devoid of self-reference loops, that knowledge is nonetheless used to refer to independent entities.

30 R. K. Merton (1949) is seminal on self-fulfilling prophesies, but his treatment considers them only as errors which may become truths. Krishna (1971), in a curiously neglected paper, produces an account close to that offered here. See also Barnes (1983), Henshel (1978).

31 I say that an act of learning is 'performative' in that it makes something which may in turn be learned of. To make something generally involves the

performance of an action or actions. Normally, we do not recognize learning, or indeed forgetting, as performances which may make or unmake states of affairs.

32 Having described a society as a distribution of knowledge I am now entitled to ask what difference exists between culture and social structure. I can find none.

Chapter 3 The Nature of Power

1 In practice, two fully differentiated systems are rarely found. On the other hand, a degree of differentiation along these lines is practically always found.

2 Note that a normative order is *constituted* by actions taking account of *all* the knowledge of a society, but it is the referent only of *some* of that knowledge. The totality of knowledge self-refers but is not entirely self-referring.

3 An idea of the possibilities of bodies of knowledge as versatile sense-making systems which need never let their users down can be obtained from Kuhn (1970) and Garfinkel (1967).

4 There is a world of difference between this modest statement and advocacy of a theory of the truth of natural knowledge as its correspondence with reality.

5 Overwhelmingly, in the sociological literature, 'power' is equated with what I call 'discretion in the use of power', and the notion of power as capacity for action is set aside in favour of the notion of power as capacity to gain compliance. This reflects the intense concern of many sociologists with relative standing in society, with themes such as 'equality', and their comparatively weaker concern with what societies can actually do.

6 That is, the agent's capacity for social action must be known under some description or other. Clearly, my, or our, concept of power need not be known in the agent's society. But what then is the 'power' which is being discussed here, in this book? Is it our conception of power, or is it that of agents in the relevant society? The answer is that 'power' in this book is our concept, a sociological concept, but defined as an aspect of their knowledge. Power in their society is not whatever they believe it to be, but what their knowledge makes it by fixing their capacity for action, and hence their power, on our definition. Any topic that is to be the subject of sociological enquiry, involving cross-cultural comparison and the systematic study of more than one social order, must be described 'externally', in the terminology of the sociologists' own society, even though it is constituted 'internally' by members of the society being studied. Power cannot be defined as whatever is taken to be power, and powerful persons as whichever agents are generally taken to be powerful, in the society being studied. If such a definition were to be adhered to consistently and uncompromisingly then power in a given society would be identified only when the written sign 'power' was encountered, or the phonetic sequence 'powr'. If, in a given society, with its own specific language and culture, 'power' just happened to be used entirely in relation to sausages, then a sociological account of power in that society would relate to sausages. Given that our interest concerns power, not

sausages, what we have to do is to describe the focus of our interest using the terms and concepts of ordinary everyday English usage, using familiar examples and instances, and then to find as close an analogy as we can for that focus in the discourse and practice of other societies. We have to start with an 'external' description or definition of something or other, and then look for aspects of practice in other societies which offer the strongest possible analogy with our description. Only in this way can sausage-like phenomena referred to with power-sounding noises reliably be avoided. In identifying power-like phenomena in other societies we are metaphorically extending use of our term 'power' away from its root or core use in the context of our own society. But once identified, these phenomena have to be described and understood more thoroughly, in richer detail: each needs to be analysed separately as it is constituted by ongoing practice in its specific context, with all its idiosyncracies and unique features. We must identify powerful agents in alien societies by analogy with such agents as they are defined and exist in our own society: our own society must serve as the familiar system from which we extend our understanding to the unfamiliar systems of alien societies. But the phenomena we seek to understand in the alien society are constituted by alien practice, not ours, and exist as features of the alien distribution of knowledge.

7   The standard conception of knowledge as accepted or acceptable belief is being deployed here, the currently accepted usage of sociologists of knowledge. The alternative conception current in philosophy, according to which knowledge is belief justified and true in some absolute sense, is not employed in this book. Curiously, however, in the present context it probably does not make a great deal of difference which conception of knowledge is used, since the knowledge self-validates.

8   Needless to say, the mistaken belief that an agent has power in society may induce a given individual to obey that agent, and hence make the agent powerful in a certain sense. But such a mistaken belief may only be sustained if the individual believer is isolated from the society, and denied the possibility of learning of it and the supposedly powerful agent's actual role in it. It is tempting to suggest that power based on mistaken belief of this kind should not be considered to be social power, just as power based solely on larger biceps than the next person, or a longer sword, is best treated as other than social power. It must be remembered, however, that belief of this kind is 'mistaken' only in the sense of being deviant. The mistaken belief about an agent's power is much like the mistaken belief that green means stop at the traffic-light. Should such a 'mistaken' belief spread and be entertained more widely, should it become institutionalized, normal and hence true, then social power would have come into existence as an aspect of a reconstituted distribution of knowledge. Knowledge about power is more vulnerable to reconstitutions of this kind than knowledge about traffic-lights. See Barnes (1983) and also Wrong (1979, p. 9).

9   In the wider context of sociological theory this failure is evident in much of the controversy over the merits of methodological individualism.

10 This is a long and fascinating story, and an endless source of materials and problems for sociologists of knowledge. For one particularly intriguing part

of the story see M. C. Jacob, (1976) and J. R. Jacob, (1977); for a sociological overview and further references see Shapin (1982).

11 The view that power is immanent in entities and emanates from entities is ubiquitous, and will remain so for reasons which I have yet to discuss. Innumerable further examples of such a view and its consequences could be cited. Durkheim's (1915) discussion of the power of the aboriginal totem is of great interest, as is Marx on the power of capital:

> The productive power developed by the labourer when working *in cooperation* is the *productive power of capital.* This productive power of associated labour is developed gratuitously, whenever the workmen are placed under given conditions, and it is capital that places them under such conditions. Because this power costs capital nothing, and because, on the other hand, the labourer himself does not develop it before his labour belongs to capital, it appears as a power with which capital is endowed by Nature – a productive power that is immanent in capital. (1867, p. 349)

12 Conceptions of power as a capacity have been criticized on the grounds that they imply that the outcomes of power struggles must be predetermined (Hindess, 1982). Such criticism is surely spurious. The capacity for action available to opponents at a given time does not serve as a sufficient determinant of the outcome of any conflict between them. The small tank may destroy the large tank, in favourable circumstances, with luck. The little army may run away and get bigger, in favourable circumstances, with luck.

13 Some nice points of philosophy arise here such as might interest those concerned to evaluate the contrasting metaphysics of free will and determinism. By acting upon the context within which another individual calculates, and making some of his choices extremely costly, it is possible to achieve discretion over, and control of, what the other voluntarily does. For neither coercion nor the imposition of costs destroy human freedom and discretion, or else every offer of two-pence halfpenny would be a fundamental threat to liberty.

14 The incident is recounted in Carr and Fusi (1979, p. 200).

15 The general premise will be that large-scale power structures must always be intelligible as the products of the actions of knowledgeable agents. Structures must not be allowed to explain themselves in terms of their own coherence or harmony or suitability for the performance of specific tasks: God has not decreed that the best conceivable social worlds will be the only actual social worlds, or even that they will be possible social worlds. Contrast this with the main extant approach to the understanding of large-scale pattern and order in society, sociological functionalism. Functionalism has turned to equilibrated dynamic systems like the human body as models in terms of which to understand society. Just as bodily processes are stable and system-maintaining, so, it is assumed, are social processes. Just as bodily organs are integrated into a functioning whole, so, it is assumed, are social institutions. Just as the body corrects external disturbance and heals when it is damaged or traumatized, so, it is assumed, does society. Just as the body is nonetheless susceptible to pathology and to the slow changes of ageing and degener-

ation, so, it is assumed, is society. If this analogy is accepted, then inter-action in any given society is treated as a harmonious, integrated, stable whole, and the existence of any part of subsystem of society is understood and explained in terms of the contribution it makes to the stable operation of that whole.

Unfortunately, although functionalism has inspired interesting and important work in the social sciences, nobody has ever been able to make it clear *why* a society should be treated as an equilibrated system with tendencies to harmony and integration. Nor has any convincing justification ever been produced for functionalist *explanations* – explanations that relate actions not to the ends and objectives of their originators, but to their unintended pattern-maintaining consequences within the system of actions as a whole. Functionalist explanation is often criticized, quite rightly, for illegitimate teleology – for assuming wrongly that the purpose served or function performed by an action within a larger system can be taken without further ado as the explanation for the existence of that action. Without our specialized educational institutions, modern knowledge-based societies would be liable to disintegrate and destabilize; without the sun, the solar system would fall apart; without feet, our legs would fray badly at the ends; but it would be wrong to *explain* feet, or the sun, or specialized educational institutions in terms of the functions they perform for the wholes of which they are, as we say, a part. Rather, we should see any functional relationships of parts and wholes as the *products* of causal processes, and as themselves in need of explanation: feet at the bottom of the body are explicable (perhaps) in terms of genetics, embryology and processes of natural selection; the sun at the centre of the solar system is explicable in terms of cosmological history and physical theory; specialized educational institutions in modern societies were, I should guess, the outcome of knowledgeable collective interactions, and should be so explained.

Unless one assumes that there is some intrinsic force or tendency, buried deep in all societies, making for harmony and integration, then functionalist accounts of societies as harmonious and integrated explain nothing; they merely point to phenomena in need of explanation. Functionalism forces an uncomfortable choice: either accept disreputable teleological assumptions about societies, or forbear from any attempt to *explain* what societies are like. In my view, it is of overriding importance to avoid any hint of teleology in explaining social interactions and institutional forms, even if this means rejecting the only extant approach to an understanding of social order on the large scale, and starting again from somewhere close to square one.

16 In terms of the contrast, soon to be introduced, between authorizing and empowering, the present discussion is of upward empowering. I am presuming that upward authorization is an empty class.

17 What determines whether an agent does or does not seek to further his interests through delegation and participation in organized action is discussed later, in section 5.2.

18 This may have been particularly the case with the socialist delegates at the centre of Michels's interests: being of modest means, it may be that they were

peculiarly vulnerable to bribes; certainly, it was conventional wisdom amongst the Greeks that the rich should be preferred for political office, since they cost the most to suborn.

19 To be fair to Michels, his contempt extends to the adulated individual as well as those prostrate before him: 'In the object of such adoration,' he remarks, 'megalomania is apt to ensue' (1915, p. 74).

20 I am thinking here of the superficially involved supporter, or the non-affiliated individual who votes for the party. The minor functionary and rank-and-file activist may represent quite different problems, precisely because of their deeper investment in the party and the very much higher costs they incur in walking away from it. Figures of this kind do indeed frequently find themselves uncomfortably sandwiched between leaders and 'the masses', often in circumstances where it has been their capacity for action which has established that very connection, and thus imbued the leadership with power in the first place.

21 One would expect a small number of leaders to act in pursuit of their collective good more effectively than a large number of ordinary members.

22 What Michels omits to consider here may perhaps be made good by drawing upon the grid/group theories of Mary Douglas (1970, 1978). For a study that makes precisely this connection see Rayner (1986).

23 The following discussion draws upon an earlier account in Barnes (1986), an account that also seeks to consider the relationship between *having* authority in the sphere of action and *being* an authority in the sphere of knowledge and cognition.

24 Absolute monarchs and despots seem to have found it expedient, just as we do today, to symbolize a change of policy by making a change of person, but their sidelining techniques were less sophisticated.

25 Thus, although he does not accept it, Wrong (1979) refers rightly to 'the familiar dichotomy of "naked" versus "legitimate" or "institutionalised" power, usually called "authority", which has become such a commonplace in the sociological literature' (pp. 39–40).

26 I use the relationship of power to authority to highlight the need for effective communication, but this is also needed if others are to know when an authority acts as authorized and when not.

27 The literature of ethnomethodology has many insights to offer here. See, for example, Garfinkel (1967) and Heritage (1984), also Clegg (1975).

28 A fine study of the use of physical resources in the cause of social control is Elias (1983).

29 Needless to say, this is to assume the absence of an agency capable of introducing any number of further tokens into the system indistinguishable from those already in use. Where a differentiated agency of this kind exists trust in money must also be related to trust in the agency.

30 There is a profound indeterminacy in the problem of fixing 'correct' spending on information. 'Full' information is infinite in cost and unobtainable, yet without 'full' information one cannot reliably calculate the 'correct' or 'economically rational' amount of information to gather, the precise amount of incomplete information to purchase at a given price for information.

31 Needless to say, alongside the distortion of free exchange in goods and powers represented by the existence of industrial hierarchies and the activities they control, there is a distortion in the free flow of finance whereby the hierarchy appropriates shareholders' profits to its own purposes, instead of looking for supplies of capital from the finance markets. Both perversions are insufficiently condemned by supporters of a free market.

32 Hobbes and Marx are the authorities here. It is intriguing to note how some followers of Marx have tended to invert the original message and assign intrinsic values to social classes.

33 Perhaps the stand taken implicitly here on the relative importance of ownership and control will prove to be misguided and incorrect, or perhaps it will prove adequate to some contexts but not to others, to Britain, for example, but not Japan, or not large multinational companies. I do not know.

34 There are other generalized systems of trust, sustaining currencies other than money. In learned professions, for example, reputation and peer recognition may serve as a form of currency.

35 This is a key theme in 'corporatist' accounts of the modern state and the basis of its stability.

36 It is also worth bearing in mind that transaction costs are minimized by arrangements of this kind. The rarity of trade and exchange up and down hierarchies or between those of widely disparate resources or position is often noted, and requires some kind of general explanation.

37 Incentives to the maintenance of collective goods are discussed in chapter 5. In most cases the boundary around the elite will be well defined and recognized as the crucial collective good which members must sustain, whereupon the elite is sociologically indistinguishable from a status group and may be considered as such.

38 This is not to assert that there is a single 'power elite' or that modern societies are generally 'elitist' rather than 'pluralist': these last terms describe alternative configurations of elites.

39 The price of this accomplishment arises for the most part from the racketeering in which elite members will indulge. Restricted confidential trading in powers is ideally suited to illicit dealing, so it is to be expected that lesser powers will be diverted systematically by elite members to covert, private or sectional interests – the accumulation of material possessions, the favourable placement of dependents, the deflection of legal and regulating agencies and so forth. Even major powers may be so diverted should circumstances allow. There is no doubt at all that membership of a well-chosen old-boy network pays rich rewards through both licit and illicit channels, and that sustaining such networks in the style to which they have become accustomed represents a major cost in practically every economy.

40 Indeed, the work-force will generally find itself attempting to offset the consequences of many of its own continuing routine actions when it engages in a strike or a protest, as indeed will the employer. Strikes and disruptions typically have the character of staged performances set against a continuing

backdrop of routine, to the constitution of which both sides continue to contribute.

41   There is a good argument here against the accumulation of truly vast powers in the hands of a single individual. Such powers come to have a low marginal utility, and access to them may be traded for trivial recompense. This makes for fine drama, as in *Anthony and Cleopatra*, but for a poor society.

42   Those I describe in this paragraph as having power through proximity are more generally described as possessing *influence*. Perhaps it is worth making a distinction between those acknowledged to possess specific powers and those able to direct powers without being recognized explicitly as having that right, between the powerful and the influential. But in practice a systematic distinction of this kind will not be easy to draw, and very little will hang upon it. Wrong (1979) simply equates power with influence exerted intentionally; Parsons (1967) develops a strong and systematic distinction between the two things.

43   This is presumably the reason why I accord no credibility to emanationist theories, and refuse to think of power as some kind of immaterial substance.

44   Luhmann (1979) offers interesting insights into the use of indicators of power to simplify understanding of power, and into how the use of such indicators may transform that which is indicated and produce a simplification therein.

45   Since there are very general incentives for calculative agents to sustain social relations based on pecking-orders and generalized deference, it must, I suppose, be very difficult technically to determine whether or not there are in addition any inherent tendencies in this particular direction.

46   No doubt this shows a way to an analysis of systems based on race or caste as systems of calculative action.

47   This conjecture concerns only interaction lying wholly within the particular bureaucratic context. Where decisions and actions have to be squared with others of comparable power in other contexts, the large-scale maps have to come out of the drawer. Where such decisions have to be justified to others later the large-scale maps will nonetheless have to be checked in advance, even if it is only to search for excuses and rationalizations.

48   Note that it is not the accumulation of powers that is being spoken of here, although the delocalization of access to power does entail some increase in power as well. Limitations of scope are at issue, not limitations of magnitude. Such limitations may of course be sustained where the expanding domains of different power-holders bump into each other. This is something of what is hoped for in a pluralist society.

Chapter 4   Divide and Rule

1   The techniques of divide and rule, which allow the threat of sanctions to be employed with maximum effectiveness, are of course already discussed extensively in the literature. See, for example, Arendt (1951, 1970); Walter (1969).

2   More will be said on collective goods, and on the specific example of bridge-building, later.

3   An additional, formal weakness lies in the fact that fear of an individual is perfectly compatible with voluntary support for him, even with slavish devotion to him.

4   Typically, deviance produces individually suffered sanctions via the direct connection, whereas compliance contributes only a very small amount to any individual's experience of sanctions through the indirect connection. Hence, for self-interested individuals, awareness of the indirect connection is not an incentive to individual deviance but only to concerted deviance. The benefits of compliance are divisible: all may go to the compliant individual. The benefits of deviance are indivisible and spread over the collective.

5   Theories of ritual tend to stress its role in creating solidarity between individuals, and to stress the extent of emotional identification with its symbols and images. But if ritual operates primarily via cognition, as I believe, then the above is but one mode in which it finds a use, and it may be deployed equally readily to degrade, to alienate, to overawe and to demoralize: moreover, these may be the effects upon participants as well as onlookers. For a penetrating analysis of the use of ritual and ceremonial in a power structure, see Elias (1983). For the basic theme of the constituting role of rites and ceremonies, see Durkheim (1915). For criticism of the functionalist side of Durkheim, see Lukes (1975).

6   Peake's novel serves well to illustrate a specific point, but strictly speaking it does not belong in the preceding section. Gormenghast does not run on the basis of coercion. Its creator presents us rather with a great floundering social organism, its ruler an integrated part of the social whole, his realm a preposterous burlesque of functional harmony. Sadly, this means that if the conception of society assumed in this book is correct, the wonderful world of Gormenghast is not a possible world.

7   Needless to say, bearing in mind the earlier discussion of authority, we have to recognize limitations and irremediable defects in any human machine. A human machine must always be to a degree unreliable and unpredictable in operation – just like a physical machine. In thinking of machines we need to free ourselves of the myths that we ourselves have made. Wittgenstein (1968) is enormously helpful here:

> If we know the machine, everything else, that is its movement, seems to be already completely determined . . . We talk as if these parts could only move in this way, as if they could not do anything else. How is this – do we forget the possibility of their bending, breaking off, melting, and so on? . . . The movement of the machine-as-symbol is predetermined in a different sense from that in which the movement of any given actual machine is predetermined. (p. 193)

8   I have attempted to discuss the proper relationship between social structure and the individual in Barnes (1977, ch. 3.2). Although the specific conception of society as a distribution of knowledge is not developed in that context the discussion still serves. Note also the following section wherein the work of

Lucien Goldmann is considered as an instance of a properly structural approach, for all its obsessive concentration on specific exceptional individuals (Goldmann, 1964).

9 This is not always so. In some New Guinea societies, for example, the death of a leader may simply mean the routine dissolution of the whole system of power relations lying under him.

10 Why should there be this concern, if rules do not determine? It is because existing rules may be used as the basis of solutions to co-ordination problems by those opposed to the ruler.

11 Needless to say, other rules are invariably recognized which exclude whole categories of powerless persons from succession, and which are not the subject of the present discussion.

12 This is another straightforward application of Schelling's (1960) notion of a 'prominent solution' to a co-ordination problem. Compare with the discussion of which bridge a society should build in ch. 5.

13 Normally this practice is adopted to make rule formally consistent with an accepted principle of heredity. But the opposite may be the case, as when Roman Emperors, on inheriting their positions, formally accepted responsibilities from the Senate in deference to Republican traditions.

14 Unless, that is, the agent in question is actually trying to contribute performatively to the general acceptance of a rule which he finds to his advantage. It may be good strategy to present oneself as firmly bound by a rule, and hence, in so far as visible behaviour is concerned, to be firmly bound by it.

15 This idea of succession rules and procedures being elaborated and developed over long periods through learning is even more clearly expressed in Burling's discussion of the Manchu dynasty. He concludes that 'Scholarly knowledge [was important] in keeping Emperors on the throne. Historical knowledge did mean power. That in the end the Manchu government weakened and fell means only that the exercise of power and its hereditary transfer are difficult problems which not even the Chinese with all their historical knowledge could completely solve' (1974, p. 122).

16 Thus, British Prime Ministers have been able to accumulate enormous personal power, primarily because of the high cost of challenging them when in office. The involvement of Britain in a number of damaging scraps of warfare, the Suez fiasco of 1956 being a particularly noteworthy example, has been very much a matter of the individual fancy of a Prime Minister; not a happy thought when several occupants of the office could serve to illustrate the role of physical pathology and mental degeneration in producing political and social change.

17 'The variety of professions in religion, when openly indulged doth directly distinguish men into parties, and withal, gives them opportunity to count their numbers.' Thus the response of the House of Commons to Charles II when he put forth his Declaration of Indulgence (Shapin and Schaffer, 1985, p. 289. Original quote, *Journals of the House of Commons*, vol. 8, pp. 442–3, 1663).

18   In his papers on power (1967), Parsons draws a fundamental distinction between negative sanctions and positive rewards, and implies that only negative sanctions can force agents to act on other than a voluntary basis. But this distinction must surely be nothing more than an artefact of how a situation is analysed, and of no fundamental importance. On the one hand, an agent is free to ignore the threat or the actuality of coercion, in just the sense that he is free to ignore positive inducements. On the other hand, if an agent is not considered to be free to ignore the threat to his life from a sword or a gun, then neither should he be considered free to ignore a threat to his life from the withdrawal of rewards. The withdrawal of positive rewards may be just as much a threat of this kind as the brandishing of a weapon: it may mean the difference between food and starvation, death and survival. Nor is there any basic difference between coercion based on force or on materials to be supplied or withheld, and coercion which uses the medium of money. Money, after all, is only a route to other things and cannot make a basic difference to the situations wherein it finds use: an extermination camp could be run as a monetary system with tokens of currency buying life.

19   The history of this development and its proper explanation are fascinating subjects for study which I set aside here. One obvious starting-point for thought on these issues is the work of Foucault (1979, 1980).

20   Note the strong distinction between 'authority' as I understand it in this book, and Weber's conception. Note also the difference between 'legitimation' as related to defining the scope of the powers of an official, a useful notion, and 'legitimation' as related to the general acceptability of institutions and the justification of entire systems of routines, an altogether more problematic notion, as I shall go on to argue.

21   Besides power, immediate capacity for action, it is essential to place the yet more speculative and problematic notion of latent power, or capacity for eventual action at some later time. However abstract and philosophical it appears, such a notion enters routinely into agents' calculations. In 1941 Japan went to war with the United States. It is hard to say precisely when military analysts in Japan realized that their project was a failure, and that they would slide into defeat, but probably this was widely recognized within one or two months, well before the point of maximum territorial expansion on the part of the Japanese forces. Yet the Pacific War began without a monstrous disproportion in the military balance of power, and the opening series of Japanese victories could only tilt that balance more and more in their direction, reducing the capacity for action of the Americans and correspondingly increasing that of Japan. What made these victories a losing run was simply the fact that they were less than utterly overwhelming. The Japanese had to triumph quickly if they were to triumph at all, for the military capacity for action of the United States would otherwise increase and multiply inexorably, well beyond anything the Japanese would be able to put forth. It was clear to all parties that the capacity for long-term military action available to the United States was truly immense, and would be realized without undue difficulty. Latent in United States society was the

possibility for further organization and reorganization, further co-operation, mobilization, application of effort, further development of technique and competence, all of which clearly implied that for Japan the only victory was quick victory.

22 I adopt a terminology common in sociology, used to refer to those who take little or no interest in the explicitly political realm and who often voluntarily disenfranchise themselves. Quite why such people are referred to as 'depoliticized', as though they had gone through some process or undergone some transformation, I am not sure.

23 It is intriguing to reflect that scarcely anyone at all in British society actually supports that lack of restraint on the flow of knowledge, information and ideas customarily regarded as essential to the full realization of human dignity and freedom. People love to censor, and to be censored. They want to have their minds shaped and ordered from the outside. Demands for openness are invariably heavily qualified with vested interest. Legislators, for example, will frequently call for 'freedom of speech under the law'.

24 'Legitimacy' in the context of the following discussion relates not to conformity with a rule or law or regulation, as in the earlier allusion to Weber on bureaucracy, but to the general acceptance of something as right and proper, or appropriate, or morally justified. There are great variations in how this conception of legitimacy is defined (see Lukes, 1986; Connolly, 1986), but the key notion is of a state of belief in the rightness or appropriateness of institutions, which in turn accounts for actions supporting them, or implying approval of or consent for them. Some authors go on to contrast 'perceived' and 'true' legitimacy, that which is indeed right and appropriate from that which is merely thought to be so. Other authors ask whether perceived legitimacy must exist only amongst elites and intellectuals or whether it must permeate through all the members of an extended social order. No doubt it is a characteristic weakness of intellectuals to exaggerate the importance of the justifications of institutional arrange-ments which they themselves labour to produce.

25 Needless to say, there may be conditions of conventionalized warfare wherein the organization of the opponent is disturbed to the minimal degree possible, and only his military resources of the moment are searched out and destroyed. Perhaps this sporting approach to war was what inspired Burke to make his remark. It is after all far from easy to appreciate that the awful ravages of European warfare in the seventeenth and eighteenth centuries still constitute from some points of view a model of restraint.

26 Some actions may perhaps plausibly be referred to as indications of attitudes and evaluations. There are actions with this kind of transparency. Take, for example, small-scale interactions where temporary hierarchies of control are rapidly constructed *ad hoc*, to facilitate particular tasks or the solution of particular problems. In sailing a boat, or climbing a mountain, or hunting game, people will rapidly and spontaneously evoke a hierarchy and concentrate discretion over action, in the interests of effectiveness and the generation of a collective good. They will conceive the hierarchy as a cognitive institution, arrange themselves to act as its components, and

implement it as a legitimate, sanction-supported structure, recognizing their own liability to sanctions for a failure to play their part therein. It is noteworthy how quickly such hierarchies may be created in small-scale interactions and how ready people are to take subordinate roles in them, often seeking such roles in preference to more powerful positions. It is noteworthy too how readily such hierarchies may be dissolved. In interaction of this kind there is often no visible clash between freedom and subordination, and no deep problem in attributing the existence of a skewed distribution of discretion to the approval of subordinates for what they have themselves helped to fashion. On the other hand, when many agents join or accommodate to an existing long-established hierarchy, a great range and variety of different attitudes and evaluations are almost invariably involved.

27 To cite a simple example, in the course of the Second World War, British people joined the army in great numbers, supported its hierarchical structure, willingly accepted their own subordination, put maximum effort into complying with orders. Yet this unity at the level of action implied no such unity in attitude or evaluation. Assessment of the army hierarchy varied enormously from deep admiration to restrained loathing. Many in its ranks found it abhorrent, regarded the vast gulf between officers and men with contempt, considered that discretion was systematically misused and power systematically misdirected. Some found in their experience of the army hierarchy their grounds for voting Labour in 1945. Willing support for the hierarchy was, as a composite phenomenon, not the consequence of its being approved, or perceived as legitimate and justified, but simply of its being. Its key advantage over all the alternative conceivable organizational strategies which might have been employed in the pursuit of the war was that it existed and they did not.

28 In developed industrial economies with elaborate monetary systems, pluralism, interdependence, representative democracy and tendencies to corporatism, power-holders are highly sensitive to demands pressed hard upon them from below, and restrained in the use they make of the capacity for action that lies to hand. For obvious reasons this is especially the case with elected members of governments and legislatures. There is no need to take seriously the myth that democratic governments act on the basis of consent in order to perceive the important consequences of universal suffrage.

Chapter 5 Unity is Strength

1 It is not that this problem of collective action can only be raised in the context of undifferentiated societies. The problem exists in modern societies, for example as the problem of why people vote; why they campaign for votes and why they give support to voting practices. It is merely that the discussion is simplified by focusing on direct provision of collective goods.

2 Although Olson introduced the free-rider problem into the context of modern economics it has a long history. David Hume considered it. Many economic

and political theorists in the European tradition highlighted examples of it. See Barry and Hardin (1982); Hardin (1982).

3 Imagine if you wish that a society of 100 people is considering whether to build the bridge. Let it be an effort involving 1000 days of labour, or 10 days per person, and let its building save future labour and hence benefit the society to the extent of 50,000 days of labour, or 500 days per person. Clearly the building of the bridge is an immense overall benefit, yielding everyone a handsome return on their investment of effort. Everyone will want the bridge built, and see the sense in building it. Yet it will be in nobody's individual interest to help with the building. For the 500 days per person of benefit is an *indivisible* benefit arising from general use of the bridge, whereas the 10 days per person of effort is private, personal effort specific to the individual. Every individual will rightly calculate that his own 10 days of effort yields him as an individual only 500/100 = 5 days of saved future effort, with the other 495 days of savings going to other individuals in the society. Hence every individual will calculate that his own particular contribution to the bridge is unprofitable, and nobody will contribute. Everyone will wait for someone else to do the work.

4 The role of group size is actually much more complex than this, and my simplified argument works only under the conditions specified, where marginal additions to costs generate marginal additions to benefits evenly. For a more extended and satisfactory account see Hardin (1982). But note that none of the complications which have to be taken account of in a detailed analysis alter the fundamental points made on the basis of the too simple treatment set out here.

5 It might be held that in the United States self-interested orientations are established as routine or customary to an unusual extent. Although such a criticism leads on into some deeply interesting issues I shall not take it further here.

6 The mere fact that collective goods are provided by stable social processes is perhaps enough to establish that the free-rider problem is a soluble one, but I make the points separately here. In his original formulation Olson considered the *voluntary* provision of collective goods, and simply assumed that they could be provided through the use of coercion, in which conditions no free-rider problem would arise. But coercion itself is arguably a collective good, or at least coercion orientated to the generation of collective goods. Such coercion has an individually borne cost which serves to generate a collective, indivisible benefit, and hence rational agents ought to free-ride and fail to provide it. Analogously, if one thinks of monetary rewards for those who generate collective goods, the problem of the source of the money arises, and if the source has to be coerced, as taxpayers generally have, then we are back with coercion as a collective good again. If collective goods cannot be provided directly, then it is difficult to see how they may be provided indirectly, other than temporarily. Olson's own suggestions on how self-interested persons might provide such goods seem inadequate as long-term expedients, as indeed Hardin shows (1982).

7 It is Jon Elster (1984, 1985) who has taken this approach most seriously, and

developed it most extensively, in what he regards as a game-theoretical elaboration of Marxism.

8 It is important to avoid the way of thinking appropriate to the labour-market where every twitch of a finger or wag of an eyebrow is to be purchased. Because all bodily motions have a price on the market it does not follow that every such motion is costly to its initiator and only worth making in return for some recompense. This would make the normal natural state of a human being a coma, and every deviation from the comatose condition a cost, which is nonsense.

An economist might perhaps assess the costs of sanctions by reference to what their application precludes or rules out: if alternative profitable activity has to be foregone in order to give time to sanctioning, then the profits lost measure the costs of sanctions. But on this basis the cost of sanctioning for many, for most of the time, is precisely zero. Few of us have lives so stuffed up with opportunity that we can give no thought to the sanctioning of others, and in any case the time expended on an act rarely varies to any great degree according to whether it is done nicely, or nastily, or with indifference. The system of implicit meaning through which informal sanctioning is carried out can operate in parallel with explicit communication and information exchange more or less cost-free.

9 If approval is intrinsically rewarding then we must expect that people will have an incentive to sanction in concert, that they will like doing it. This seems reasonable. People seem to enjoy the collective application of both positive and negative sanctions, honouring and degrading. It is easy to fail to see, perhaps because we have no wish to see, the sheer pleasure that is derived from the collective application of negative sanctions. We have abolished public executions and turned our prisons into fine and private places, but the collective expression of disapproval is still a part of the staple of social life – and choruses of anger and outrage are like choruses of other kinds in that they are generally made up of volunteers who give their services freely for the joy of participation.

10 Note that mutual sanctioning to sustain knowledge and mutual sanctioning to encourage actions are not separable activities. People develop knowledge of society from their observations of those actions that are sanctioned and those that are not. That which aligns cognition is also that which aligns action. Mutual sanctioning, we might say, underlies the continuation of culture, or form of life.

11 Those social theorists who refuse to treat communication and cognition in purely instrumental terms have a point. For all their wonderful optimism and romanticism, writers like Arendt and Habermas offer a more accurate account of interaction than may be constructed from an 'economic' perspective. Yet it remains useful to think of human activity with an 'economic' framework, since it so often provides a useful worst-case scenario.

12 We are altogether too prone, both in our formal and our informal thought, to attribute collectively orientated, individually unprofitable actions to irrationality and psychological fixation. Consider the suicide-bombings of

Muslim fundamentalists, often spoken of as evidence of 'fanaticism' and fixed commitment. These bombings further a collective good for the fundamentalists. More interestingly, they further it in the most 'rational' way as far as both group and individual are concerned. Suppose a thousand casualties must be inflicted upon the well-equipped Western enemy. One approach is to march into battle in the usual way. Another is to establish a public norm of obedience with sanctions so comprehensive that life becomes intolerable in the face of them – and then to give the task of delivering the bombs to whoever draws the short straw. The overall chances of death from the second approach are far less than from the first. The second approach is the humane approach, which minimizes death and suffering on one's own side. Indeed, the Shiite strategy is likely to be the most humane in most military operations, not our own Western approach of weak control and weak sanctioning. Why, then, take for granted their 'fanaticism' and our 'rationality'?

13   It is worth considering here Emile Durkheim's celebrated description and explanation of religious practices. In his account of aboriginal totemism, which served him as a paradigm for religion in general, Durkheim (1915) saw the ultimate object of veneration as society itself and the totem as a mere substitute, a representation of the true object of worship that reflected incomplete knowledge on the part of those involved. But perhaps there is more to be said in favour of aboriginal totemism, and indeed of religion generally as a cognitive system, than even Durkheim was able to discern. In venerating a totem, and making it the central focus of their celebration and ritual, the worshippers may perhaps in some sense have been venerating their society, but they were venerating no particular society. No rules, norms or institutions were explicitly involved. Not even a general description of a particular society, or verbal references to specific features of a particular society, made an appearance. And perhaps this was, in a sense, a necessity. Perhaps members could only share in an act of veneration if they failed to specify what it was they venerated. Perhaps speech in this context had to be the enemy of unity and community. Perhaps any verbal rule, any account of social order, any hint of what was being venerated, would have generated disputation, a lack of solidarity, however slight, among those who all alike were committed to their society and saw its fate as their own. If this is so then the totem was well chosen as the focus of ritual, and the celebration and veneration of the totem was the very opposite of fetishistic action. Aboriginal totemism may then be seen to serve not merely as a paradigm of religious practice, but as a profound representation of the nature of our sociability. Note how this would help to account for the major point which Durkheim himself fails to throw light on – the absence of society as an *explicit* point of reference in religious practice. Durkheim's postulate of incomplete understanding of the object of worship is ultimately unconvincing here.

14   I have not discussed altruistic or universalistic calculative action, since their existence simply makes the general argument all the easier. Needless to say, there is no need to treat the contrast of self-interest on the one hand and

altruism or universalism on the other as a contrast between calculative orientation and moral, 'conscience-driven' orientations. People may simply act out of sympathy with others, taking their good into account in their calculations rather than or as well as their own. There is nothing at all strange in an individual who identifies as a member of a community, supporting it, opposing its enemies, acting in its defence without undue concern with the niceties of individual profit and loss, and yet who, far from making a fetish of its central professed norms and values, actually opposes them and conducts his own life in defiance of them. It is a fundamental mistake to equate identification with a society and concern with the furtherance of its collective good with acceptance of most, or indeed any, of its central rules, norms or values. Indeed, in modern societies many of those who evince the strongest concern with our collective good are particularly prone to wholesale denunciations of our entire form of life.

15 Before a collective project can be sanctioned and hence achieved there must be a plan for its execution, a plan to unite the sanctioners. But not all sanctioning activity needs to be based on a plan, or any other agreed conception of appropriate public action. Where an individual agent acts to the clear disadvantage of everyone else, whatever the relationship of the act to recognized norms or plans, he creates an identity of interest within the rest of the community and is likely thereby to provoke collective disapproval. Social control on a completely *ad hoc* basis may proceed in this way much of the time.

16 Is there, here, an additional incentive for the individual to participate in the provision of a collective good? Suppose an individual thereby gains a chance of fine-tuning the nature of the indivisible benefit. What kind of an incentive is this, and how would it condition the calculations of a rational agent?

17 'Polya processes' provide valuable mathematical analogies for the social processes involved in the emergence and maintenance of stable cognitive institutions, and indeed stable institutions generally (Polya, 1931; Arthur, 1984).

18 Presumably, where there is pluralism, multiple hierarchies, checks and balances between power-holders, the rake-off will be smaller in consequence. In any case, it is hard to argue from an economic perspective that the price paid for co-ordination is too large, given what occurs when such co-ordination is lost. The various hierarchies engaged in the routine production of collective goods are the institutional capital of a democratic society. Like other capital it has been accumulated over many generations. Like other capital it may be used much or little, well or badly. Like other capital its destruction undoes the work of all the many generations and effects an impoverishment from which quick recovery is impossible.

19 Boundedness of context is a factor rightly emphasized in much recent anthro- pologically orientated work. See for example Douglas (1970, 1978, 1986); Gross and Rayner (1985); Rayner (1986).

20 Peasant society was surely highly organized, not atomized, although it might perhaps be argued that it was organized, or appeared to be organized, more from above than from within. But perhaps this was the consequence of the

long period of time over which peasant communities had existed, in contrast to the newly established working-class communities. Marx lived at a crucial but unusual time in the development of industrial working-class communities. As time passes, they too increasingly have the appearance of being organized from above, more than from within.

21 These are standard, well-recognized points, which may be recapitulated briefly because many extensive discussions already exist. They are not, however, points which can yet be taken for granted: there remains a tendency to equate wants or desires with interests.

22 Again, the problems of explaining collective action solely by reference to interests are well known and extensively discussed. Employer and employees may share an interest in supporting a strike by a competing employer's employees. Employers are in competition with each other and therefore often find themselves with opposed interests. Employees are similarly placed as competing purveyors of labour. Reference to interests, even when interests are understood as implying 'potential courses of action', are not sufficient to explain why labour has organized against capital and vice versa and why organization along these lines has been overwhelmingly more important and extensively developed than alternative possibilities.

23 Workers are thrown together in the newly industrializing areas, but capitalists are not. Hence it is actually more difficult within Marx's frame of reference to account for solidarity and collective action amongst employers and property-owners, who, it might be thought, can readily avoid mutual sanctioning and free-ride on the collective action of others furthering the capitalist good. The difficulties involved here are highlighted nicely by Elster (1984), who struggles with them energetically but not wholly successfully. The ingenuity, not to say the whimsical and ironical character of much of Elster's argument stands as testimony to the recalcitrance of the problem he seeks to solve. The collective good of capitalism, he asserts at one point, was favoured precisely because individual capitalists lacked the power to further their own individual good. Capitalism became economically preponderant, but capitalists were not able immediately to secure political power. This long remained in the hands of the old landed aristocracy, or else, as in France, passed to bureaucrats and functionaries, who had an interest in the overall productivity of capital but no considerable interest in any specific component thereof: thus, at the heart of the great capitalist Leviathan the bourgeoisie is 'delivered from the danger of its own rule' (Elster, 1984, ch. 2, section 8). There is, of course, another hypothesis which demands to be considered here, the hypothesis that some of the collective goods of employers and capitalists have become increasingly perceived as coextensive with the collective good as a whole, and are now supplied, in the last analysis, for that reason. Such a hypothesis is consistent with the fact that such goods are now mainly supplied through the mediation of the state, and those who have greatest discretion in the direction of the state apparatus are elected on the basis of universal suffrage.

24 Religious practices may, of course, be imposed upon a community from the outside, or 'from above', as a part of the business of control. Here again,

though, the concern may be to pre-empt independent organization as such, rather than organization for anything in particular. Religious order may thus be pressed upon communities rather like empty projects and activities are pressed upon armies or labour-forces, simply to sustain the status quo. It is a commonplace to explain vast ancient monuments or tombs in terms of a need to keep large masses of human beings organized. Even apparently functional entities like Hadrian's Wall have been accounted for in this way, on the assumption that it is dangerous to park an army unless one leaves the engine running.

25 A key problem in the organization of dissent is often that of establishing the dominance of just one project. Strategic assassinations may be helpful here, or atrocities directed against the established order to provoke retaliation, polarize the situation and destroy an entire range of 'moderate' and 'reformist' programmes. At the ideological level, debate between leaders is one part of the business of competition and rivalry. Sociological theories have occasionally taken on a performative role in such debates, finding use to 'demonstrate' the inevitable success of a political programme, and thereby helping to contribute to and constitute its success. On some occasions the leaders of political movements have developed their own sociological theories. No doubt as the power of an agent increases, the performative significance of what he says increases correspondingly. Powerful agents are generally well aware of this. Thus, practically no senior Western politician would ever feel able to agree openly with such a banal truth as 'violence often pays'. Note too the political and legal use of an obscurantist distinction between 'speaking' and 'inciting'.

26 For power-holders to mobilize latent power they must sanction each other for their collective good, which makes it necessary for them to interact more intensely with each other and to erect stronger boundaries around the contexts within which they interact. But if the powerful interact more with each other they will interact less with others; if they separate themselves off they allow a similar separation to their enemies; if they emphasize their own identity they emphasize that of those they exclude; if they concentrate their own actions upon a single specific enemy they concentrate opposition around that same enemy. For the powerful to maximize their capacity for action they must assist the opposition in maximizing theirs.

27 For systematic theorizing based on Weber, see Collins (1979, 1986).

28 Metaphors linking natural and social order have generally been treated with suspicion in the social sciences. They have been thought to exaggerate the durability of social order. This danger should now be past, given our improved understanding of natural order, and two-way traffic via the metaphor should now be encouraged as safe and productive.

29 Durkheim's famous explanation of totemic religion is not functionalist but intellectualist. Throughout his late period Durkheim is interested in the cognitive role of classifications more than in their functional side-effects. Totems are representations developed 'not to facilitate action but to advance understanding'. 'The Australian does not divide the universe between the totems of his tribe with a view to regulating his conduct or even to justify his

practice' (Durkheim and Mauss, 1963, pp. 81-2). The totem is an attempt to represent reality, to make sense of certain kinds of experiences associated with collective life. Consider, however, that everything which Durkheim asserts in this connection concerning the aboriginal totem may be asserted equally well, with no qualification or reservation, of his own concepts of 'society' and 'social pressure'. This adjustment more or less yields the position adopted and developed in the main text.

30   'Durkheim, as all those who knew him testify, was always, above all, a moralist' (Lukes, 1973, p. 320).

31   I shall simply expound Weber on the nation-state without regard for how far the relevant materials are ironical. This is indeed a fascinating question, but one for Weber scholars only.

32   The uniform legal framework of the nation-state, extending as it does over a large area and population, is often thought of as making it an advantageous arrangement for capitalists. For this, and other sources of vested interest, see Gellner's fascinating treatment (1983).

33   Weber sets the modern nation-state in a chain of social evolution extending back to much cruder and simpler 'communities of violence', generally all male, all dependent on the same kind of intense emotional arousal.

34   Thus recognized membership of a nation-state, recognized nationality, gives the individual member the prestige of nationality, much as the prestige of any other generally possessed category transfers to individual possessors – ethnicity, language, ancestry and so forth.

35   It is arguable how far Weber sees the political community as *necessarily* having to justify and legitimate itself in this way. For an interpretation of Weber pressing him very strongly in this direction see Collins (1986).

36   For all the formal distinction made by Weber, ethnicity and nationality remain clearly related in practice (Weber, 1968, pp. 921-5).

37   It is hard to understand orientations to nationalism generally, in the context of sociological theory. Anthony Giddens's (1979) discussion of *Central Problems in Social Theory*, for example, not only lacks any extended discussion of 'state', 'nation' or 'nationalism' but actually omits to list any of these terms in its index, even though they do often make an appearance in the text.

38   Collins, for all his insistence upon success as the basis of legitimacy, actually makes extensive reference to the power and significance of stateless 'nations' and ethnic groupings, in order to elaborate a theory of the growth and decline of states (1986, ch. 8).

39   This is as close as Collins comes to the point of view being advocated here. But he takes care to insist upon the necessity of legitimation, even if it is generated only intermittently: 'Ultimately this is the lifeblood (or should one say the heroin fix) of politics' (1986, p. 161).

BIBLIOGRAPHY

Aitken, M. and Mott, P.E. (eds.) (1970) *The Structure of Community Power*, New York, Random House.

Arendt, H. (1951) *The Origins of Totalitarianism*, New York, Harcourt Brace Jovanovich.

Arendt, H. (1970) *On Violence*, New York, Harcourt Brace Jovanovich.

Arthur, W. B. (1984) 'Competing Technologies and Economic Prediction', *Options*, 2, pp. 10–13.

Axelrod, R. (1984) *The Evolution of Cooperation*, New York, Basic Books.

Bachrach, P. and Baratz, M. S. (1962) 'The Two Faces of Power', *American Political Science Review*, 56, pp. 947–52.

Bachrach, P. and Baratz, M. S. (1963) 'Decisions and Nondecisions: an Analytical Framework', *American Political Science Review*, 57, pp. 641–51.

Barnes, B. (1977) *Interests and the Growth of Knowledge*, London, Routledge and Kegan Paul.

Barnes, B. (1982) *T. S. Kuhn and Social Science*, London, Macmillan.

Barnes, B. (1983) 'Social Life as Bootstrapped Induction', *Sociology*, 17, 4, pp. 524–45.

Barnes, B. (1984) 'The Conventional Component in Knowledge and Cognition', in Stehr, N. and Meja, V. (eds) *Society and Knowledge*, New Brunswick, Transaction Books.

Barnes, B. (1986) 'On Authority and its Relationship to Power', in J. Law (ed.) *Power Action and Belief*, London, Routledge and Kegan Paul, Sociological Review Monograph 32.

Barry, B. and Hardin, R. (1982) *Rational Man: Irrational Society*, Beverly Hills, Sage.

Becker, H. S. (1964) 'Personal Change in Adult Life', *Sociometry*, 27, 1, pp. 40–53.

Berger, P. and Luckmann, T. (1966) *The Social Construction of Reality*, London, Allen Lane.

Bhaskar, R. (1979) *The Possibility of Naturalism*, Brighton, Harvester Press.

Black, M. (ed.) (1961) *The Social Theories of Talcott Parsons*, Englewood Cliffs, Prentice Hall.

Bloor, D. (1983) *Wittgenstein: a Social Theory of Knowledge*, London, Macmillan.

Bonjean, C. M., Clark, T. N. and Lineberry, R. L. (1971) *Community Politics: A Behavioral Approach*, New York, Free Press.

Burling, R. (1974) *The Passage of Power*, New York, Academic Press.

Carr, R. and Fusi, J. P. (1981) *Spain: Dictatorship to Democracy*, 2nd edn, London, George Allen and Unwin.

Clegg, S. (1975) *Power, Rule and Domination*, London, Routledge and Kegan Paul.

Clegg, S. (1979) *The Theory of Power and Organization*, London, Routledge and Kegan Paul.

Collins, H. M. (1985) *Changing Order*, London, Sage.

Collins, R. (1979) *The Credential Society*, New York, Academic Press.

Collins, R. (1986) *Weberian Sociological Theory*, Cambridge, Cambridge University Press.

Connolly, W. (ed.) (1986) *Legitimacy and the State*, Oxford, Basil Blackwell.

Dahl, R. (1957) 'On the Concept of Power', *Behavioral Science*, 2, pp. 202–3.

Dahl, R. (1961) *Who Governs?*, New Haven, Yale University Press.

Douglas, M. (1970) *Natural Symbols*, London, Barrie and Jenkins.

Douglas, M. (1975) *Implicit Meanings*, London, Routledge and Kegan Paul.

Douglas, M. (1978) *Cultural Bias*, London, Royal Anthropological Institute, Occasional Paper 35.

Douglas, M. (1986) *How Institutions Think*, Syracuse, Syracuse University Press.

Durkheim, E. (1915) *The Elementary Forms of the Religious Life*, tr. J. W. Swain, London, George Allen and Unwin.

Durkheim, E. (1933) *The Division of Labour in Society*, tr. Graham Simpson, London, Macmillan.

Durkheim, E. and Mauss, M. (1963) *Primitive Classification*, tr. R. Needham, London, Cohen and West.

Elias, N. (1983) *The Court Society*, Oxford, Basil Blackwell.

Elster, J. (1978) *Logic and Society*, London, John Wiley.

Elster, J. (1984) *Ulysses and the Sirens*, Cambridge, Cambridge University Press.

Elster, J. (1985) *Making Sense of Marx*, Cambridge Cambridge University Press.

Fleck, L. (1935) *Genesis and Development of a Scientific Fact*, Chicago, Chicago University Press; (English tr. 1979, F. Bradley and T. J. Trenn)

Foucault, M. (1979) *Discipline and Punish*, New York, Vintage.

Foucault, M. (1980) *Power/Knowledge*, New York, Pantheon.

Garfinkel, H. (1967) *Studies in Ethnomethodology*, Englewood Cliffs, Prentice Hall.

Gellner, E. (1983) *Nations and Nationalism*, Oxford, Basil Blackwell.

Giddens, A. (1968) '"Power" in the Recent Writings of Talcott Parsons', *Sociology*, 2, pp. 257–72.

Giddens, A. (1979) *Central Problems in Social Theory*, London, Macmillan.

Giddens, A. (1984) *The Constitution of Society*, Cambridge, Polity Press.

Goldmann, L. (1964) *The Hidden God*, London, Routledge and Kegan Paul.

Gross, J. L. and Rayner, S. (1985) *Measuring Culture*, New York, Columbia University Press.

Hardin, R. (1982) *Collective Action*, Baltimore, Johns Hopkins University Press.

Hart, H. L. A. (1961) *The Concept of Law*, Oxford, Oxford University Press.

Henshel, R. L. (1978) 'Self Altering Predictions', in Fowles, J. (ed.) *Handbook of Futures Research*, Westport, Greenwood Press.

Heritage, J. (1984) *Garfinkel and Ethnomethodology*, Cambridge, Polity Press.

Hesse, M. B. (1974) *The Structure of Scientific Inference*, London, Macmillan.

Hindess, B. (1982) 'Power, Interests and the Outcomes of Struggles', *Sociology* 16, pp. 498–511.

Hobbes, T. (1651) *Leviathan*, quotations from 1962 edn, London, Fontana.

Hunter, F. (1953) *Community Power Structure*, Chapel Hill, University of North Carolina Press.

Jacob, J. R. (1977) *Robert Boyle and the English Revolution*, New York, Franklin.

Jacob, M. C. (1976) *The Newtonians and the English Revolution, 1689–1720*, Hassocks, Harvester Press.

JOURNALS of the House of Commons (1663) London.

Kripke, S. A. (1982) *Wittgenstein on Rules and Private Language: An Elementary Exposition*, Oxford, Basil Blackwell.

Krishna, D. (1971) ' "The Self-Fulfilling Prophesy" and the Nature of Society', *American Sociological Review*, 36, 4, pp. 1104–7.

Kuhn, T. S. (1970) *The Structure of Scientific Revolutions*, 2nd edn, Chicago, Chicago University Press.

Law, J. and Lodge, P. (1984) *Science for Social Scientists*, London, Macmillan.

Lenski, G. (1966) *Power and Privilege: A Theory of Social Stratification*, New York, McGraw-Hill.

Lewis, D. K. (1969) *Convention*, Cambridge, MA, Harvard University Press.

Luhmann, N. (1979) *Trust and Power*, New York, John Wiley.

Lukes, S. (1973) *Emile Durkheim: His Life and Work*, London, Allen Lane.

Lukes, S. (1974) *Power: A Radical View*, London, Macmillan.

Lukes, S. (1975) 'Political Ritual and Social Integration', *Sociology*, 9, 2, pp. 289–308.

Lukes, S. (ed.) (1986) *Power*, Oxford, Basil Blackwell.

Lynn, J. and Jay, A. (1986) *Yes, Prime Minister*, London, BBC Publications.

Manicas, P. T. (1987) *A History and Philosophy of the Social Sciences*, Oxford, Basil Blackwell.

Martin, R. (1977) *The Sociology of Power*, London, Routledge and Kegan Paul.

Marx, K. (1845) *The Holy Family*, English tr. 1956, London, Lawrence and Wishart.

Marx, K. (1848) *Manifesto of the Communist Party*, English edn 1952, Moscow, Progress Publishers.

Marx, K. (1852) *The Eighteenth Brumaire of Louis Bonaparte*, English tr. in *Selected Works*, 1958, London, Lawrence and Wishart.

Marx, K. (1867) *Capital*, English tr. 1958, London, Lawrence and Wishart.

Merton, R. K. (1949) 'The Self-Fulfilling Prophesy', in *Social Theory and Social Structure*, New York, Free Press.

Michels, R. (1915) *Political Parties*, New York, Free Press.

Mills, C. W. (1956) *The Power Elite*, New York, Oxford University Press.

Mills, C. W. (1959) *The Causes of World War Three*, London, Secker and Warburg.

Ng, S. K. (1980) *The Social Psychology of Power*, London, Academic Press.

Olson, M. (1965) *The Logic of Collective Action*, Cambridge, MA, Harvard University Press.

Parsons, T. (1937) *The Structure of Social Action*, New York, McGraw-Hill.

Parsons, T. (1951) *The Social System*, New York, Free Press.

Parsons, T. (1967) *Sociological Theory and Modern Society*, New York, Free Press.

Peake, M. (1946) *Titus Groan*, London, Penguin.

Polanyi, M. (1958) *Personal Knowledge*, London, Routledge and Kegan Paul.

Polya, G. (1931) 'Sur Quelques Points de la Théorie des Probabilités', *Annales Institute H. Poincaré*, 1, pp. 117–61.

Poulantzas, N. (1973) *Political Power and Social Classes*, London, Sheed and Ward.

Rayner, S. (1986) 'The Politics of Schism', in J. Law (ed.) *Power Action and Belief*, London, Routledge and Kegan Paul, Sociological Review Monograph 32.

Richards, M. P. M. (ed.) (1974) *The Integration of a Child into the Social World*, Cambridge, Cambridge University Press.

Schelling, T. C. (1960) *The Strategy of Conflict*, Cambridge, MA, Harvard University Press.

Schutz, A. (1964) *Studies in Social Theory, Collected Papers*, The Hague, Nijhoff, vol. 2.

Shapin, S. (1982) 'History of Science and its Sociological Reconstructions', *History of Science*, 20, pp. 157–211.

Shapin, S. and Schaffer, S. (1985) *Leviathan and the Air-Pump*, Princeton, NJ, Princeton University Press.

Thibaut, J. W. and Riecken, H. W. (1955) 'Some Determinants and Consequences of the Perception of Social Causality', *Journal of Personality*, 24, pp. 113–33.

Thomason, B. (1982) *Making Sense of Reification*, London, Macmillan.

Vygotsky, L. S. (1962) *Thought and Language*, Cambridge, MA, MIT Press.

Walter, E. V. (1969) *Terror and Resistance*, London, Oxford University Press.

Weber, M. (1947) *The Theory of Social and Economic Organisation*, Chicago, Free Press.

Weber, M. (1968) *Economy and Society*, New York, Beckminster Press.

Wieder, D. L. (1976) *Language and Social Reality*, The Hague, Mouton.

Williamson, O. E. (1975) *Markets and Hierarchies*, New York, Free Press.

Wittgenstein, L. (1964) *Remarks on the Foundations of Mathematics*, Oxford, Basil Blackwell.

Wittgenstein, L. (1968) *Philosophical Investigations*, Oxford, Basil Blackwell.

Wrong, D. (1979) *Power: Its Forms, Bases and Uses*, Oxford, Basil Blackwell.

INDEX